ALL AMERICAN

ALL AMERICAN

★ ★ ★

Why I Believe in Football, God, and the War in Iraq

ROBERT P. McGOVERN

★ CAPTAIN, U.S. ARMY ★

WILLIAM MORROW

An Imprint of HarperCollins*Publishers*

ALL AMERICAN: WHY I BELIEVE IN FOOTBALL, GOD, AND THE WAR IN IRAQ. Copyright © 2007 by Robert P. McGovern, Captain, U.S. Army. All rights reserved. Printed in the United States of America. No part of this book may be used or reproduced in any manner whatsoever without written permission except in the case of brief quotations embodied in critical articles and reviews. For information address HarperCollins Publishers, 10 East 53rd Street, New York, NY 10022.

HarperCollins books may be purchased for educational, business, or sales promotional use. For information please write: Special Markets Department, HarperCollins Publishers, 10 East 53rd Street, New York, NY 10022.

FIRST EDITION

Library of Congress Cataloging-in-Publication Data

McGovern, Robert, 1966–
    All American : why I believe in football, God, and the war in Iraq / Robert McGovern.—1st ed.
      p. cm.
    ISBN: 978-0-06-122785-1
    ISBN-10: 0-06-122785-4
    1. McGovern, Robert, 1966– 2. Lawyers—New York (State)—New York—Biography. 3. Judge advocates—United States—Biography. 4. September 11 Terrorist Attacks, 2001—Personal narratives. 5. World Trade Center Site (New York, N.Y.) 6. Rescue work—New York (State)—New York—Biography. 7. United States. Army. Judge Advocate General's Corps—Biography. 8. New York (N.Y.). Office of the Special Narcotics Prosecutor—Biography. 9. War on Terrorism, 2001—Personal narratives. 10. Football players—United States—Biography. I. Title.

KF373.M3954A3 2007
973.931092—dc22
[B]   2006052148

07 08 09 10 11 WBC/RRD 10 9 8 7 6 5 4 3 2 1

To our children, those already born and those yet to be born. May we be brave enough to face the challenges of our age with courage and determination so that they may have the chance to live in peace with their neighbor and with God.

★ CONTENTS ★

★ ACKNOWLEDGMENTS ★

There were so many incredibly talented and giving people who helped to make this book possible. First and foremost among them is Terry Golway. Without Terry's help and assistance from the very beginning, I could not have maintained the stamina and discipline necessary to complete this book. Like so many of the great teachers and coaches I have had in my life, Terry guided me with care and kindness throughout the writing process and enabled me to convey my thoughts and experiences with clear purpose and meaningful direction. More than anyone else, Terry made this book a reality.

I also want to thank Maureen O'Brien from HarperCollins for all of her support and mentorship. Maureen was the first person to reach out to me with the idea of writing this book and I can't thank her enough for believing in me and the story she helped me tell. This book is the direct result of her initiative and constant motivation. I will be indebted to her for life.

The publication of this book could not have happened without the tireless efforts of a large number of fantastic individuals at HarperCollins. Their contributions cannot go unacknowledged. Thanks must go to Stephanie Fraser, Judy DeGrottle, Kyran Cassidy, Seale Ballenger, and Samantha Hagerbaumer for all their hard work. A very special thanks must also go to Jim Walsh for getting me together with the great people at HarperCollins.

A book like this could not have been possible but for the hard work and dedication of some of my fellow soldiers in the United States Army. Thanks go to Colonel James Quinn, Colonel Flora Darpino, Lieutenant Colonel Frank Misurelli, and Sergeant First Class Eric Reinhardt for their professionalism and dedication. I will always be grateful to them and to the United States Army for giving me the complete freedom to speak my mind about the people and the issues that matter most to me.

Thanks are due to Lieutenant Colonel Kevin Boyle, Captain Rob Stelle, Captain Micah Pharris, Captain Frank Rangoussis, and Romona Parker from the Trial Counsel Assistance Program. These great colleagues and friends gave me the encouragement and assistance I needed during the months and months it took to write this book at night and on weekends.

I also have to say a word about my ex-wife, Marianne Aiello. Although our marriage did not survive the strains caused by war or even the ones caused by ordinary life, I am still truly thankful for our time together. I am the person I am today, in part, because I have known her. I will always be thankful to her for her unwavering support during my deployments and for our years in

New Jersey and New York. I pray that nothing but happiness and joy come to her, Pam, Newk, Joseph, Vincent, and a very, very special little girl named, Alie Rose Newkirk.

I want to thank my good and dear friend Ron Cami. I could not have written this book without Ron's help. He has been a source of incredible strength and wise counsel to me for over twelve years now. His help and advice regarding this book and regarding life itself have served to make me a wiser and more thoughtful person.

I received inspiration and constant encouragement from my family and close friends for which I will always be grateful. In particular, my twenty-four nieces and nephews have brought me great happiness and laughter all my life. I cannot imagine the world with out each and every one of these precious souls and I want them to know how important they are to me. Thank you, Brian, Lindsay, Kevin, Sheila, Katy, Annie, Grace, Max, Michael, Hunter, Riley, Melanie, Emily, Lizzie, Sean, Amanda, Delainey, Mackenzie, Brendan, Erin, Colin, Griffin, T.J., and Timmy.

Finally, I must thank the most incredible woman in the world. She came into my life when I thought I would never find true happiness or unconditional love. She has turned my life around and has shown me that no challenge is too great, no obstacle too large if you are with the one you love and you both place your faith in God. I am so thankful to God for bringing her into my life. I love you, Kelly.

★ A NOTE TO THE READER ★

We're living through a tough time in America today. Our military forces are deployed all over the world. Lots of people, maybe including yourself, oppose the war in Iraq. Our country is divided over exactly how we should use our military forces and how best to direct our fight against terrorists and those who seek to destroy us.

I understand that not everybody is going to agree with the opinions I express in this book. That's great: That's why I love this country and why I'm proud to serve the greatest nation on God's green earth. You are free to disagree with me, and even better, you're free to disagree with our leaders. That kind of country, that kind of system, is worth fighting for.

I didn't write this book to make those divisions worse. I know Americans on both sides of this issue love their country. I want you to know that I don't doubt for a second the motives or integrity of anyone who opposes the Iraq war. I only ask that as you read this book you afford my thoughts and my opinions the same respect. I also wrote this book to get a few things off my chest: to tell you about some heroes I've met along the way, and to encourage all of us to hash out our differences in a civil manner. We should talk to each other as friends, just like neighbors sitting in a local tavern or on a park bench. You may disagree with me, I may disagree with you, but at least we're talking to each other.

You might wonder about the use of *All-American* in the title. First of all, let me say off the bat that I'm not talking about myself here. I'm not a perfect man. I've been through a divorce, and I have more than my share of flaws. So don't think for a minute that I'm claiming to be some perfect all-American type.

What is an all-American anyway? As a former college and professional football player, I've met a few people who were named *all-American* based on their ability to catch a pass or level a quarterback or block a linebacker. But as a kid from New Jersey who was taught by great parents and wonderful teachers, as a former assistant district attorney in Manhattan, and as an officer in the United States Army, I've met some real all-Americans—quiet, unassuming, heroic people who inspire students, protect us from crime, and defend our values.

They are all-American in every sense of the phrase. I chose this title in part to pay tribute to these all-Americans I've been lucky enough to meet and work with through the years. I also chose it to pay special tribute to the men and women of our armed forces, especially those in the 82nd Airborne Division. That famous unit happens to be called the All American Division. The 82nd has a great tradition of courage, honor, and service—truly all-Americans. You'll meet some of them in this book.

One thing many of my heroes have in common is a deep, abiding faith in God. I share that faith. After all I've seen in Afghanistan and Iraq, after prosecuting ruthless drug dealers here at home, and terrorists overseas, yes, I still believe in God, and in His goodness. I don't blame God for the troubles and tragedies of the world. But I see God's presence in how decent, God-loving people react to those tragedies and troubles. I saw God on the campus of Holy Cross College. I saw Him in the faces of rescue workers at Ground Zero. I saw him working small miracles in the villages of Afghanistan and Iraq.

War and violence can shake our belief in God. But it can also assure us that only a loving God would create men and women who would risk their own lives in service to others. Yes, I still believe in God.

And, yes, I believe more than ever in the moral goodness of the United States and its people. I'd like to think we all do, regardless of how we feel about the war in Iraq or about politics in general.

—Robert P. McGovern,
Captain, U.S. Army,
December 2006

ALL AMERICAN

CHAPTER ONE

★ ★ ★

September 11, 2001

A FRIEND OF MINE WAS GETTING MARRIED ON SUNDAY, September 16, and he wasn't the only one who had to get his act together in the days before the wedding. I was looking frantically for my old tuxedo. It was a formal wedding, so all the men had to have one. I eventually found it in an old suitcase I'd buried in the back of a closet. I tried it on. Size 48L, the same size I wore when I was a linebacker in the NFL in the early 1990s. Only it looked ridiculous on me now. I weighed twenty pounds less than I did when I was playing with the Chiefs, Steelers, and Patriots, so I looked like a little kid trying on something he'd found in his dad's closet.

I had to get the monkey suit altered and cleaned up pretty fast. So I brought it to the tailor's shop near my apartment on

Manhattan's Upper East Side. They told me to come back on Tuesday morning—Tuesday, September 11, 2001.

Getting this chore done would mean I'd be late for work that morning, but I knew that wouldn't be a problem. As an assistant district attorney in the office of Manhattan D.A. Robert Morgenthau, I had spent the last few weeks working with the New York Police Department on an undercover investigation of a violent drug gang. I had put in a lot of hours on this case, so I was pretty sure nobody was going to be too upset if I showed up a little late that morning.

AS I WALKED to a nearby subway station, I noticed traces of smoke in the air to my left, toward downtown. I heard somebody in the street say that an airplane had hit the World Trade Center. Like most of us that morning, I figured that a small plane had somehow lost its way and plowed into one of the towers.

I got off the subway at the City Hall stop, which is just a few blocks south of the D.A.'s office in Foley Square. The stairs lead north, toward Foley Square and away from downtown. From the darkness of the subway station, I started walking up the stairs to the sunshine. But with each step, I saw more and more people gathered around the subway entrance. As I emerged I saw hundreds of people standing in the street. I could see their faces, filled with fear and bewilderment. Their heads were tilted up, their eyes staring at some object in the sky behind me. Some of them had tears in their eyes.

I turned around. There was a horrible, sickly gash in the north tower of the World Trade Center. Smoke was pouring out of the gash. "Holy shit! That was no small plane," I thought. My head then snapped to the left to see the south tower. It seemed like smoke was seeping out of every side of that huge steel frame just above the midway point. The smoke was clinging to the sides as it slowly rose toward the top.

This was far, far more awful than I'd imagined during the subway ride downtown.

After a few minutes, I overheard some guy to my left talking about how he was inside the north tower when the first plane slammed into it. I looked away from the burning towers to hear what he was saying, and as I did, I heard a deep rumbling sound. I looked back toward the south tower and saw it collapse.

People were pushing past me as they fled the falling debris. I just stood there, dumbstruck.

I snapped out of it when I saw a huge cloud of dust and debris whip around the corner of a building directly in front of me. I turned and joined the river of people running north away from the danger. As I ran, I kept repeating to myself, "The tower is gone. I can't believe the tower is gone."

When I was clear of the collapse zone, I stopped running and began to make my way to my office. I was still in shock but knew I had to check in with my colleagues to let them know I was okay. Sirens pierced the air—ambulances, fire engines, police cars, all heading to the World Trade Center site. Through the confusion and chaos, I made my way to 80 Centre Street and up to my office on the sixth floor.

I was assigned to the Office of Special Narcotics in a building located directly across the street from the D.A.'s offices at 1 Hogan Place, and shared an office with an A.D.A. named Jon Shapiro. We were more than just colleagues—the two of us both served as reservists in the Judge Advocate Generals Corps, better known as JAGs. That we both served part-time as military prosecutors meant one weekend a month and two weeks a year. I was Army and he was Navy, so aside from the normal ribbing we would give each other about our poor judgment in picking a branch of service, it was a perfect fit.

Thanks to our military training, Jon and I knew the first order of business was to make sure our colleagues were safe. Everybody, luckily, was accounted for. We evacuated the office, and I walked home through the war zone that Manhattan had become.

During that long walk uptown, I saw men and women moving as if in a trance, their clothes covered in dust. We were modern war refugees, as shell-shocked as the men, women, and children who fled the Nazi blitz in 1940.

What kind of monsters had carried out this act of mass murder? What kind of barbarians had brought such misery to innocent people? As I made my way uptown, the numbness of shock gave way to a simmering fury. I wanted to hit back. I wanted to kill whoever was responsible for this slaughter. And I wanted to do something, anything, to help the rescue workers already picking through the rubble of the World Trade Center.

Back home, I heard somebody on the radio say that people with military training were needed downtown. That's all I needed to hear. The following morning, I got up at six o'clock as usual, but this time I put on my military uniform instead of a suit. I was certain there would be people trapped under the debris downtown, and every free hand would be needed to move the rubble. I didn't bother to call the office to explain why I wasn't coming to work anytime soon. With downtown Manhattan sealed off, there was no office to go to anyway.

I took the subway to Canal Street, just about a mile from the smoking pile that already had been dubbed "Ground Zero." The NYPD and the city's emergency responders had set up an outer perimeter along Canal Street. The tens of thousands of people who worked south of Canal were not getting past the checkpoints set up along the street, which runs across Manhattan from the East River to the Hudson River. If I had been wearing my usual office attire, I'd have been stopped, too. But I was wearing my military fatigues, called BDUs, which is short for Battle Dress Uniform. As I approached the checkpoint, a police officer waved me through.

It was devastating to see how much had changed in less than twenty-four hours. At this time a day earlier, downtown Manhattan was filled with office workers emerging from subways, getting out of cabs, lining up for a coffee and doughnut from a sidewalk vendor, reading through the city's tabloids. Now, everywhere I looked, I saw only military personnel, or firefighters, or emergency medical technicians, or police officers—some of them dressed in body armor and carrying automatic weapons. Thousands were dead, and for all we knew thousands more lay injured below the ruins of the Twin Towers. It was hard to believe, but New York really was a war zone.

The New York City fire department clearly took charge of the site, even though there was a substantial National Guard presence in the streets. I think everybody understood that the FDNY had suffered horribly the day before, losing 343 members— including most of its top command. So the military, the police, and other emergency personnel quite naturally deferred to the FDNY's authority.

Even though I'd watched news footage of the wreckage, nothing could have prepared me for what I saw as I approached the site. I walked to the spot where I'd seen the towers fall, on Park Row near City Hall. An inch of fine dust covered the street—like the morning after a snowstorm. Ground Zero itself was a smoking pile some seven stories high. The buildings' unique facade was broken into pieces, looking like darts stuck in the ground.

I looked for somebody who seemed to be in charge, finally finding a fire-department battalion chief. I asked him, "What can I do?" He just looked at me and pointed over to the pile, where hundreds of people were lined up, passing buckets of debris from hand to hand. It was that primitive—the site was too dangerous for heavy construction equipment. Instead, people were digging through the remains of two of the world's tallest buildings with their bare hands.

I worked the pile for twelve hours on September 12. Every now and again, you'd hear somebody yell, "It's going to collapse, clear the pile"—meaning the pile above us or underneath or even a nearby building was in danger of giving way. We'd all climb down off the debris pile and start running for our lives, but of course, we had no idea if we were moving away from the danger, or going directly toward it. In any case, it usually was a false alarm.

At one point that afternoon, I was holding a rope with several other people as some firefighters lowered themselves one by one down the side of a pit made up of twisted steel and debris. They were searching for bodies while nine of us remained at the top holding the rope that would eventually pull them back up. About twenty other people were digging through rubble nearby. Someone yelled, "It's gonna collapse . . . It's gonna collapse! Get off the pile now!"

The look on everyone's face said it all. We were scared. Everyone who was digging nearby started running off the pile. The guys in the pit began scurrying back to the base of the rope to try to climb up to safety. About four or five of the guys holding the rope with me took off and never looked back. I now know what they mean when they say panic is like a virus—I could see it spreading across the pile, and I could also feel it trying to infect me, too.

I was scared, really scared. I didn't know what was going to happen. Was the pile I was standing on going to give way and swallow me up? Was the wall of debris to my left going to fall over and crush me? Was one of the huge skyscrapers just across the street going to collapse on top of me?

Then I heard a voice coming from down in the pit. It was a firm voice, but a calm voice. The voice belonged to a fireman. He was a thin, distinguished-looking man in his late forties maybe early fifties. He had salt-and-pepper hair and his navy-blue pants and light blue shirt were still amazingly clean and pressed. He was trying to calm one of the younger firefighters in the pit. The kid wanted out of that pit and he wanted out now. He was trying desperately to find a way up and out.

"Everything's gonna be okay," the senior guy said. "You're gonna live. It's gonna be okay." I was as nervous as that kid; I was just doing a better job of hiding it. That firefighter's quiet bravery calmed down the younger guy, and had the same effect on me. I looked behind me at another guy who was helping hold the rope. "We're staying, right!" I said. It wasn't a question. It was a statement of fact. He looked back at me and said, "Yeah, we're staying!" The two other guys with us then turned and nodded, too. We were staying. So we anchored ourselves, and began to pull each firefighter up the side of this huge pit until they all made it out.

It had been another false alarm, but for me there was nothing false about it. For a moment I felt that overwhelming fear that drove those other men to drop the rope and flee the pile. I am ashamed to admit that I had the same urge. But even though the thought crossed my mind, I knew I couldn't run. I knew I had to stay and help. Those men in the pit were counting on us to pull them out, and thanks to the courage and leadership of one man— whose name I will never know—we didn't let them down.

Later that day, I heard somebody yell, "Got one." Again, it was amazing how quickly the unthinkable—the gruesome— became routine. When somebody yelled "got one," we soon realized what that meant: somebody had found a body, or more to the point, a piece of a body. On one occasion a guy working near me picked up a hand and a piece of a forearm. Those were the first recognizable human remains I saw.

A little while later I was standing next to a firefighter who turned to me and said, "Here's one." I looked at him and asked, "Where?" "Right there," he said, pointing to some object directly between our feet. I didn't see anything that looked like a body, but then, I was looking for something intact. As I peered closer, I saw something that looked like a bloody slab of meat covered in a fine layer of dust. I couldn't tell what part of the body it was, but it belonged to a person. A real human being. The firefighter pointed out the barely recognizable fabric from the white shirt the person must have been wearing. As I stared at it, I could barely make out the small strips of torn cloth that were now so inextricably tangled with the shredded human flesh as to make them almost indistinguishable and completely inseparable.

It was a horrible sight, and for a moment I wondered if I could handle it. I was supposed to be some big tough NFL linebacker.

I'd played against guys like Hershel Walker, Marcus Allen, John Elway, and Lawrence Taylor. I had even been in a few fights in my day.

I was tough enough for anything, I thought. But I wasn't sure if I was tough enough for this.

I'd never seen anything like this before. I didn't want to touch it—that person. I just knelt there next to the firefighter and quietly watched him as he gently slid his hands under the remains and lifted them into his arms. Then he placed them into the body bag I was holding open. I zipped it up and handed it to the next guy in the line. I watched the bag as it was handed down the line until it disappeared into the back of an ambulance. I carried that image with me as I left the pile that day and headed back home.

The destruction in the twin towers, the damage caused to surrounding buildings, and the body count, which figured to be, in the words of Rudy Giuliani, "more than we can bear," made me more pissed off than I'd ever been in my life. All Americans know exactly how I felt, because they felt the same way.

The pictures you saw on TV couldn't capture the atmosphere at Ground Zero. The smell of human remains mixed with concrete, steel, and plaster was unbearable. The more carnage I saw, the more I wanted to strike back at the murderers who were responsible for this.

I knew about Osama bin Laden and his murderous ideology long before 9/11, in part through my work in Mr. Morgenthau's office. Most Americans were unaware that Osama bin Laden had been indicted in Manhattan for ordering terrorist attacks on American targets in the 1990s. Not surprisingly, the indictment that was handed down on November 5, 1998, alleged bin Laden and Al-Qaeda had engaged in a long-term conspiracy to attack

U.S. facilities overseas and to kill American citizens. In indicting bin Laden, the grand jurors found evidence that he and Al-Qaeda were attempting to obtain components to nuclear weapons and had made efforts to produce chemical weapons as far back as 1993. Contrary to a great deal of public opinion today, this same federal grand jury also found evidence that Al-Qaeda had forged an alliance with the government of Iran and reached an agreement to work cooperatively with Saddam Hussein himself, particularly in regard to weapons development.

Osama bin Laden and Al-Qaeda had been trying to provoke a war with the United States for years, and now he had one. He had joined a list of despots who made the mistake of thinking that America was too soft and too unprepared for war.

When a German U-boat sank the *Lusitania* on May 7, 1915, prior to our entry into World War I, and when the Japanese fleet attacked Pearl Harbor on December 7, 1941, the enemy hit us first and hit us hard. In both of those wars, like on 9/11, we lost the first battle and suffered a bitter defeat. But the enemy had underestimated our resolve, and lived to regret their actions.

As I went to bed that night, there was no question in my mind that what happened at the World Trade Center was not only an act of mass murder. It was an act of war, a war that had started with attacks as far back as 1998 in Africa and one that would not go away with mere indictments and criminal trials. It was time to take the gloves off.

THE FOLLOWING DAY I was assigned to work on the northwest portion of the site. A bridge connecting the Trade Center to the World Financial Center, across West Street, had collapsed, and I was asked to search the area for human remains. I was working with a firefighter who, at one point, said he saw a corpse in the twisted wreckage below us. We both tied ropes around our waists and climbed down the side of the pile.

I wound up landing near the body—if you want to call it that. I could see the torso and shoulder area that made up most of the remains. Although there was no head, attached to the top of this mangled torso and shoulder was a small patch of skin that was once a scalp. They looked to be the remains of a man. From what I could see of the very small patch still clinging to the scalp, he had straight, black hair. For some reason, I am not exactly sure why, it made me think he was Asian.

His left hand was detached but lying next to the torso. I noticed that he wore no wedding ring. It's odd, I know, but I said to myself, "Good. Maybe he wasn't married. That way he has no wife, no children who were waiting for him to come home on Tuesday evening." Of course, he might have been married, and he certainly might have had children. I was just trying to find some way to make myself feel a little better. But really, that didn't matter. What mattered was his life—two mornings earlier, he had been one of us. He had a life, he had friends and relatives, he loved and was loved in return. Now he lay where the crumbling twin towers had deposited him when men who claimed to be serving their god flew an airplane into his building.

I went to pick him up gently, and as I did, his liver and intestines spilled out onto my right forearm. Horrified, I immediately pulled my arm away. The firefighter with me asked, "Hey, can you handle this?" I looked at him, took a deep breath to gather myself, and nodded my head up and down. "Yeah," I said.

I picked up the torso and remaining shoulder and placed them in the body bag that had been lowered down. I then picked up his hand. After that I placed a foot that was lying nearby in the bag. I looked around to see if I was missing anything else before I left. Something caught my eye. It looked like bones attached at a main joint. At first I thought it was the skeletal remains of his other hand. I heard a voice say, "It's his ribs." The firefighter I was working with startled me—I hadn't realized he was watching.

Torn muscles, tendons, and flesh still clung to the jutting bones. I returned my gaze to the bones I held in my hand and nodded quietly in recognition. I placed the last remaining pieces I could find into the half-empty bag and slowly zipped it up. We then lifted the remains out of the pit.

When I made my way back into the daylight, I decided I needed a break. I walked over to the World Financial Three building, where they had a kind of first-aid and makeshift sleep area. These aid stations began to spring up in several locations around the site so people could catch a little sleep or eat one of the premade ham sandwiches sitting out on the tables wrapped in plastic to keep them clean. I found a quiet spot on the end of one of the cots in the sleep area and sat there for forty-five or fifty minutes, staring straight ahead, thinking about that guy with the straight black hair and no wedding ring. I thought about how his family didn't even know his fate yet. I thought about how much they must miss him and how worried they must be about him. I thought about how hard it was going to be for them when they found out.

I wondered if his family was one of the thousands who posted pictures of their missing loved ones all over the city and on light posts and storefronts hoping to hear something—anything— about their fate. Did they check the hospitals like many people

did hoping to see if he was miraculously alive but just uncon-
scious and unable to communicate? Or did they know from the
first moments that he was gone forever? Did they, like many, re-
sign themselves early on to his fate when he didn't call and he
didn't come home, didn't walk through the door that night?

I really hoped that maybe, just maybe, by finding his body, I
had enabled a grieving family to gain some closure, some peace.
I really wanted to believe that something I did down there would
amount to some good. It just didn't seem like there was anything
good that would come of all this. Maybe it helped. I don't know.
After a little while, I stood up and walked back out onto the pile.

EVERY NIGHT WHEN I returned from the site, I called home to
my parents to let them know I was okay. And every night, it
seemed, I found out about friends whose lives had been lost or
altered forever on that bright September morning. You couldn't
live in New York or New Jersey and not know somebody who
would never be the same after 9/11. It seemed like someone from
every part of my life had either been killed or lost a close family
member. It seemed liked no one escaped the loss.

Sean Lynch worked at the investment firm of Cantor Fitzger-
ald, which lost hundreds of employees on 9/11. I had known
Sean for ten years, through a mutual friend, Dave Murphy. A
couple of times a month, I'd meet up with "Lynchy" and "Murph"
and another friend of ours, Tom Kelleher, for beers after work.
Lynchy was a single guy and a real ladies' man. He was young,
athletic, with blond hair and a movie-star smile. Throw in a little
Irish charm and a level of self-confidence that was unaffected by
female rejection and you had a winning combination. He grew

up in Lynnfield, Massachusetts, and he was a graduate of Boston College.

Lynchy, Murph, Tom, and I had a lot of fun together running around the streets of Manhattan till all hours of the night in our late twenties. When I heard that Lynchy was dead, I thought about the last time I'd seen him, just a few days earlier, over beers. We hadn't seen each other in a while, so when he arrived, Lynchy came up to me and punched me in the chest—it was his way of saying hello. He usually followed it with a big laugh and a "Hey, McGovs. How you doing?"

I'd been putting in some long hours at work and was pretty grumpy. Lynchy's punch didn't hurt, but I just wasn't in the mood. "C'mon, Lynchy," I said. "Cut the crap!"

When I heard he was dead, all I could think about was how mad I'd been at him that night—the last night I saw him. Now he was gone. I was comforted by the fact that we were able to laugh about it before the night ended, but I still couldn't forgive myself for making such a big deal over such a petty little thing.

Bill Pohlmann was an assistant deputy commissioner for the New York State Department of Taxation and Finance, although I knew him as a lieutenant colonel in my first Army reserve unit. He was a kind and scholarly man who made you wish you had him as your grandfather.

On September 11, he was in his office on the eighty-seventh floor of the south tower when the first plane hit the north tower. He, like many of his colleagues, remained in their offices by choice or because they were told that leaving the building would only cause problems for the firefighters and emergency relief personnel arriving at the scene. Pohlman was last seen drinking coffee in a break room with two of his colleagues when one was called away. The colleague who left went to meet his wife, who also worked in the building. They had agreed after the first terrorist attack on the towers in 1993 that if it ever happened again, they would find each other and leave the building together. That's what they did.

Bill Pohlmann, fifty-six years old, married with grown children, remained in his place. I can only imagine the horror he must have felt when he saw United Airlines Flight 175 bearing down on his building—if he even knew at all.

Then there was Nellie Anne Casey. She was a beautiful and friendly thirty-two-year-old merchandise planning manager for TJX Cos for eight years before deciding to have a baby. She and her husband, Mike, had also gone to Holy Cross College in the late 1980s. On September 11, 2001, Nellie and Mike were still basking in the joy of their newborn baby girl, Riley, who had arrived in this world only a few months earlier.

TJX is an off-price retailer of apparel and home fashions and Nellie had recently returned to work after giving birth to Riley. On the morning of September 11, she was scheduled to fly from Boston to Los Angeles on business. She backed out of the driveway to her home in Wellesley, Massachusetts, and waved to her husband, who was holding their beautiful daughter. Nellie was leaving her newborn for the first time.

Nellie boarded American Airlines Flight 11 at Logan International Airport. Just before 9 that morning, American Airlines Flight 11 crashed into the north tower of the World Trade Center.

The families of Sean Lynch, Bill Pohlman, and Nellie Casey will never fully recover from the loss they suffered that day. I can only imagine the pain they felt and still feel from losing a loved one in such a calculated and brutal manner. My prayers are with them always. Although I had several family members who worked in lower Manhattan, my family was spared the loss felt by the Lynch, Pohlman, and Casey families.

My brother, Mike, worked in the Deutsche Bank building located directly across the street from the south tower in their offices at 130 Liberty Street. He was a manager in the finance department for Deutsche Bank. He had been with them for little over a year and had only recently been transferred to lower Manhattan from their midtown office. Mike is probably my closest sibling. We slept in the same room growing up and played on a lot of the same sports teams. He is an incredibly intelligent, athletic, and funny guy. He is also as kind a human being as you are ever going to meet.

Mike and his wife, Kristy, had just had their first child, Hunter, on August 27. After taking about a week off, he returned to the office on September 10. Not surprisingly, Mike had been late getting started on the morning of September 11 because of his newborn baby. Mike was standing on the dock in Hoboken across the Hudson River in New Jersey. The Hoboken Ferry left the dock each morning carrying commuters to their offices and other work places all over Manhattan. That is where he was when he learned that the first plane hit the north tower.

As he stood there in the bright morning sun watching smoke rising from the north tower, he noticed an airplane that seemed too big in the sky flying unusually low for that area. He didn't think anything of it at first. He too thought the plane that hit the north tower was a relatively small one and that it was an accident. Then he saw this jetliner turn hard left and, only moments later, bury itself in the south tower. "Oh my God!" he thought to himself. He was in shock. His employees were in the big black building that the second plane just flew directly over on its way into the south tower.

Mike ran over to the ferry boat that was just pulling into the dock. He had to get into the city and to his office, he thought, so he could check on all of his people. The ferry was already filled to capacity with people fleeing the now besieged city. As he attempted to board, the ferry driver yelled, "Hey buddy, where the hell you think you're going?" Mike looked back at him and yelled, "I got to get over to Manhattan. I have to get to my office." The heavy-set ferry driver with the black mustache and a no-nonsense delivery stopped him in his tracks. "Buddy, Manhattan is closed." Mike stopped pushing his way through the crowd and just stared back at the ferry driver. He couldn't believe his ears—this was like no other day.

My brother-in-law, Peter Hill, worked for J. P. Morgan at their offices located on 60 Wall Street just a few blocks from the south tower. Earlier that morning, Pete had made his way to work like he usually did taking the commuter Path Train from Hoboken directly into the World Trade Center. He emerged and walked to his office unaware of the approaching danger. He was a managing director for J. P. Morgan's municipal finance department and he was in charge of approximately one hundred people. After the first plane hit the north tower, he, like so many others, found himself waiting, watching, and wondering what to do about the horrible tragedy that was unfolding before his eyes. Pete was staring out his office window looking at the burning north tower when he too saw what appeared to be another airplane flying incredibly low and heading south—away from the towers. This plane was just off of the tip of Manhattan Island when he noticed it start to make a long, banking left turn and begin heading back north toward the city. In disbelief, he watched as the plane suddenly increased its air speed and tipped its wings slightly as it plowed headlong into the south tower.

Why do some people live while others die? Why was my family spared when other families were not. Why does God allow good people to be taken from us so early? These are some of the hardest questions any of us will ever try to answer. I can only say that I believe God calls each one of us home at our own special time. That each one of us has a good and decent purpose in this life and that God gives us enough time to fulfill that purpose before he calls us to our final rest.

I don't presume to know the full purpose for which God gave us Sean Lynch, Bill Pohlman, and Nellie Casey but I think I know a few of them. I knew Sean to be a good and caring son, a trusting brother, and an incredibly loving uncle. He was also a good friend to some jerk who got mad at him the last time he saw him. Bill Pohlman was a loyal husband and proud father. He was also a warm and encouraging superior officer to a young inexperienced Army First Lieutenant who could barely find his way around a courtroom. And Nellie Casey was a wonderful wife and the loving mother of a beautiful little girl. What greater purpose could one ask for?

I lost friends that morning. Others lost husbands, wives, sons and daughters. I can't imagine that kind of grief, that kind of loss.

I grieved for my friends, and for all those who lost loved ones. But grief wasn't enough. I wanted revenge. The people responsible for all this loss, all this pain, had to be wiped out before they did it again. My country, I knew, could not stand by and call this carnage a "tragedy." Yes, it was tragic, all right. Tragic in the way Pearl Harbor was tragic.

In other words, it was more than just a tragedy. It was an act of war. And it demanded a warlike response.

I RETURNED TO Ground Zero each day to continue digging. On Friday, September 14, I was walking back with some firefighters and construction workers to the pile after taking a break when we came across some yellow police tape blocking our path. Was the area unsafe? I asked some of the other workers nearby what was going on. One guy told me that no one could pass through right then because President Bush was on his way to the site. Security personnel were basically creating a path for the president and his party to follow.

I was glad to hear that the president was coming because, frankly, some of the volunteers at the site were beginning to wonder if he was going to show up at all. We all heard the reports that it might be too dangerous for the president to travel to New York City so soon after the attack. The huge pile of debris was very unstable and the site was actually still burning in some areas. There was also concern that there might be another terrorist attack. Based on these circumstances, the Secret Service had advised President Bush to stay in Washington, but he refused.

President Bush knew he needed to get to Ground Zero and see for himself the destruction inflicted upon his fellow citizens. In the ruins of the World Trade Center, in a piece of Manhattan instantly turned into sacred ground, those of us who saw the carnage firsthand believed that our commander in chief ought to share our outrage.

As we stood there wondering if we were even going to get a glimpse of the president, someone in the advance team approached me and some guys standing with me. "Would you guys like to meet the President?" he asked. "Sure," we replied.

We were escorted under the yellow police tape and asked to stand in a line near the remains of 7 World Trade Center. I stood there with some construction workers and a police officer. We said nothing to one another. We didn't know one another and probably never would, but we were now about to experience something that none of us would ever forget. That seemed to be happening a lot the past few days.

After a few minutes, we saw the president coming toward us in his motorcade. They pulled up and the president, Mayor Giuliani, and Governor George Pataki climbed out of a big black Suburban. Senators Hillary Clinton and Charles Schumer arrived a few minutes later. They all looked somber and deeply moved. The president was dressed in dark slacks and a gray bomber jacket, not the usual suit and tie. His face was taut, and he seemed older than he looked on television. He shook the hands of a few firefighters, police officers, and construction workers who were standing across the street from us. Then he made his way over to our side.

When the president approached me, I saluted him as any soldier should when approached by the commander in chief. I was also the only military person there, so it seemed like the thing to do. He saluted me back. No smile, no twinkle in his blue eyes. I saw the face of a man who was determined to right a horrible wrong.

We gripped each other's hand and he looked me in the eye and thanked me for helping. I thanked him for coming, but then, for some reason, I didn't stop with that. I blurted out, "We're ready, sir." I don't know why I said that, and in retrospect, it was a crazy thing to say. Here I was, a reservist—and a JAG officer, not a combat soldier. Who the heck was I to tell the president of the United States that "we" were ready?

But that's how I felt. I wanted him to know that his military was up to the task. I had been in the Army Reserve since 1997, and that allowed me to see just how good our armed services are. But I wasn't a combat soldier. I was too old for that. I joined the Reserves after my NFL career ended, in part because I wanted to remain part of a team, but mostly because I love my country and wanted to serve. My father served as a Marine. My grandfather served. I wanted to serve too.

It was time for me to do my part. That's how I'd felt as a twenty-nine-year-old law student when I signed up. That's how I felt at Ground Zero in the presence of my commander in chief. And that's how I still feel now.

Still, I wasn't regular Army, and I'd never heard a shot fired in anger. Yes, I had been part of a war-game exercise about a year before 9/11, and I served for a few months in South Korea with the Special Operations Command there. But that didn't make me a professional, frontline soldier. It just made me what I was—a reservist who was proud to serve alongside some real soldiers in the regular Army.

So when I said, "We're ready, sir," to the president, I was awkwardly trying to let him know that I had seen these great men and women in action and I knew what they were capable of. I knew they were up to the task of capturing and killing the men who were responsible for September 11 and for protecting us from future attacks. I knew it in every fiber in my body—I knew it my bones—and I just wanted him to know it, too.

At first the president just nodded silently and moved on down the line, but after shaking a few other hands, he stopped, and then walked back over to me. I was startled, but I remembered to return to the position of attention as he approached. What was he doing? Did I say something wrong? The president then put his hand on my left shoulder and looked me right in the eye. "I know you're ready," he said. "And we're going to hit more than just dirt this time, too!"

Of course, I knew what he was talking about—the failed attempt to take out bin Laden in 1998, when our cruise missiles hit nothing but dirt in Afghanistan. He had said exactly what I was feeling at that very moment—what I think most Americans were feeling. We had been hit hard and now it was time to hit back.

The president then surveyed the destruction of 7 World Trade Center with Mayor Giuliani and Governor Pataki. A few minutes later, he and his party returned to their motorcade. The cars passed near where I was standing, and as the president passed, I saluted the motorcade. I could see him inside the car. He returned my salute. By this time, a huge crowd of rescuers was gathered at the far end of the street—hundreds of people held back by just police tape and wooden barricades that outlined a path just wide enough for the motorcade to pass through on its way to the next destination. As the president's Suburban disappeared into the throngs of people gathered to see him—pumping their fists and cheering—I couldn't help but feel an incredible sense of patriotism. As I slowly followed up the street on my way back to the pile, I was struck by the sound of the crowd chanting "USA! USA!"

A few minutes later, Bush visited another work party just east of where I was. That's when he captured the world's attention by throwing his arm over a retired firefighter, grabbing a bullhorn, and vowing that the people who knocked down the World Trade Center would soon be hearing from us. I didn't see that famous scene unfold firsthand, but when I saw it on TV, I let out a cheer. "Damn right!" I said out loud. Those bastards would pay for what they did.

And like most Americans who heard the president's promise that day, I wanted those bastards to hear from me, too.

THE DAY AFTER the president's visit to Ground Zero, I was told, gently, that my services were no longer needed. Command structures were now in place and the recovery effort would be more formal. Those of us who'd come individually or in groups of two or three were thanked and sent on our way.

But September 11 and the days that followed had changed me forever. I wanted to be a part of whatever the commander in chief and his aides were planning. I wanted to do whatever I could to avenge the horror I saw at Ground Zero, to avenge the crime committed against my country and against my friends.

On Monday, I returned to work in the Manhattan D.A.'s office and called the headquarters of my reserve unit, a civil affairs battalion based in Connecticut.

"Are we mobilizing," I asked. I was fired up and ready to go. I expected to hear that we were getting ready to move out.

"We'll get back to you on that," came the reply.

So I waited. Over the next few weeks, as the shock wore off and as friends buried their dead, our work in the D.A.'s office took an unexpected turn. Before 9/11, I was helping to prosecute drug cases. Some pretty basic stuff. But now drug cases had a more urgent meaning. There was ample evidence that a lot of drug organizations were tangentially related to terrorist groups or run by people known to have ties to terrorists. Some so-called legitimate businesses that were really fronts for drug operations were used to launder money for terrorist groups or those affiliated with them. In turn, these groups and individuals would return the favor.

It was a match made in hell, but by focusing our drug investigations on these gangs, we hoped we might be able to do our part in this newly emerging war front. That, for the moment, satisfied my urge to do something to help my country.

All the while, I was hoping to do more. I loved working for Mr. Morgenthau, one of the greatest district attorneys in American history. I loved the work I was doing. But after 9/11, I wanted to put on a uniform and do whatever I could to get the terrorists out there who were working day and night to destroy my country. Finally, I heard the Army was looking for some JAGs to mobilize and go to Fort Bragg in North Carolina, home of the Airborne and Special Operations Forces. It seemed like the perfect place to go. These troops were bound to be the frontline soldiers of our new war.

I was curious about what kind of work I'd be doing at Bragg. Would I be helping with targeting decisions or the laws related to the treatment of prisoners? Maybe it was more war gaming, like I had done already?

"They want you to work at the tax center," some guy told me.

"The tax center?" I replied. I must have heard wrong.

"Yeah, the tax center," came the reply. "The work involves advising other soldiers about their tax returns. They also want you to advise on financial matters, review contracts, and do some general legal work related to paternity suits and divorces."

It wasn't the kind of work I wanted to do. It wasn't the kind of work I imagined doing when I was working the pile at Ground Zero. However, I knew it would be a foot in the door—after paying my dues in the tax center, I'd get the chance to deploy overseas. That would be only a matter of time.

I asked for a leave of absence from the D.A.'s office. It was a hard thing to do, because you don't walk away easily from a legend like Robert Morgenthau. I was happy with the work I was doing, and was learning how to be a first-rate prosecutor.

Still, my country was calling, and I had to answer. Mr. Morgenthau graciously granted me a leave, and I arrived at Fort Bragg in January of 2002.

Even as I helped soldiers with legal and financial issues, I raised my hand every time some unit here or there needed a JAG overseas. And every time I did, someone would politely say, "Thanks, but no thanks." I figured they weren't planning to send the reservists right away, so I just needed to keep doing my job and wait for my turn. That's where my NFL experience came in handy. I was used to sitting on the bench.

Then in November of that year, my turn finally came. I was told I would be deploying to Afghanistan with four other JAG officers as a part of the second rotation for the Combined Joint Task Force 180. As a JAG in a combat zone, I'd be responsible for giving legal advice to officers planning major offensives against our terrorist enemies. Not the same as actually killing them, but better than being on the bench.

On November 3, 2002, I boarded a C-17 airplane at Pope Air Force Base and began my journey to Afghanistan.

A year had passed since the attacks on September 11, but I was finally getting my chance to do something. I knew it wouldn't be kicking in doors or throwing hand grenades. I was thirty-six years old and a lawyer. I was not going over there to use my muscle as I'd done when I was playing football. Now I had to use my mind to make a difference.

And making a difference was all I wanted to do.

CHAPTER TWO

★ ★ ★

Our Defining Moment—
"If there must be trouble let it be in my day,
that my child may have peace."—*Thomas Paine*

WHEN I WAS A FOOTBALL PLAYER, THE MEDIA DIDN'T exactly crowd around my locker. I was a linebacker, after all. I made a few good plays now and again, but ultimately, I was just another linebacker, not a star running back or a flashy wide receiver or, God forbid, a quarterback. I just went out and did my job and hoped that it was good enough.

So I don't want you to think I've written this book to bring attention to myself as a soldier or a football player. I'm not a hero—but I've seen plenty of them in Iraq and Afghanistan. I'm too old to be jumping out of helicopters, but I've met people who do it all the time. I didn't risk my life in major combat operations, but I was in a command center monitoring the actions of our brave men and women in the field and offering them real-time guidance in the rules of engagement.

I am merely a witness to their incredible bravery. I am a messenger carrying their story to you. For me, the war on terror isn't something I've heard about on television. It's not something I read about in the newspapers. It's something I've lived through, it's something I've seen firsthand.

It's something I believe in. And it's something I want to share with anyone who'll listen—and, especially, with those who refuse to listen.

Throughout my life, I've been lucky enough to cross paths with inspirational men and women whose names you'll never know, whose work gets done out of sight of the global media, whose values represent all that we wish for in our country. I'm talking about the magnificent men and women I've had the honor to serve with in the United States military and the brave NYPD undercover cops I worked within the D.A.'s office. I'm talking about teachers who inspired students to develop the minds God gave them, about priests and football coaches who preached and lived the gospel of service. I'm talking about the courageous firefighters who showed me how to find the strength I needed to sustain myself at Ground Zero. I'm talking about our parents, brothers, sisters, family, and friends who inspire us by their devotion, personal sacrifice, and undying loyalty to the ones they love—us. These are the people who deserve our praise and admiration. They're the people the media ought to be talking about. These are the people whose stories you ought to know. Why you don't is a question I can't begin to answer.

Or maybe I can. As a young boy growing up in New Jersey, as an NFL linebacker, as a prosecutor in Manhattan, and as an Army officer in Iraq and Afghanistan, I have had the rare privilege and opportunity to observe these unsung heroes who walk among us every day. I have seen them in schools, on playing fields, on crime-ridden city streets, and in hostile foreign lands and I have never ceased to be amazed by their professionalism, courage, and dedication.

These unique and sometimes unlikely heroes come from many different walks of life, but the common thread is that they each embody qualities that truly deserve our admiration and respect. By honoring and emulating Americans who possess these very best qualities of humankind, we will instill those same qualities in future generations.

This book is my opportunity to honor these great people. I only hope that their stories will have the same impact on you as they have had on me. They truly are incredible examples of how to live ordinary lives in extraordinary ways.

I'VE ALSO WRITTEN this book because I believe we live in a pivotal moment in our nation's history. We are currently engaged in a desperate struggle against forces of hate and repression all around the world. This is a struggle that will, most likely, last for years or even decades to come and it is one we must win or risk losing everything we've gained as a nation and a civilization. As I write these pages, the focus of this great struggle is our ongoing military operations in Iraq and Afghanistan. I feel passionately that Americans simply don't realize the good work being done in their name in those two countries. I saw it firsthand, and now I want to tell you about it.

I returned home from my tours in Iraq and Afghanistan convinced that Americans need to know that we're doing the

right thing in both of those countries, and that the war that terrorists have declared on us has only just begun. It will not be
limited to Iraq and Afghanistan, for even as I write, Iran and
Syria are carrying on a proxy war of terror against Israel in
Lebanon and Gaza. In writing this book, I'm speaking only for
myself. But, indirectly, I hope to serve as an advocate for the
troops I've met overseas and at home, men and women whose
motives are the same as those brave, aging former soldiers we
salute as part of "the greatest generation."

Why don't we cherish today's soldiers as we did during World
War II? Take a look at some of those old newsreels from the
mid-1940s—the media really understood and appreciated GIs in
a way they don't today. I think some of us are just scared by
what's going on in the world today, and I understand that. Like
I said, I'm no hero. I get scared. I was scared working that pile at
Ground Zero. And I was scared in Afghanistan and Iraq, too.
But we live in a dangerous world at a dangerous time. It's okay
to be afraid, as long as we don't give in to that fear, or make
stupid decisions based on that fear. We all need to hear the calm
voice of that brave firefighter at the bottom of a pit at Ground
Zero. "It's okay. Everything's going to be okay."

I believe that is true, because I believe we're doing the right
thing and that we are succeeding in the war against terrorism
and extremism in Iraq and Afghanistan.

NOT LONG AFTER I joined the Combined Joint Task Force 180
in Afghanistan, I was given a terrible, heartbreaking assignment.
Even though it involved a tragic incident, it revealed a positive
side of the war that you won't see on television.

On December 14, 2002, nine young boys were scavenging scrap metal on a mountainside used by U.S. Special Forces to train the Afghan Army in mortar fire. It was common to find young kids in the fields we used for training, because they often found stuff, like scrap metal, they could sell at their local marketplace. On this day, as usual, before the exercises began, troops went into the area and announced in English and in the native language for that area, Pashtun, that everybody ought to stay clear because firing was about to begin. Unfortunately, these kids chose to ignore the repeated warnings. The mortar shells started falling, and four of the nine boys were killed.

We set up an investigation immediately. We found that the troops at the range had followed all safety procedures, and that this tragedy could have been prevented only if the boys obeyed our instructions. But kids are the same all around the world. They didn't take the warnings seriously.

I was assigned to help direct our response, and was ordered to meet with members of our embassy staff to discuss the tragedy. I traveled to our embassy in Kabul with a soldier named James Merrill, a specialist. He was an incredibly hardworking and intelligent young man who had maturity and wisdom beyond his years and schooling. Simply put, Specialist Merrill could handle any type of mission, including one requiring immense diplomatic—and human—sensitivity.

During our convoy ride to Kabul from our air base in Bagram, Specialist Merrill and I discussed what we could do to show our sympathy to the four families who lost their boys. Merrill suggested that we fund a humanitarian effort in the village where the boys lived. That way, he said, perhaps some good might come of this terrible event.

After arriving in Kabul, our convoy made its way through that city's tightly packed streets to the embassy. I met with personnel there and passed along Specialist Merrill's suggestion. They approved it immediately.

A meeting was arranged between our party, the families of the children, and the elders for the village where the boys lived. They greeted our party respectfully and extended us the traditional offer of a cup of tea before discussing the tragedy. They were clearly upset, and told us that even when no one was at fault, their customs and traditions required that the parties involved express an appropriate level of sorrow. I expressed my sincere condolences to the elders and the families, and then I assured them that the United States would do all we could to properly remember and honor the four fallen boys. By the time the meeting ended, we all agreed to repair and restore the local school in memory of the four boys. The project took several months, but when the day came to dedicate the rebuilt facility, I was unable to attend. I sent Specialist Merrill in my place. That only made sense—it had been his idea in the first place.

I asked this young soldier to offer our government's sympathy to the families of the boys, knowing they would be in attendance. I knew Specialist Merrill could handle this very delicate assignment with great sensitivity. My only regret was that I couldn't attend myself. And after hearing Merrill's account of the ceremony, I regretted my absence even more.

After Specialist Merrill expressed our sorrow to the families, one of the fathers who lost a son rose to speak. The crowd sat there silently, as you might imagine. With tears running down his cheeks, this grieving father spoke of the long years of war his country had known. He talked about the cruelty of the Taliban and of their guests, Al-Qaeda. His voice was barely more than a whisper, and his fellow villagers had to strain to hear him.

"All my life, my country has only known war," he said. "Then the Americans came and we now know peace. I may have lost a son, but it is the price I have to pay for having peace in my country." By the time he finished speaking, there wasn't a dry eye in the place, including Specialist Merrill's.

Our efforts in both Iraq and Afghanistan can be summed up in this one incredible story. We are not an invincible nation with the power to wave some magic wand and make all wrongs into rights again, and sometimes our presence or even our actions have unintended consequences that we all wish we could undo. But it is equally clear that the United States is a force for peace in the world. Our presence in both of these countries will, in the end, bring about a greater good for everybody, ourselves included.

I don't think enough Americans realize this, or appreciate it. I think it's time they did.

When I flew in helicopters over villages in both countries, I often saw little kids come running out of their homes to wave at us as we passed over. They were smiling and laughing as they waved, and we waved back.

Doesn't that tell you something? It should. Here's what it tells me: If the parents of those kids thought that Americans were evil, would they allow their children to go running out of the house to wave at our helicopters? Not a chance. If those kids thought we were the enemy, that we were coming for them, then they'd be cowering in their homes, waiting for us to pass. They'd be hiding from us. They'd be afraid.

Instead, these kids come out to welcome us and cheer us on.

That's the truth about what American military men and women are doing in Iraq and Afghanistan and it is all the proof I need to know that there is a bright and peaceful future just over the horizon for both of these countries.

I really believe that.

MY MOTHER ALWAYS said that I played with toy soldiers just a few years longer than most other kids. I suppose that was an early sign of my interest in the military. But I wasn't the only person in my large family—I have six brothers and two sisters— who respect and admire the armed services. My father was a Marine in the 1950s, which I always found pretty impressive. But my mother, well, she would have been one heck of a drill sergeant. Of course, how could she have been otherwise in a house full of enough kids to field a baseball team?

The night before I turned eighteen years old—this would have been 1984—I went out for a bit of a celebration with friends. I got home late, as you might have expected. But I had nothing to do the following morning—a Saturday morning—so I had planned to sleep in.

My mother had other ideas. At about six o'clock or so, she charged into my room and ripped off my blankets. She'd done that before, but this time I really wasn't ready for such a rude awakening. "Ma, what are you doing?" I managed to growl. My head was still on the pillow, and that's where I wanted it to stay for a few more hours.

"Get up and put on your clothes," she said. "You're eighteen years old, and you have to register for the draft today."

"Today? Why today? I have thirty days to register. C'mon, Ma." Oh, man, I was not a happy guy. My mother was right—back then, you had to register with Selective Service when you turned eighteen. But I was right, too: you had thirty days.

"Listen, no son of mine is going to be a slacker," she said, hovering over me and daring me to protest. Just like a drill sergeant.

"You know, Ma, a lot of mothers would be crying about this," I said with a smile on my face. "They'd be saying, 'Oh, son, I don't want you to be drafted. I don't want you to go to war.' But not you, Ma. You can't push me out the door fast enough."

I knew that line of reasoning wasn't going to work. Because I'd known for years that my mother wasn't like a lot of other mothers.

My dad is the same way, as you might expect of an ex-Marine. Actually, as the Marines say, there is no such thing as an ex-Marine. So put my father down as a Marine. He fought the Cold War in uniform during the 1950s and served in Greenland as well as over in Europe and at sea. I remember once, when I was a grammar school kid in the 1970s, I asked my dad if the United States could ever be friends with the Soviet Union. I suppose a lot of parents might have given some touchy-feely answer like, "Oh, yes, son. We are all the same, after all." Not my dad. "Nope," he said. "That'll never happen."

My mother, however, was even tougher. I suppose she had to be, with my father working long hours in the family trucking business he inherited from his father. She is not afraid to call wrong by its name. After September 11, 2001, I overheard her saying that we ought to turn those terrorist training camps into parking lots. That's why I love her. That's why, when I think about it, I'm very much my mother's son.

I guess you could say it runs in our family. My mother's dad, Edward Markey, was a cop in West New York, New Jersey, who did the right thing by turning down a chance to make a lot of money serving as a bagman for some bad cops and politicians in Hudson County, at the time one of the most corrupt counties in America. The way my mother tells the story, her father never considered the offer for a minute, and when he turned it down, his career went downhill. It's funny—he was considered untrustworthy because he was honest. I remember hearing stories about my mother's father from an early age, and always regretting that I never met the man. He died years before I was born. But somehow, through my mother's strong sense of right and wrong, I think I've come to know my grandfather. I'm certainly proud of him, and proud to be his grandson.

I'm also proud to say that I am my parents' son. They've made me what I am today—although I like to joke that I'm not always sure they want to take the credit for it! They taught me the determination I needed to make it to the NFL, they encouraged me to develop a strong sense of right and wrong, which made me a good prosecutor in civilian life as well as in the military, and they reminded me that I was obliged, as a person born with many blessings—being an American citizen, for one—to serve my fellow men and women whenever and wherever possible. And, on that last point, if I didn't get what my parents were preaching, the Jesuit priests who taught me at the College of the Holy Cross in Worcester, Massachusetts, and those at Fordham University Law School were delighted to reinforce the theme. And I'm glad they did.

★ ★ ★

I TELL YOU these stories to help you understand why I feel the way I do. I, like my mom, think we need to call wrong by its name, and it bothers me deeply when I hear so many negative news stories regarding our efforts in Iraq and Afghanistan. It seems like the only time you ever hear anything about Iraq and Afghanistan is when we receive the terrible news that a U.S. soldier has been killed or that the democratic process in either of these two countries has hit some snag. I do not want to minimize for a second the importance of reporting on the loss of each and every American soldier during a war. I know, like every soldier knows, that the loss of every single American life is a tragedy. I believe it is equally important, however, that the American people be completely informed about the progress of our military operations in those countries.

We are in the middle of a fierce national debate about the course of the war in Iraq and Afghanistan. Ultimately, we are going to have to decide as a nation and a people if we should continue our current military path or abandon these people and pull out. I believe it is imperative that the American people be allowed to make a fully informed and thoughtful decision. For that reason, I believe it is incumbent upon the news media who regularly comment on the progress of the war to provide both the positive and negative aspects of the conflict. Unfortunately, from much of the content and tone in the majority of reports I have heard on the war, it seems to me that the media have failed in this professional duty.

When questioned directly, I have heard news reporters and TV anchors attempt to justify the seeming disparity in coverage by blaming the demand for higher and higher ratings. They explain that the public's desire for juicy news stories trumps any call for balanced coverage regardless of the subject matter. In defending this industry practice, reporters often point to the daily news coverage of any big city in America as an example of their dilemma. This coverage is usually dominated by stories about rapes, robberies, and murders. The public, they claim, just doesn't want to see the positive stories. The phrase "If it bleeds, it leads" comes to mind.

However, this analogy is completely misplaced when talking about covering a war on foreign soil. We don't watch the nightly news coverage of crime-plagued cities with an eye toward abandoning them and relocating their entire populations somewhere else.

Whenever we are engaged in a war, we are simultaneously engaged in an important debate over the propriety of that war. Today is no different. We must decide if our military operations in Iraq and Afghanistan are worth continuing. The media today figure prominently in that debate—a debate that will direct the future course of our nation and impact the lives of millions of Americans. In light of this, I think it is imperative that the news media provide an unbiased and accurate picture of the war to the American people.

If the media were to do otherwise, it would only serve to remind us of another war that was hotly debated in this country and, arguably, wrongfully influenced by the news media. No, I am not referring to the Vietnam War. I am actually talking about the news coverage leading up to our entry into the Spanish American War. Reporters in that era stoked up the patriotic passions of millions of Americans in favor of war with Spain by printing highly inflammatory stories about the Spanish and the harsh treatment they administered to their Cuban protectorate. This one-sided media coverage, culminating in accusations that the Spanish government was behind the sinking of the U.S.S. *Maine* while it was moored in a Cuban harbor, led to our entry into that war and it is now widely recognized as a shameful blemish on the otherwise proud history of journalism in America.

YOU HAVE THE right to know all the facts. And I believe if you know all the facts, you will come to agree that we should be in Iraq and Afghanistan and we will succeed there if we just have the courage to see this thing through to victory.

Although our current struggle is being fought on many fronts and in many locations around the world, it is the same basic conflict regardless of our theater of operations. Just like the Cold War, our current conflict is not a struggle over geography—it is a struggle between two competing ideologies. It is critically important that we view this struggle as our fathers and mothers saw the struggle with communism and as our grandfathers and grandmothers saw the struggle with fascism and Nazism. Today, like back then, the idea of freedom and democracy is once again at war with the ideology of hate and oppression.

We entered Afghanistan to defend ourselves against the terrorist organization that launched the September 11 attacks and the Taliban regime, which harbored them and gave them sanctuary. This sanctuary enabled Al-Qaeda to train and equip its members in preparation for attacks on the United States. Both of these illegitimate entities were responsible for the murders on 9/11, and our military action in Afghanistan was a legally and morally justified response.

Learning from the example of Afghanistan, we rightly concluded that any state that harbors a terrorist is as culpable as the terrorist himself. To conclude otherwise after seeing the carnage in New York, Washington, D.C., and Pennsylvania would be just plain irresponsible in my opinion. Like Afghanistan, our military action in Iraq was a justified attempt to defend ourselves against a regime that had connections to Osama bin Laden as far back as 1993 and was still harboring terrorists like Iman al-Zarqawi, Abu Nidal, and Abu Abbas . . . just like the Taliban had done for Osama bin Laden and Al-Qaeda. Given the horrible and costly lessons learned from our inaction prior to 9/11, it is inconceivable to me how we could allow Saddam Hussein to continue harboring these and other terrorists and just hope for the best.

In light of Saddam Hussein's refusal to let United Nations inspectors verify the presence or absence of chemical, biological, or nuclear materials, and his continued support of terrorists, we had no choice but to ensure he could not use WMD or provide safe harbor to those who would. As with the Taliban, we even gave Saddam the opportunity to step down from power peacefully. With all this evidence and the experience of September 11 still fresh in our collective memories, we really had no other logical choice.

I truly believe our decision to attack Iraq was an act of last resort. Inaction that appeared reasonable or practical prior to September 11 seems completely incomprehensible and reckless today. I am sure we would all agree that if we could go back in time and send U.S. military forces into Afghanistan in advance of the September 11 attacks, we could have stopped the most devastating surprise attack our country has ever seen and saved thousands of lives. I am sure we would also agree that if the nations of Western Europe had stood up to Hitler instead of trying to appease him, maybe twenty million Russians, six million Jews, and hundreds of thousands of U.S. soldiers would not have died in World War II. Using these examples from history as our guide, we now know a preemptive attack is justifiable, as, sometimes, it is the only way to save lives.

Can you even imagine if we had not acted against Saddam and another terrorist attack was launched where some or even all of the terrorists involved came from Iraq? What if they used chemical, biological, or nuclear materials that were stored in Iraq? The same people objecting to military intervention in Iraq today would be blaming the president for failing to protect us from a known and identifiable threat. In fact, those very same accusations were made in the weeks and months following the attacks of September 11, 2001, against both the Bush and Clinton administrations. Those critics still complain that our government failed to take the necessary preemptive action against a known rogue state like Afghanistan. Whether Saddam possessed the necessary weapons to inflict great harm on the United States in March of 2003 is largely irrelevant because he clearly had the intent. In a post–9/11 world, waiting until Saddam's military, chemical, biological, or nuclear capability matched his sinister intent was not a reasonable option.

MAKE NO MISTAKE about it, we are succeeding. Despite what the news reports say, our military and political efforts in both Iraq and Afghanistan are alive and doing well. It makes me think of the famous quip of Mark Twain, who said, "The reports of my death have been greatly exaggerated."

Afghanistan successfully drafted and enacted a constitution, elected a parliament and president, and rejoined the community of nations. Iraq is on this same sometimes rocky yet no less certain path to democracy. Iraq enacted a constitution, elected a parliament, and recently elected a president, two vice presidents, and a prime minister. The new democratically elected government of Iraq consists of members from every major religious faction in the country today. This newly formed government is a sure sign that true democracy is taking root in Iraq and that the Iraqi people, through their freely elected representatives, are well on their way to firmly establishing the rule of law in their country.

THESE THINGS, HOWEVER, take time and patience. In the months and years to come, there will be pitfalls and roadblocks on the path to democracy for both Iraq and Afghanistan. New conflicts may arise elsewhere in the world, or in other nations in the Middle East. But that does not mean we should hit the panic button. These bumps in the road are not unusual, nor do they spell disaster for democracy and peace in this area of the world.

We have seen other countries through this same journey. U.S. occupation forces were in Japan for approximately ten years after the end of hostilities in World War II. At that time, Japan was an extremely fanatical enemy who believed that their leader was actually a god. Can you think of any more difficult a challenge than enabling a society of this nature to embrace the concept of democracy? I am sure many critics of that day said it could not be done. Sound familiar? Well, today, Japan is one of the world's most stable and prosperous democracies. It is also one of our closest allies. The same holds true for Germany after World War II.

U.S. military forces have also remained in South Korea since the end of fighting in that country in 1953. We still have approximately thirty thousand troops stationed on or near the border between North and South Korea holding off a potential attack by North Korean forces. Does this mean South Korea has failed or that we are propping that government up? Of course not. The presence of our troops in South Korea has had the effect of making South Korea one of the strongest economies in the world. In comparison, the people of North Korea are starving to death at the hands of yet another ruthless dictator. Our continued presence in South Korea is a necessary reminder that the process to democracy is a slow one and that all free nations making this journey need help and assistance along the way.

These democratic success stories show us that what we are doing in Iraq and Afghanistan is not unique and that success is possible. In fact, the success of Japan, Germany, and South Korea shows us that the only real danger of failure for U.S. policy in the Middle East is if we heed the recent calls to pull our troops out and go home. Victory will only slip away from us if we lack the resolve to see these two emerging democracies succeed like their Korean, Japanese, and German counterparts.

THE THOUGHT THAT both Iraq and Afghanistan are failed or failing states because they are having difficulty forming a representative government does not account for the example of our own great experiment in nation building at home. The United States declared its independence from Great Britain in 1776. However, we were unable to enact a Constitution until 1789.

Nor do the incidents like the prosecution of a Muslim convert to Christianity in Afghanistan foretell a grim reception for Jeffersonian principles in the Middle East. We have also seen our share of injustices perpetrated against individual human rights. Remember that for the first ninety years of our democracy, we subjected vast segments of our population to forced slavery. The continued existence of slavery in our own country during its early formation was a critical challenge to the moral fiber of our democracy and it eventually had to be resolved by a huge and costly conflagration. Can you think of anything more unstable than this? Does that mean we are not a legitimate democracy? Does that mean we were not capable of handling democracy? Of course not.

The United States was not destroyed by our early divisions and today we are the best example of a true democracy the world has ever seen. The difficulties currently faced by Iraqis and Afghans will not destroy them, either. Iraq and Afghanistan are succeeding and it is our duty and responsibility to give them the time and assistance they need to do it. President Dwight Eisenhower stated in his first inaugural address that "history does not long entrust the care of freedom to the weak or the timid." We are at a time in history when we must stand up to the challenges that confront our nation and the safety of all freedom-loving people. Only by remaining loyal to our core values in the face of great danger will we be able to protect what our forefathers risked their lives to establish for us 230 years ago.

★ ★ ★

THE DEBATE OVER how we meet this challenge dominating our nation's discourse, and the outcome, will determine our nation's future.

I wrote this book because I want to have this debate and I want you to be fully informed before you decide what you think we should do in Iraq or anywhere else. I also want you to hear about the heroic men and women who are serving us every day far from the spotlights and cheering crowds. They are the true "all-Americans" for whom this book is named. Football players and other pro athletes are often great role models for our children, and when I was in the NFL I saw a lot of terrific examples of sports figures who truly exemplify the best of what America has to offer. But I want you to hear about the other heroes—the men and women who go about their day quietly and selflessly protecting us, teaching us, and inspiring us. I have had the honor to get to know many of them throughout my life and I want you to get to know them, too.

Chapter Three

* * *

Family, Faith, and Football—
Growing Up an Irish Catholic Kid in New Jersey

WHEN YOU'RE THE SEVENTH OF NINE CHILDREN, AS I was, you learn a few important lessons at a very early age. You quickly realize, the world doesn't revolve around you, which helps to explain why I find writing this memoir more than a little disconcerting.

You also learn that if this large enterprise called the McGovern family is going to get anything done, you have to cooperate. You can check your selfishness and your introspection at the door, thank you very much, because there are more important things that need to get done. These lessons certainly helped prepare me for a career in the military.

I know it's fashionable these days to complain about how bad your parents were, but I can't say that. Howard and Terry

McGovern, my dad and mom, were fantastic parents who built their lives around their seven boys and two girls. I'm happy to say that's still true, all these years later.

My parents were high school sweethearts growing up in West New York, which is, in fact, in New Jersey. Built on the heights overlooking the Hudson River and the West Side of Manhattan, West New York was a thriving little city during my parents' childhood, known throughout the world for its embroidery industry.

As I mentioned before, my mother's father was a police officer in West New York in the late 1930s. He died in 1963, three years before I was born, but I heard so much about him I feel as though I knew him, and I certainly am proud of him. I've often thought about how tempting that offer to become a bagman must have been for my grandfather. He wasn't getting rich walking a beat in West New York, and he had six mouths to feed at home, four of them children's. My grandfather wasn't being asked to do anything more than deliver money from one crooked official to the next, but he didn't do it. He said, "No!"

Of course, there was retribution. He was taken off his beat and relegated to some nowhere desk job deep in the bowels of city government. Although he eventually made his way back up to detective, his career in the department never went anywhere because he refused to play the game. Years later, he wound up leaving the force and running the welfare office in West New York. As the county "poor master," he provided help and assistance to people in need in Hudson County. My mom still recalls how my grandfather would often bring welfare recipients home with him to join his family for Thanksgiving, Christmas, or even Easter dinner. "They had nowhere else to go," he would say. So my grandfather made sure they weren't alone on the holidays. No one should be alone on the holidays.

I've always taken pride in these stories about my grandfather. Here's a guy who could have made a better living for his family if he did what a lot of other people were doing in Hudson County. But he refused, and he had to know that there would be consequences. He saw no alternative. He was a good cop and a good guy. He had children at home and he was going to make sure he raised them right. He didn't do it with long-winded sermons or meaningless gestures. He set the example. He led from the front.

There's more to the story, though. My grandfather had served with the 107th Artillery in the early 1930s. He was a sergeant back then and his job was to teach soldiers how to fire the howitzer cannon. During World War II, he was in his forties and a second lieutenant. He had two punctured eardrums courtesy of the polluted waters of the Hudson River and, I'm sure, from firing a lot of howitzers. He was also the father of four children.

Nevertheless, he tried to volunteer after the Japanese bombed Pearl Harbor. He wrote letters to the Army brass, to congressmen—even to President Franklin Roosevelt. Somebody always responded with a nice letter thanking him for his patriotism and telling him they'd get back to him if his services were ever needed. Of course, they never did.

I remember reading those letters as a young man and being so impressed by my grandfather's sense of duty and his determination to do whatever he could at a time when his country and his way of life were in danger. Thinking about him now, I like to think I am a lot like him. I never met the man, but I completely identify with him and what he was trying to do. I know exactly how he must have felt when people were putting him off—that's the reaction I got after 9/11, when I was trying to find somebody who would take me on as a full-time soldier. Like my grandfather, I knew I wasn't going to be in the trenches, but like him, I just wanted to do something for my country.

As a soldier, a cop, and a social worker, my grandfather dedicated his entire life to helping people and serving his country. If you ask me, that makes him a man of character and integrity. A man of service and sacrifice. He was a man I could be proud of. A man we all could be proud of.

Given how closely I identify with my mother's father, I guess it's no surprise that I consider myself to be very much my mother's son. I have a great relationship with my father, but I take after my mother.

She, more than anyone, made me who I am. I think like her. I laugh like her. I have faith and go to church because of her influence on my life. I am in awe of her strength and her devotion. People say you can see God in some people because of the way they live their lives. I see God in my mother every day.

Looking back on my childhood, I don't know how my mother did it. She had nine kids in a span of about eighteen years. Math isn't my strong point, but even I can figure this one out: she was giving birth about once every two years. And seven of those kids were boys. Can you imagine?

Childbirth became so routine that when my mother was getting ready to deliver one of my older siblings, my father drove her to the hospital, dropped her off, and went to work. What a different world it was back then! My dad and his two brothers owned a warehouse in New York City, where they shipped merchandise like children's clothing and books to all sorts of outlets on the East Coast.

My dad drove three hours every day from New Jersey to Brooklyn and back again while working long hours so he could feed his nine growing children and give them the life he wanted them to have. When I was very young, my mom figured out that I was bothered by my dad's absences. He left for work at around five o'clock in the morning and didn't come home until well after I was asleep. That was bad enough, but at around this time, he had been working on the weekends, too.

I hadn't seen him in a while and apparently I was showing signs that I missed him badly. My mom let my dad know how I was feeling. The following morning, and for many days afterward, he made sure to stop by my bed before he left and each evening when he got home to give me a hug and a kiss.

He may have been a tough Marine, but deep down he was one big softy. He eventually lost his "tough-guy" image completely when my sister Betsy accused him of being a nerd. In his defense, he confessed, "I am not a nerd. Although I may have nerdish tendencies."

You can't possibly explain to kids today what it was like for the eleven of us to pile into a station wagon with three rows of seats—no seat belts, of course—and drive a thousand miles to Florida, which we did. I remember my father behind the wheel, a big cigar in his mouth and his window wide open—thank God. The drive took over twenty hours and usually lasted two days. One thing you can be sure of: at any given moment during that ride, one or more of us was crying or complaining.

"Are we there yet?"

"How much longer till we get there?"

"Tell Dave to stop touching me!"

"Who ate all the brownies?"

"Pipe down back there! We haven't even left New Jersey yet!"

Running the McGovern household took a certain military precision—and discipline. Every morning my mother would do a kind of reveille to get us all up. We'd get a couple of chances, but if we weren't out of bed by my mom's third pass, she'd bring out a water pistol or a cold wet rag. That'll get your attention, which, of course, was the whole idea.

Getting the attention of your children becomes increasingly harder as the years go by. What terrified you at the age of six doesn't necessarily get the job done when you're twelve. So my mother had to change her tactics accordingly, if only to keep her sanity. One night when I was on the edge of adolescence, my friend Mark Casey slept over at our house. He, my brother Mike, and I shared a room. Talk about a recipe for disaster.

We were upstairs, and I was talking my head off while my parents had some neighbors over for dinner. That was mistake number one. My mother made a couple of trips upstairs to get us—mostly me—to shut up, but did I listen? Not a chance. Mistake number two. My mother then grabbed a broom handle and started banging on the dining-room ceiling, right below my bedroom. That didn't really do much to scare me, either. I actually thought it was pretty funny. So I kept goofing around and talking my head off. Mistake number three.

The next thing I knew, the bedroom door flew open. Standing in the door frame was the silhouette of Dirty Harry, disguised as my mother. And she was armed . . . armed with shoes. Lots and lots of shoes. I crouched in the far corner of the room, and now I was terrified. I barely blurted out a panic-stricken plea to God in heaven when she opened fire. Shoe after shoe—sneakers, wing tips, you name it, and she was heaving them in my direction. I tried to take cover, but there was no escape, no place to hide.

My mom kept me pinned in the corner dodging her patent-leather projectiles and praying for mercy. With each launch, she'd utter a single word, until she delivered her message: I! (shoe) TOLD! (shoe) YOU! (shoe) TO! (shoe) BE! (shoe) QUIET! (shoe)!

I was pretty scared, but my friend Mark was absolutely horrified. He took cover in a corner of the bedroom, trying to make himself as small a target as possible. My brother Mike was doing the same in another corner. But I was the only one in her crosshairs that evening. This was a side of "Mrs. M." that Mark had never seen before. Then again, neither had I. I'm just glad I lived to tell the tale.

Thankfully, my mother's aim wasn't very good. As the attack drew to an end because my mom was running out of ammo, I calculated that she had missed her intended target—me—entirely, although there were a few close calls. But just as I began to feel the satisfaction of a man who thinks he has escaped the hangman's noose, she fired one last round.

It clipped me in the elbow. It stung pretty bad, but luckily for me, my mother couldn't follow up the assault. There were no more shoes. After the barrage came to an end and I surveyed the damage, I assured myself that it was my mother who got the worst of it. She had just painted the room, and now there were scuff marks all over the walls. "That'll show her," I thought.

While my mother ruled the house with an iron fist and lousy

aim, my father played the role of provider and breadwinner. Again, that's not to say he had no influence over us, but he saw his role as keeping a roof over our heads and food on our table.

His own father was a classic American success story. As a kid growing up in the early 1900s on Thirty-ninth Street in Manhattan's Hell's Kitchen, my paternal grandfather, George McGovern, worked for a guy who delivered packages with a horse and buggy. This was at a time when most people couldn't afford one of those newfangled Model T automobiles being made by some guy named Henry Ford. So he made his rounds the old-fashioned way, which, for him, was the only way.

When the boss died, his widow quickly realized that she was not going to take up the reins in his place. They had no children of their own, so she gave the horse and buggy to my grandfather. It was 1914 and he was all of fourteen years old. He was also still in the fourth grade. Which meant, apparently, he wasn't much of a scholar, and he knew it. So he left school and started his own delivery business.

By the time he retired and passed the business to his three sons, including my father, G. T. McGovern Trucking and Warehousing was one of New Jersey's largest trucking companies.

As I was growing up, my father often told me that I was welcome to join him and my brothers in the family business. Again, I'm no math whiz, but this is another one even I could figure out. Being the seventh of nine children, would there really be anything for me to do? I figured the only thing left would be to have me account for the number of broomsticks in the cleaning-supply closet. So while I appreciated the offer, I knew I'd probably have to find some other line of work.

★　★　★

BY THE TIME I arrived in 1966, my parents had left the urban world of Hudson County for the suburban, almost rural charms of River Vale in Bergen County. When I was about four, we moved to Oradell, where most of my family still live and the town I consider my home.

My parents couldn't have picked a more pleasant place for their children to grow up. The town has grown over the years, and the surrounding area has been built up, but in the 1970s, it was like living in some small town in New England. For a while, ours was the only house on the block. It was a ten-room Colonial with brick face, aluminum siding, and plenty of yard space.

But our monopoly on Schirra Drive didn't last very long, because lots of families were leaving New Jersey's cities in the 1970s. Pretty soon my siblings and I had plenty of kids to play with and fight with. Their parents had left behind the old neighborhoods of their own childhoods, whether those neighborhoods were in New York City or in cities closer to home like West New York, Jersey City, and Paterson. In places like Oradell, these middle-class parents had their own homes and yards, and their kids had trees to climb and ball fields to play on. It was a great place to be a kid, and a parent.

It seemed like every family on the block was large and Catholic—churchgoing Catholics. To this day, I attend Mass every Sunday. Mass enables me to spend time each week in the presence of God and to thank him for all the blessings he has bestowed upon me and my family. But I certainly don't think that going to church makes me better than anybody else. In fact, the reason I worship God regularly is that I know I'm a sinner and shouldn't be allowed out without proper guidance. I've relied on that guidance every Sunday since childhood. My father said it best, "I don't go to church because I think I am better than everyone else. I go to church because I know I am not."

Most of the families in my neighborhood were either Irish or Italian. The Caseys lived next door and had seven children. Some other neighbors had eight and even ten kids—enough to field two basketball teams, which was just as well, because life for most kids in Oradell revolved around sports. Sure, we had a few hangouts like Smitty's Convenience Store in our little downtown, but for the most part, Memorial Field was the center of adolescent social life. We weren't always there for ball games—the town sponsored concerts and other activities at the field. But for the most part, when somebody told me, "Hey, meet us at Memorial," it meant we'd be playing some sport or other.

And that's how my parents wanted it. They didn't care what game we were playing, as along as we stayed out of trouble and weren't watching television. My father told us, "I don't ever want to come home and catch somebody in the house in the afternoon watching the boob tube."

That was a great rule, and it still is. But then again, we were smart enough to know that Dad never came home early in the afternoon, and if my mother was out, well, who would be the wiser if we flipped on some mindless TV show at three-thirty or four o'clock?

When I was about eight or nine, I got the courage to put that theory into practice. I got home from school; it was a nice day, but instead of going outside with my buddies, I flipped on Bugs

Bunny or some similar after-school cartoon. Life was good, until I heard a car pulling into the driveway. It was my father. My father never came home before six o'clock.

"Holy crap! What's he doing home?"

I was caught dead to rights. There was no escape, at least by conventional means. I turned off the TV, scurried to a room in the back of the house, opened a window, waited until I heard him opening the back door, and then I made my exit out the window into the yard. I walked around to the front of the house, went in, and pretended to be surprised when I saw my father. "Oh, hey, Dad," I said. "What are you doing home? I just got back from the Caseys' house. Yeah, we've been hanging out, playing ball all afternoon."

He must have believed me, because if he'd thought I was lying, well, that would've been worse than if he'd caught me in front of the TV. But whatever punishment he meted out, I know one thing: he would not have raised his voice. He was not a guy who yelled and screamed. His has a quiet kind of strength. I saw him really lose his temper only once, when I was a junior in high school and the proud owner of a brand-new driver's license. I borrowed his car, went to a party where I had a few beers, and drove home. He caught me, and he let me have it. And he was right.

With nine of us to nurture, love, and discipline, my parents needed to have rules and had to enforce them—the first part doesn't work without the second. So we learned early on that we were expected to be active, both the boys and the girls. We weren't pushed into any particular sport, just as long as we were playing or doing something constructive. But it soon became apparent that a pattern was forming. One by one, I watched my older brothers go off to become pretty good football players or golfers for

Bergen Catholic High School, which had one of New Jersey's top athletic programs, and then go on to play for Holy Cross.

I knew pretty quickly that I wasn't destined to make the PGA Tour like my brother Jim, who made it to the big time in 1993. When I was still a young kid, I went out to play a practice round that lasted only as long as it took for me to throw three clubs into a tree (they never came down—what goes up doesn't always come down, at least, not when you're talking about golf clubs). At that moment, I realized that any athletic future for me lay in blocking and tackling—not chipping and putting.

So I focused on football from an early age. When I turned ten, I had my first chance to play on the town's Pop Warner football team. I was pretty sure I knew exactly which position I wanted to play, so when my dad asked, I told him. "I want to play center," I said. When he asked why, I told him I wanted to play the same position as my older brother Jack, who was the starting center on the Holy Cross football team that year. I looked up to Jack and I wanted to be just like him.

However, I quickly realized something about the center position I hadn't thought of before the start of the season. When it's your job to snap the ball to the quarterback, you are completely vulnerable to the noseguard lined up across from you on every play. I soon found out that every time I snapped the ball, I was getting clobbered by a defensive lineman before I could even pick up my head to see who was doing it. "This stinks," I thought.

By my second season, I managed to become a fullback—a much better arrangement. Carrying the ball for touchdowns and cheers seemed like much more fun than picking dirt out of my teeth after every play.

Even though I was pretty sure football was my game, I still

knew I'd have to work hard to be as good as my brothers Jack, Bill, and Jim, all of whom distinguished themselves in high school. Jack and Bill went to Holy Cross on full athletic scholarships. Jim went to the University of Arkansas on a golf scholarship before turning pro, winning the 1993 Shell Houston Open and finishing fifth in the Masters that same year. My younger brothers also excelled in sports. Mike played football and golf for Lehigh and Dave led the University of Massachusetts Minutemen to the I-AA Yankee Conference championship as a freshman quarterback in 1990. I wanted to be able to look all of them in the eye someday knowing that I was as good as they were.

One of the most important men in town was a guy named Doug Parcells. He was in charge of Oradell's recreation department, which meant that he was pretty much a god to us kids. I got to know Doug, or Dougie, really well when I was growing up. If there was a game being played anywhere in Oradell, Dougie Parcells was there, either as an umpire or a referee or just as an interested spectator. Dougie was an incredibly funny and warm man who devoted his life to children. He maintained all the ball fields and made sure the Oradell sports train ran on time. Every kid who grew up in Oradell in the 1970s and 1980s knew and loved Dougie Parcells. If they built statues for people who made kids laugh and enjoy their childhood, there should be a huge one of Dougie Parcells right smack-dab in the middle of Memorial Field.

Dougie's older brother is Bill Parcells, who was a local legend even in the 1970s, long before he was a coach in the National Football League. Back then, Bill Parcells was a local kid who had played college football and was making a career as a college coach. For jocks like me and my brothers, that seemed like the coolest life imaginable. But I didn't know Coach Parcells at all back then—he was more than twenty years older than me and was well on his way to fame and fortune by the time I came of age in Oradell. It would take another fifteen years until our paths would cross.

MY MOTHER SAVED most of my report cards from Assumption Parochial Elementary School in Emerson, New Jersey. It's funny seeing them now—the consensus of my grammar school teachers was summed up in a single phrase, repeated in grade after grade: "Robbie talks too much in class." I guess I did. Check that—I know I did. And I still do.

Like a lot of my friends, I went to Catholic school even though the local public schools were some of the best in the state. For us, public school simply wasn't an option. My parents raised their children to believe in God and they wanted their kids to have the benefits of religious instruction from an early age. I guess this shouldn't come as a surprise, since my mother grew up in a deeply religious household.

Her brother, Earle Markey, is a Jesuit priest. He was an All-American basketball player for Holy Cross who was drafted by the Boston Celtics in 1954 but chose to enter the priesthood instead. Can you imagine that? I guess when the Big Man drafts you to play on His team, there is no renegotiating that contract. My mother told me that she always knew my uncle Earle was going to become a priest. She described for me how he would pretend to say Mass for them all in their living room when she was growing up. He would use the radiator for the altar and some white bread for the Eucharist. My mom served dutifully as the altar girl for these services. I guess that makes her kind of a trendsetter in that area, doesn't it?

My uncle Earle spent approximately ten years studying for ordination—the Jesuits don't make it easy on anybody—until he finally realized his lifelong dream of becoming a servant of God in 1963. Uncle Earle spent several years, from 1957 to 1960, in Ateneo de Zamboanga in the Philippines as a missionary and again in Ateneo de Manila from 1966 to 1970. He would travel to distant and isolated villages to bring spiritual guidance and comfort to those who needed it most. He also taught in schools and universities in the Philippines while still managing to squeeze in a few pickup games of basketball every now and then.

Upon returning from Asia, Father Earle served as principal of St. Peter's Preparatory High School in Jersey City until 1976, when he made his way back to Holy Cross. He has been ministering to and serving his fellow men and women on Mount St. James ever since.

Though we didn't know it at the time, the 1970s were kind of the last years of the golden age of Catholic education, at least in the Northeast. Schools were bursting at the seams. New schools, new wings, new gyms were being built all across New Jersey. And just like it's fashionable to portray parents as control freaks or brutal dictators, it's equally fashionable to deride Catholic education. Even if you're not Catholic, you've heard about the supposedly brutal nuns, the repressed priests and brothers, the creativity-killing principals who were more interested in order than in learning.

Well, again, I beg to differ. I received a marvelous education from grammar school to law school in Catholic institutions. My mother may have been the most influential person in my life, but the nuns, brothers, priests, and lay teachers who taught me from the time I was six to the time I was twenty-six certainly had a lot to do with making me who I am today.

I had wonderful teachers from the very beginning of my education. One of the most memorable was a Franciscan educator named Brother Christopher, who taught me in sixth grade. He seemed at the time to be about a hundred years old, although in reality he was probably half that. He lived the true spirit of the Franciscan order: he was kind, gentle, and deeply spiritual. There wasn't a materialistic bone in his body. He came into class every morning, picked up a piece of chalk, walked over to either the left or right corner of the blackboard, and wrote three letters: T R Y.

He never said anything, never drew any attention to this ritual. He just did it, and then moved on to the lesson of the day. I think he was waiting for one of us to ask him what this was all about, and finally somebody did toward the end of the year.

He had his answer ready, and I never forgot it. "That's the key to life," he said gently. Brother Christopher wasn't the kind of guy who gave bombastic sermons. That's what made his preaching so effective. "You have to try. No matter what you do in life, you have to try. Nothing will happen if you sit around waiting. And if you blame everybody else for what's going wrong in your life, if you constantly come up with excuses for your bad behavior or poor performance, you'll get what you deserve. But if you try, you will succeed. Not every time, but more often than not."

That was it. That's why he wrote those three letters on the blackboard every morning. And I never forgot that lesson. It was one of those moments early in life when you realize that you've just learned something you'll never forget. And I haven't.

There were other teachers like him: Sister Faye Marie, my

third-grade teacher, a sweet and patient woman whom we worshipped because she was so obviously a good person who cared about each one of us. Again, you don't hear much about people like Sister Marie, Brother Christopher, and my uncle Earle in the popular culture. Instead, you hear about tyrants and sadists, mostly from people who, frankly, hated their Catholic school experience. Some of these stories even come from people who actually never set foot in a Catholic school.

One of the sad things about Catholic elementary school, though, is that after eighth grade, people tend to go their separate ways after spending eight years together. Some kids go to public high school, others scatter to this Catholic high school or that one. For my part, I really didn't have a choice in the matter. The McGovern boys had a tradition: we went to Bergen Catholic. It was an all-boys high school founded in 1955 and it was less than a mile from my house. I guess I always knew that BC was my destiny, but I figured I'd tease my mom a little. I told her I was thinking about St. Joseph's and Don Bosco, which were two of Bergen Catholic's big rivals.

"Yeah, yeah, yeah," my mom replied. "You're going to Bergen Catholic."

That's how decisions got made in the McGovern house. And the system worked out pretty well.

THE ONLY UNPLEASANT memories I have from childhood have nothing to do with parents or teachers or even siblings. The general state of the world was pretty bad in the 1970s, and it was hard not to realize that, even if you were a kid. This was the era of gas-station lines, odd- and even-day rationing, government paralysis, inflation, scandal—it was just a rotten time.

I was fascinated by history and politics in grammar school, and still am. So I probably was a little more aware of these things than some of my buddies. I remember as president of my eighth-grade class putting up yellow ribbons during the Iran hostage crisis. I remember the long lines at the gas station and the general feeling that things seemed to be falling apart all around us.

I was listening to the radio one morning while brushing my teeth—it's a vivid memory—when a news announcer read a bulletin saying that an attempt to rescue the hostages in Iran had ended in failure. Helicopters crashed in the desert night, soldiers were dead, and the mission was aborted. I was crushed, and I never forgot that feeling. That's why I became a huge Ronald Reagan fan in 1980.

As far as I was concerned, everything seemed to be going wrong in the world until President Reagan came into office. During the seventies, it almost seemed like *patriotism* was a dirty word, and, in any case, there wasn't much going on that made you feel especially good about the state of things in America. Inflation and unemployment rates were in the double digits, interest rates were nearly 20 percent, and there was a progressive income-tax rate of 70 percent. Can you believe that? They even had a mechanism for tracking all these horrible figures. They called it the "Misery Index."

But President Reagan drastically lowered income-tax rates, which revitalized our floundering economy. His stewardship brought inflation down, and unemployment dropped as well. A 1990 Commerce Department study showed that U.S. manufacturing productivity tripled during the 1980s, and consequently, interest rates returned to manageable levels. All the while, government funding for things like health care and housing increased by 63 percent and 65 percent, respectively.

One of the many positive consequences of this newfound economic strength was an increase in American charitable contributions, which almost doubled during the Reagan years. Donations to charities went from $64.7 billion in 1980 to a record $102.3 billion in 1989. With Reagan, everything changed and it changed for the better.

I also remember thinking, "Yeah, we're not taking it on the chin anymore." Ronald Reagan broke the grip of the OPEC oil moguls and returned worldwide crude oil production to normal levels, which ended the oil crisis. Our American hostages in Iran returned safely, and we even liberated the tiny island of Grenada from communist oppression. How did he do all this? In part, because he returned our military to prominence by providing the necessary funding to properly train, equip, and field a fighting force our country could be proud of.

I never again want to feel the way we did in the 1970s, when we doubted our confidence at home and seemed helpless to influence events abroad. When we worried more about upsetting the "Arab street" than standing up for what we believe in. It seemed like in the 1970s, we always needed to apologize for our foreign policy. President Reagan didn't apologize for our foreign policy because he knew we didn't have to. He recognized the two simple truths about the world: every nation must and should stand up for its own rights and the safety of its people, and the United States is the world's best hope for freedom.

★ ★ ★

WHILE THE WORLD around me seemed to be going to the dogs, well, there was always football. I loved the game. There's no other way to describe it. I loved football—I loved the competition, I loved the contact, I loved the thought process that goes into every well-designed play on either side of the ball.

It went without saying that I'd play football at Bergen Catholic. My brothers already were football legends by the time I got there, and more than anything else, I was determined to live up to their legacy.

I remember my first day of practice for the freshman team. Now, I'm just a few weeks out of grammar school, and I'm still carrying around memories of gentle Brother Christopher and kind Sister Faye Marie. I'm still pretty naive. I'm lying on the ground on my back, stretching, and all of a sudden this figure is standing over me. The sun's behind him, and he's basically towering over me, so all I can see is this dark silhouette. But I know it's Coach Pete Blazer. He's got a cigarette in his hand—he always had a cigarette in his hand.

Now, I'm on my back, completely vulnerable, and the coach is standing over me. And he looks down at me and says, "McGovern, just because your brothers were All-Everything here doesn't mean you're shit to me."

All I could see was this giant hovering over me. "Yes, sir," I said. "I understand, sir. I don't even like my brothers, sir. I hardly even talk to them."

If I didn't get the point, my father summed it up pretty nicely. He took me aside before that first season and said, "You'd better be ready for football, because if you're not, the shit's gonna hit the fan." I guess he was sending me a message, but all I could think was: "Oh my God. My father said a curse word." I had never heard him say a curse word in his life.

Then I realized what he was saying. "This high school football is serious stuff," I thought.

I made the team my freshman year, and played a lot as a sophomore, mostly as an offensive tackle and a defensive end. I moved to outside linebacker for my junior year, which was fun, especially when I scored two touchdowns as a defensive player in a game against one of our big rivals, Hackensack High School.

But for the last game of the season, I was told to play middle linebacker. I wasn't out on the field two minutes when a light went on. I remember thinking, "Yeah, this is what I was meant to do." As a middle linebacker, I was involved in every play. I had a chance to make a tackle on every carry. When I was playing outside linebacker, if the other team ran a sweep in the other direction, away from me, I wasn't involved in the play. As a middle linebacker, my job was to pursue the ballcarrier. I loved it.

I was lucky enough to be playing for a great defensive coordinator, a guy named Joe Leverchio. He was one of those tough-but-fair coaches, and definitely old school. He spotted me once warming up for a game and wearing baseball batting gloves with the fingers cut off. I have no idea where I got this idea from—I probably saw some NFL guy on TV wearing them. If you look at NFL linemen and linebackers today, they all wear them. But at the time, they were pretty unusual, and Coach Leverchio wasn't much for unusual things.

"What the hell do you have on your hands?" he asked me.

"Well, they're my gloves, coach." I kind of thought they looked pretty cool.

"Get those things off your hands." Coach didn't think they were cool. I got rid of them. I loved him for stuff like that, because he had no patience for prima donnas, for any kind of crap. He made me into a linebacker by reminding me that it was my job to get dirty and make the play. The bloodier and dirtier you were, the more he liked you.

"You're either gonna get hit or you're gonna hit somebody, but either way you'd better be ready," he'd tell us. The message he sent was plain and simple. Be prepared and do your job. It's a lesson I still take with me wherever I go. It's a message every soldier has to keep in mind.

We had some pretty good teams during those years, but we lost in the state championship my junior and senior years. That just about killed me. My brothers, after all, not only were great players, but their teams were state champs. And mine were second best, which haunted me. I felt like I had failed. I had to make changes.

After my senior season, I knew I had to get serious about the next stage of my life. I wanted to go to college, and I wanted to play college football. I decided to skip the basketball season my senior year because I usually lost about ten pounds during the season, and at 215 pounds, I knew I couldn't afford to lose any weight.

Besides, I wasn't much for hoops anyway—I was the guy they put in late in the game to foul people. And to prove my point, during my first three years, we were just average. My senior year, with me in the grandstands and not on the court, the basketball team went to the state championship. I improved the team by not playing. It wouldn't be the last time.

I decided to use this free time during the basketball season to work out with my best friend and cocaptain on the football team, John O'Brien. We both desperately wanted to make it to the college level in football and we knew we had to devote 100 percent of our efforts to a training regimen if that was going to happen. Each summer during high school and even during our college years, O'B and I worked out together, pushing each other harder and harder in the gym, on the track, or doing agility drills. We were trying to reach our potential as athletes and we motivated each other to keep going when everyone else around us seemed to be running off to parties or hanging out at the Jersey shore.

O'B was a sought-after recruit our senior year for obvious reasons. He was six feet four inches and 235 pounds. Thinking of a future after sports, however, John wisely turned down numerous college scholarships from less academically inclined schools and accepted one from Villanova University. As an outside linebacker, O'B became a Yankee Conference standout and was named as the team's captain his senior year. More impressive is the fact that John graduated from Villanova in 1989 and went on to receive a master's degree as well as a law degree and is now a successful attorney in New Jersey.

By contrast, as my last months in high school began to wind down in the spring of 1985, I had a problem. Nobody was offering me a scholarship to play football, which meant that nobody wanted me. That wasn't in the plan, so I was getting worried. I knew I wasn't big enough to play at a I-A level—Notre Dame or Michigan or Ohio State. But I figured some smaller school at the I-AA level would offer me something. After all, three of my brothers had gotten full athletic scholarships. That meant I had to get one, too.

But nobody was calling. I didn't understand that. One day I

bumped into a college coach and I asked him why I wasn't getting any offers. "Oh, your coach told us you were a step too slow," he said.

What the hell? I couldn't believe it. Most high school coaches talk up their players, try to sell scouts on his guys. But my head coach said I was a step too slow? I couldn't and wouldn't believe it, until I confronted him. Amazingly, he admitted that he had been telling college scouts exactly that—I was a step too slow. "Rob, I gotta keep my credibility up," he said. "I'm not one of these coaches who says his players are the greatest thing since sliced bread."

I was furious. College coaches deal with high school coaches all the time. They expect that every high school coach is going to talk up their players—not undersell them. So when a college coach hears a high school coach telling him, "McGovern is a step too slow," all they really hear is "McGovern stinks!"

"You're supposed to be going to bat for me, coach," I pleaded.

"No, Rob. I gotta keep my credibility."

"Look, you're entitled to your opinion, but would you please stop killing me?" I stormed away. I just couldn't believe it. My own coach was telling colleges not to bother looking at me.

I knew I wasn't the greatest player in the world, but I also thought I had enough talent to play college ball at the I-AA level, like my brothers.

All along I figured my best shot was at Holy Cross, where my brothers went. The Cross had been a national powerhouse decades ago, but it couldn't compete with the big state schools anymore. Still, the school played a respectable schedule against teams like Lafayette, Bucknell, Army, and some of the Ivy League teams.

The deadline for scholarships came and went, and I got nothing. I was devastated.

"Is this it?" I asked my father. "Is it gone for me now?" My father knew a little bit about the process after having three sons go through it already. "Nah," he said, although I'm not sure he believed it. "Schools will offer one player a scholarship; when he turns it down, that school can offer it to somebody else." I thought, "Maybe that somebody else will be me." That would mean I wasn't anybody's first choice, but I didn't care. I just wanted a chance.

All along, I had been talking to some people at West Point. The idea of playing there and then going on to serve in the military intrigued me, which came as no surprise to my mom. And it looked like West Point saw something in me that nobody else did. So I was ready to listen.

The coach recruiting me, Charlie Taaffe, even visited our house one night to talk with my parents and me. Unsure of how the process worked, I informed Coach Taaffe that I hadn't lined up a recommendation from my congressman yet. He let me know that there was still plenty of time if I decided West Point was for me. In the middle of this conversation, the phone rang: it was Kevin Coyle, an assistant coach at Holy Cross.

"Hey, Rob," he said, "I wanted to let you know we haven't been able to locate a scholarship for you just yet. No guarantees, but I'm working on trying to get you a half scholarship. So what do you think?"

All of a sudden I'm in a pretty good negotiating position. "Well, coach," I said, "don't worry about it. Coach Taaffe from West Point is in the living room right now, and I think I'm gonna go there."

There was a long pause. "Well, don't make any decisions tonight. You should sleep on it." We hung up and for the first time in a long time I felt good about the sometimes cold and calculated business of college athletics.

The following morning, Coach Coyle left a message asking me to call him. By an amazing coincidence, he told me, the head coach, Rick Carter, came into his office just after we spoke and told him that he had an extra full scholarship available, and it was all mine if I wanted it. Years later, over a beer, Coach Coyle insisted that he'd wanted me all along, that the offer from West Point had nothing to do with the offer I finally received from Holy Cross.

"C'mon, coach!" I said. "Don't give me that crap. I was the last guy you gave a scholarship to. Just admit it." We had a laugh, but he disputes my theory to this day. I was one of his top guys, he says.

So like my brothers before me, I received a scholarship and went to Holy Cross. So far, so good—I was going to get my chance to play college football and my parents did not have to pay a dime to send me, either. With nine kids, it would have been impossible to send all of us to a private college like Holy Cross. As my dad likes to say, "You can't get blood from a stone." So four of us getting full athletic scholarships to college really lightened my parents' financial load. It also felt good to finally be able to give something back to the two people who had given so much to me all my life.

FOR AS LONG as I could remember we'd been making the four-hour drive to Holy Cross to visit one of my older siblings, or watch them play at Holy Cross's football stadium, Fitton Field, just off Interstate 290 near the Mass Pike. But it's one thing to visit my sister Patti or my brothers, or to go there for basketball camp, like I did when I was in high school. It's another thing to be moving there, at the age of eighteen. Even though the place was familiar, I had the usual anxiety of any kid who's about to leave home for the first time.

My father drove me there in the family station wagon. I had a duffel bag filled with T-shirts and jeans and not much else. Of course, the highways were all familiar to me—I'd made this drive lots of times. But it had always been a round-trip journey. This time, it was one-way.

When we reached my dorm, I grabbed my duffel bag and got out. My father rolled down his window.

"Okay," he said. "See you later. Don't forget to give your mom a call." And off he went. He didn't even get out of the car. It was his way of handling the situation. To make it seem like no big deal and to keep me from embarrassing myself. I don't know if I appreciated this then, but I know I do now. My father is the most important male figure in my life. He showed me how to be quiet but strong, firm yet fair, tough yet gentle. I just stood there in the parking lot and watched him drive away, threw the duffel bag over my shoulder, and headed for my dorm.

Just like any other day. Except that Holy Cross wasn't Oradell, and the dorm wasn't the McGovern house, and my parents weren't in charge of my life anymore.

I was.

Chapter Four

⋆ ⋆ ⋆

Holy Cross and the Jesuits—
"To whom much is given,
much is expected."—*Luke 12:48*

AS I LOOK BACK ON MY CHILDHOOD AND EARLY ADULT-
hood, it's not hard to figure out where and how I developed the
beliefs I have today—beliefs that I relied upon in Iraq, Afghanistan, and in my current position as a JAG based in Virginia.

When I was a kid, and a young college student, my parents
and teachers emphasized the importance of serving others—
friends, neighbors, and strangers. I joined the Army to try to help
others at home and abroad, to do my small part in the struggle to
bring freedom and democracy to people who haven't had it.

It's no surprise, I suppose, that when I think of the path that led
me to the Army, I think back to the training I received from the
Jesuit priests at the College of the Holy Cross from 1985 to 1989.

The campus of Holy Cross is built on a hill overlooking the old industrial city of Worcester, Massachusetts, the traditional dividing line between the eastern and western parts of the state. The Jesuits founded the school in 1843, and for more than a hundred years, it was a male-only institution. It was a place where students wore jackets and ties to class, studied the classics in Latin, and were expected to be at Mass on Sunday. By 1970, the school dropped the dress code and started letting women attend along with men—thank God. Today, more than half the students who attend Holy Cross are female—a figure, I'm sure, that was not overlooked by the young men who attended HC. I know it wasn't overlooked by me.

Early on, the school's academic reputation attracted the children of ambitious, upwardly mobile Catholic families from New England and elsewhere. The school's athletic reputation attracted some of the best high school athletes in the country as well, like the legendary NBA stars Bob Cousy and Tommy Heinsohn. Holy Cross was a national powerhouse back in the 1940s, which was the golden age of Catholic college sports. Schools likes Boston College, Georgetown, Fordham, and that other college out in South Bend, Indiana, all were big-time players along with Holy Cross.

But the school's football tradition is also inextricably linked to one of the worst tragedies in American history. On November 28, 1942, Holy Cross beat the number one team in the country, Boston College, our archrival and fellow Jesuit school, 55–12. It remains one of the greatest upsets in college football history. Later that night, some fans were celebrating at a nightclub called the Cocoanut Grove in Boston. A fire broke out, and within fifteen minutes, 491 people were dead. Ironically, when Boston College lost, the team canceled its planned victory party at Cocoanut Grove. Otherwise, the death toll might have been even higher.

By the time I got to the Cross, the school had downgraded its football program to I-AA, which meant that we no longer played the big powerhouses, except Boston College. But that great rivalry had become pretty lopsided. Heisman Trophy winner Doug Flutie put BC on the map. So by the mid-1980s, we literally weren't in the same league. Still, we continued to play each other until my junior year, but it was pretty clear that the 1940s were over and that there would be no more stunning upsets.

That said, the Cross fielded some darn good teams in the 1980s as one of the founding members of the new Colonial League, now called the Patriot League. In 1983, a couple of years before I arrived there, we went to the quarterfinals of the I-AA championships after winning the Lambert Cup as the top Division I-AA team in the East. Our only loss was to BC (it was Doug Flutie's junior season), which went on to play in the Liberty Bowl. Our coach, Rick Carter, was the NCAA's Division I-AA coach of the year. My brother Bill was a starting defensive back that year and he led the team with six interceptions. We won the Lambert Cup again my sophmore, junior, and senior years. In 1987, my junior year, we were ranked as the number 1 Division I-AA team in the nation. This time, head coach Mark Duffner was the I-AA coach of the year.

Holy Cross was, is, and always will be a school where success on the athletic field takes a backseat to academics and service. And that's how it ought to be. While I enjoyed playing football, I also received a first-rate education and some valuable lessons about life at Holy Cross. As a history major, I found professors who shared my passion about stories from the past and the lessons they teach us in the present. To this day, I celebrate my birthday by stretching out on a sofa, eating my favorite meal, meat loaf—that's right, I said meat loaf—and watching the History Channel. I have to admit, though, that majoring in history wasn't the most practical decision I could have made. I figure with a history degree, you can do one of two things: you can teach, or you can be a game-show host. But that didn't matter to me—I loved learning about world history, and Holy Cross allowed me explore that to my heart's content.

Ironically, two of my most memorable classes were not in history, but in nineteenth- and twentieth-century art—a topic I knew nothing about and had little interest in. I took the first class, in nineteenth-century art, only because I needed three credits in art and, well, that class was open and available. Within a matter of days, the instructor, a Jesuit priest named Father John Reboli, immersed us in the world and the style of the great masters of the age. Believe me, I was an unlikely art-history student, but this wonderful priest's enthusiasm and love of his subject matter motivated his students and made us appreciate the history, technique, and philosophy behind works of art that we might ordinarily take for granted. That's why I signed up for a second course.

To this day, I still can talk with more than a bit of knowledge about some of the great artists Father Reboli introduced me to, like Monet, Manet, Renoir, Munch, and Picasso. Father Reboli is still teaching art history at Holy Cross today, opening the eyes and minds of countless young people to the beauty and culture that are all around them. Just like he did for a jock like me so many years ago.

That's what education in the Jesuit tradition is all about, and why schools like Holy Cross have played an important but misunderstood role in educating generations of Catholic kids—and these days, many non-Catholic kids, too. Today, as I write, my alma mater has personal connections to three U.S. Supreme Court justices: Clarence Thomas is a graduate of the school; Antonin Scalia's son, Paul, graduated from the Cross before going into the priesthood; and Chief Justice John Roberts's wife, Jane Sullivan Roberts, also is a graduate. Clearly, the Jesuits and lay faculty at Holy Cross are doing something right, never mind how the football team is doing.

I treasure the education I received at Holy Cross more now than I did at the time—but then again, I'm not the only one who feels that way, I'm sure. I was one of those guys in the dorm pulling all-nighters during final exams. During the last week of any semester, you could usually find me up all night cramming like crazy because I was too lazy to study before it was almost too late. It wasn't until I went to law school—when I was older and wiser—that I realized school was a lot easier when you studied all along and knew the material.

One thing I couldn't avoid, and didn't want to, was the school's insistence on service. I think that's the aspect of my education that I treasure most. I don't remember most of the books I read for class, but I do remember the Jesuits telling me that I owed something to my fellow men and women. They hammered home that message all the time. "You need to give something back"—I must have heard that message a thousand times. "To whom much is given, much is expected." I heard that one over and over again, too.

Going to a school like Holy Cross reminded me of how lucky I was, and that those of us who are lucky are expected to help those who are not. Notice the wording: the lucky are *expected* to help those less fortunate. That's how the bar was set at Holy Cross: service was *expected*. It was not considered an option. It was not regarded as a nice little extra to put on your résumé when you were looking for your first job.

I have been given so much in life. A fantastic family, devoted teachers and coaches, and I was lucky enough to attend a great academic institution on an athletic scholarship. My time at Holy Cross reinforced in me the belief that since I had received so many blessings from God, I had a duty to use those gifts for a good and decent purpose.

When I meet my Maker, He is not going to ask me how many tackles I had or how many games I won. He is going to say, "Rob, what did you do with the talents I gave you? Did you use them to help others or to gain profit and praise for yourself?" Ultimately, how I answer that question will determine if I have earned the reward of eternal salvation. That is why I consider it an obligation to develop my body, my mind, and my spirit each day.

Because I am so blessed personally, I also realize that I have an obligation to help others in whatever way my limited talents allow. I learned these lessons first from my parents and my teachers when I was a kid. But it was driven home at Holy Cross.

Down the hill from campus, a Holy Cross student can find plenty of opportunities to put service into practice. Worcester is an economically struggling town of about 170,000 people, a place where there were once plenty of manufacturing jobs. The factories and mills are gone, and the railroads don't matter anymore. Worcester needs help adjusting to the postindustrial global economy.

The football team had a terrific program called the Little Crusaders. On Sundays, after a game, we'd visit the children's wards of the local hospitals, where we always got a wonderful welcome.

Dan Allen was an assistant coach, the leader of the team's outreach program, and the founder of the college's chapter of the Fellowship of Christian Athletes. He was one of the finest human beings I've ever met. A college football coach's life is hectic enough, even at a I-AA program like ours, but Coach Allen, Coach A, as we liked to call him, gladly spent hours in the Worcester community every week. He arranged the hospital visits and all our other outreach work. He was the cajoler, the guy who reminded us about our obligations to something other than ourselves, our studies, and, of course, our team.

I can still hear his voice as he made his way around the locker room after a practice. "C'mon, who's going over to the hospital tomorrow," he'd yell out in a tone that made it clear that this was just as important to him as a good performance on the field. You'd hear guys say, "Ah, coach, I gotta go to the gym tomorrow." Or, "Coach A, I gotta go meet some people somewhere." He'd heard it all, and his reply was always the same: "C'mon, you guys. It takes forty-five minutes of your time." He was one of those people on campus who reminded you that whatever you had on your plate wasn't all that important compared with the plight of kids in a hospital, or of families struggling through each day in parts of Worcester. Coach Allen lived the Jesuit idea of service—he didn't do it to get good press. In fact, the press wasn't invited along for our service outreach programs and nobody ever wrote about this stuff.

Coach Allen was promoted to head coach after I left. He became ill in 2002 and missed the entire season. In August 2003, he announced that he had a mysterious disease called multiple chemical sensitivity. He lost control of his body from the neck down, but in an act of unbelievable courage and determination, he coached from a wheelchair during the 2003 season. He died, at the age of forty-eight, in May 2004.

I will never forget how much love and compassion Coach A had for the children in those hospitals and for the kids who played for him during my years at Holy Cross. Years later, his battle with a debilitating disease and his spiritual strength in the face of his own mortality served as a testament to the power of faith in conquering fear. I will never forget him as long as I live. He left us far too early, but his impact on me and all those who knew him will live forever. He may not have been named to an all-American team as a football player, but he earned that honor as a human being.

AS FAMILIAR AS I was with Holy Cross, I still had some adjustments to make, socially, academically, and athletically. The toughest adjustment of all, I have to say, was getting used to seeing women in the classroom. After eight years of all boys at Bergen Catholic High School and Assumption Grammar School, it really was a shock to see a woman at the desk next to me. "This is awesome!" I thought. "There are chicks all over the place." I quickly surmised that this was going to be a great adjustment to make, although I can't say for certain whether that sentiment was mutual.

What this meant, however, was that I couldn't go to class looking like a mess and smelling worse. Throughout grammar school and high school, I was tethered to a tie in the class-room. In college, I figured I'd be liberated from the oppression of the uniform look. I had this idea that I'd be going to class in sweatpants, looking like I'd just gotten out of bed. I'd be at liberty to express the slob within me. Instead, I walked into my first class and thought, "Oh, man, I gotta start dressing up again."

I'm pretty sure nobody noticed the change, none of the people who were supposed to notice anyway, but at least I tried.

One thing I didn't have to adjust to, because I was familiar with it, was the shadows of my siblings at Holy Cross. And I didn't think that was a bad thing at all, even though they had pretty big shadows. As I mentioned before, my brother Bill was a Division I-AA all-America selection as a defensive back and led the nation in 1985 with eleven interceptions. My brother Jack was a four year starter before graduating in 1980. And my brother Tom played on the golf team until he graduated in 1978. My sister Patti graduated in 1982. An athlete in her own right, she also had the additional responsibility of keeping the McGov-ern family's cumulative grade-point average at a respectable level. No easy task, I might add.

My attitude was pretty simple: I had to be as good as they were. Yes, I felt a lot of pressure to live up to this tall task, but I didn't resent it, or them. I found the pressure to be a great moti-vator, especially on days when it would have been easy to dog it at practice, skip the gym, or blow off class. It may sound weird or twisted, but the truth is, that's all I wanted as a young man. I wanted to be able to hold my head up when I was in a room with my family.

I was lucky enough to make the team as a freshman and played a little bit on special teams. I wasn't a star, not by a long shot, though I held my own on a team that finished 4–6–1. But the best part of my freshman year had little to do with football, and everything to do with family. My sister Betsy is about twelve years older than me, so she was out of the house and on her way to Boston College while I was still in grammar school. Because she wound up staying in Boston after graduating, she was more like an aunt who showed up on Christmas and Easter than my sister.

But during my freshman year, I visited her at her home in Ashland, Massachusetts, where I had a long dinner together with her and my brother-in-law, Steve Budra. As I drove back to Worcester I was thinking, "Wow, my sister's a really great person." I never knew that. Until that night, I really didn't know her. I couldn't believe I was nineteen years old and I was just finding out what a great person my sister was. I guess that is just one of the crazy things about being in a big family.

Today, she's a breast-cancer survivor.

Betsy was diagnosed with the disease when I was in Iraq in 2005. She went to doctors, underwent treatment, and worried about the future of her two daughters and loving husband if the unthinkable became reality. Through it all, she had an incredibly positive outlook. She didn't blame God or lose heart. Instead, it was clear that her faith was still intact as she surrendered herself entirely to God's providence.

As my deployment went on, she would e-mail me with messages telling me how proud she was of me and how hard it must be for me. I couldn't believe what I was reading. Here she was fighting for her life and all she could do was tell me how proud she was of me. I was the one who was proud. Proud to have a sister like her to show me the true strength and courage of the human spirit. Had I not gone to Holy Cross, chances are Betsy would have remained a distant figure in my life, instead of the big sister I've come to love and admire.

I also got to know my brother Bill a lot better, because he was hired as an assistant coach after my freshman season. Bill and I had lots of great conversations about family, football, and life. He pushed me to work on getting faster and stronger and on using my mind on the football field. His presence made me even more determined to squeeze my body for every ounce of talent I had. I wanted his respect all the more, if that were possible.

In February of my freshman year, I was working out in the field house when I saw my brother walking toward me. He looked awful.

"What's wrong?" I asked. I was sweating pretty good. I was in the gym lifting weights with the other guys on the team during one of our scheduled off-season workout sessions. The weights were clanging and the music was blasting through the gym, but it all seemed to fade away at the sight of my brother's face as he walked toward me.

He hesitated for a second. "It's not good," he said. And that's all he would say. He walked away.

I found out a couple of hours later that our head coach, Rick Carter, had hanged himself in his home a few hours before. His twenty-one-year-old son, who was a student at Holy Cross, found his body. Coach Carter was only forty-two and had been battling depression, although no one on the team knew. For many of us, Coach Carter's suicide was the first time we had to deal with sudden death. It sounds trite, but it truly did remind us of what's really important in life. Football meant nothing compared with the Carter family's tragedy. In addition to his older son, Carter left behind a wife and a twelve-year-old son.

Moments like this really stop you in your tracks. They put life into perspective and help you realize how precious each day we have on earth truly is. I often get wrapped up in the hectic pace of my life and lose sight of the really important things, like family, faith, and enjoying the people around me. To this day, I try to remember that every success I am lucky enough to have in life is a gift from God. Coach Carter's tragic death helped me to realize that.

That message, that lesson, has only become more important for me. Many Americans say that 9/11 reminded them of what was really important in life. I hope that's still true, but I also know that very few soldiers need to be reminded that life is filled with heartbreak and tragedy. In Iraq and in Afghanistan, I saw how life can change for the worse in an instant. Coach Carter's death was an early lesson in learning about life's real priorities. That lesson was reinforced in the streets of Baghdad and in the mountains of Afghanistan.

GIVEN THAT AS a kid I played with toy soldiers long after my friends had moved on to other toys, it's not surprising that I was fascinated by the military even after I passed up a chance to go to West Point. One of the highlights of my college career was our annual game with the Black Knights of Army, one of the nation's most storied college football programs.

Although Holy Cross, as a Division I-AA program, wasn't exactly a football factory, I kept telling myself that if I worked hard, I'd get a shot at the NFL. It was crazy—I mean, what scouts would be booking flights to Worcester to watch me play? And the odds of getting noticed even by accident were pretty slim, since most of the schools we played weren't exactly big-time. I don't know where I got off thinking that somebody would notice me. Call it the foolishness of youth.

I did have two things working in my favor, though: Holy Cross had pretty good teams during this time. And in a related story, we also had a sensational running back named Gordie Lockbaum, who was a Heisman Trophy candidate in his junior and senior years. Looking back, I realize that I wound up getting my shot at the NFL because of Gordie Lockbaum. During my junior year in 1987, his senior year, scouts actually were coming out to see our games. I got noticed by accident, I guess.

And those scouts saw some pretty good football. We went 11 0 in my junior year, thanks mostly to Lockbaum, and we got a shot at national exposure when ESPN covered us on a Thursday night when we beat Villanova 39–6. But probably the most memorable game I played that year was against Army at West Point. Army still was a I-A program in the late 1980s, and they always drew fifty-five thousand people to their games, by far the biggest crowds we ever saw.

They had a tough, physical team, and win or lose, you could count on getting banged up against them. Plus, West Point is such a great place to watch or play football. The campus is filled with great tradition—I mean, this is where history was made, and still is being made, every day. One of my favorite spots on campus is the statue of General George C. Patton, who finished last in his class at West Point. I love where they put his statue: in front of the library, a place Patton apparently didn't visit very much when he was a plebe.

As game time approached, we were out on the field before the coin toss, getting psyched up, slamming one another, screaming at one another—the usual football thing. Then we heard the PA announcer say that Mrs. Douglas MacArthur was coming out to midfield to toss the coin. "Wow," I said, "I didn't know she was still alive." She was quite elderly and frail-looking, but still, she was spry enough to walk out to midfield with an escort and chat with the captains before tossing the coin. I remembered, as I watched her, that she was quite a bit younger than her husband, the great General Douglas MacArthur, who died in 1964.

I don't remember whether we won the coin toss or Army did. But I do remember watching Mrs. MacArthur as she walked toward the sideline, a living part of our history. She was leaning on the arm of her escort while the fans cheered for her and all that she and her husband meant to America.

While this was going on, we got into a big circle to get ready for kickoff. And we were screaming like football nuts: "Who do they think they are?" and "Let's kill 'em." We did a quick cheer, and with our adrenaline flying high, we turned and started charging toward our bench. We were screaming and hollering and doing the whole college football thing. It was great. We were psyched. There were seventy of us running toward the sideline and raging mad.

Unfortunately, we didn't notice that a certain frail elderly lady was still making her way off the field. She had her back to us, and we didn't see anything but the heads in front of us. All of a sudden we all came to a stop, and it was like human bumper cars—I smashed into the guy in front of me, and got smashed into by the guy behind me. It turned out that Coach A realized that we were about to trample Mrs. MacArthur to death. He sprinted out to the field, eyes bulging, arms flailing, screaming "Stop! Stop!" Thankfully, he got there just in time and we managed to avoid killing a national icon.

Oh, did I mention that we won that game 34–24? We kicked their butts, and loved every minute of it. But we also knew that the guys on the other sideline were more than just college football players—they were soldiers, future officers, men who'd agreed to serve their country after graduation. You couldn't help but respect that. West Point was one of the biggest games on our schedule all year, but the biggest contest these cadets prepared for was not the kind played out on some neatly manicured football field.

The men and women of the U.S. Military Academy volunteered for a life-and-death struggle that would one day require my high school friend, Mike Minogue, to climb into a Bradley Armored Fighting Vehicle for the 24th Mechanized Infantry Division and head out across the Iraqi desert to kill the enemy waiting for him in 1991. That was no game like I was playing and there were no points for second place.

I WAS CAPTAIN of the team during my senior year in 1988, and we had a pretty good season even though we started 1–2. Without Gordie Lockbaum, who graduated the year before and finished third in the Heisman voting, we weren't the same team. All in all, though, we were pretty respectable. We didn't lose a game after our slow start and still managed to win the Lambert Cup trophy as the number one team in the East.

The NFL was still my dream, but I wasn't dumb enough or arrogant enough to think it would happen automatically. Even though I worked hard on improving my speed and agility, I knew the odds of being drafted were pretty small. And even if I were to be drafted, which was unlikely, there was absolutely no guarantee that I'd actually make it. Lots of guys get drafted every year—and lots of guys never make it through training camp.

I thought about law school. That seemed like the natural progression because I liked hearing myself talk, not that anybody else considered it such a pleasure, and because law was a field where people actively competed against one another. I'm not talking about corporate law. I'm talking courtroom law: Defendant v. Plaintiff; Prosecutor v. Defense Attorney. I figured I would enjoy the competition, it seemed like the perfect fit. I would be taking on an opposing attorney, fighting it out in a court of law. One guy wins and one guy loses. It was exactly what I was looking for in a life after football.

One day late in my senior year I got a call from a guy named Ron Waller. He was a retired guy who did some scouting every now and again for NFL teams. He told me who he was and that he wanted to see me work out because the Kansas City Chiefs had expressed some interest in me.

That was fine with me, but I wasn't about to get my hopes up. Mr. Waller could come and see whatever he wanted to see, but ultimately, I was a small linebacker from a I-AA program who, I knew, was not your stereotypical linebacker in the NFL. This was the age of Lawrence Taylor, when linebackers weighed 250 pounds and ran like gazelles. I was small and from a fairly un-known school. Not a good combination.

Mr. Waller drove from Delaware to Worcester to see me. We had a terrific chat before starting the workout. We stood in the field house and talked about the past football season. But we also found ourselves drifting into a deeper conversation. I don't know if it was his plan or not, but we both discussed things like our upbringing and its impact on our work ethic and great figures in history we admired and why.

Mr. Waller was a gray-haired gentleman whom I opened up to immediately. He spoke plainly but always with a purpose. However, that's not what made it easy to talk to him. It was the fact that he listened. He listened to me with as much attention and care as he spoke. He responded with questions that really forced me to think about why I felt the way I did. Without real-izing it, he slowly had me revealing more and more about what made me tick.

Dressed in gym shorts and a T-shirt, I walked with Mr. Waller across the field house into the center of the running track. At this time of year, the track was a buzz of activity with kids preparing for the spring track season. As we walked from the wrestling mats where we had been talking to the centerline painted down the middle of the field house to help divide up the intramural basketball and volleyball courts, I tried to mentally prepare my-self for what was about to happen. I had done this for a few teams already, so I knew the drill, so to speak.

Mr. Waller had me do a bunch of common agility drills de-signed to test my lateral movement and vertical leap. Every now and again he'd throw me a curveball by having me do a drill I hadn't seen—or practiced—before.

The air hung thick and moist in the field house that day, as it always did. My T-shirt was soaked with sweat as I raced back and forth and back again from line to line, trying to shave a tenth of a second or maybe even two-tenths off my time. All the while Mr. Waller stood quietly, clicking the stopwatch that was hanging around his neck and jotting down notes in a tiny green notepad he pulled from his back pocket.

During one test called the shuttle drill, where I was running back and forth and back again like a hamster in a maze, Mr. Waller looked at his stopwatch. "Yeah, that's okay," he said, "but why don't you do it over again and try it this way?"

I was kind of stunned. Did I just hear what I thought I heard? Wasn't he supposed to be *testing* me? Instead, he was giving me tips on how to improve my time. I was beginning to realize Mr. Waller wasn't the typical coldhearted scout who shows up, says little more than "What's your height and weight, kid?" and then leaves before you have time to say, "Please give me one more chance? I know I can do better."

No, he was actually coaching me. He was trying to make me realize my potential by making me faster, quicker, better. I got the feeling that Ron Waller was on my side.

So I tried the drill his way, and it seemed to work. Later on, we walked over to the gym to do the bench press, which was a standard part of the workout. You bench-pressed 225 pounds as many times as you could. I was always pretty good at this one. I did it twenty-one times, and then, on my twenty-second attempt, my arms were shaking and I couldn't lock them out to get credit for one last rep. I was really pushing it—I was huffing and puffing and groaning and sweating, trying to get that one extra rep.

The guy who was spotting me—hovering over me to make

sure I didn't hurt myself—grabbed the weight and put it back on the rack. I was done at twenty-one.

Mr. Waller looked at me. "All right," he said, "twenty-two."

"Twenty-two," I thought. "Mr. Waller, I want to kiss you." Wisely, I didn't express this sentiment out loud.

We finished the workout, Mr. Waller took his last notes, we said good-bye, and that was it. I figured this might be my last football moment.

As draft day approached, I hooked up with an agent, Brad Blank, just in case. This was before the draft became a made-for-ESPN extravaganza, with experts going on and on about who might draft whom and why. It was a two-day draft, with all the big prospects picked, of course, on the first day. I didn't pay a whole lot of attention because even if by some miracle somebody drafted me, it wasn't happening on the first day.

I did get a call that day, though, not from a team, but from my agent, Brad. "Stay by the phone tomorrow," he said.

"Brad, I appreciate the heads-up," I said, "but nobody's gonna draft me. I'm just hoping somebody will sign me as a free agent." That was Backup Plan A: wait until after the draft, see what teams still need a small linebacker from an I-AA program, and maybe catch on as a free agent. Backup Plan B was law school and a career as a prosecutor.

Brad insisted that I stay by the phone.

I hated the idea. It meant having to waste the whole day sitting in my dorm room, staring at the walls. This, of course, was the backward age when most people didn't have cell phones. So if you were expecting a call, you couldn't take your phone with you—you had to wait by your phone.

Brad insisted that I stay by the phone. So I did, for a few

hours anyway. It was pretty boring—and it's not like I could tune in to ESPN to see how the draft was going.

After a few hours, I left my dorm room on the first floor and walked up a couple flights of stairs to my girlfriend's room on the women's floor. We just sort of hung out—I remember having a football in my hand and throwing it up and down, just to pass the time. Then the phone rings in her room: it's my roommate, a guy named Gerry Trietley who actually gave himself the nickname "T-Bomb." He was a noseguard on the team, a big, hulking guy of about 290 pounds. He was also one of the team's leading practical jokers.

"Hey, Rob, you have to get down here," he said. "The Chiefs are about to draft you."

You know, there's a time for jokes, and this wasn't the time. I was not amused. "Yeah, yeah, go to hell, T-Bomb," I said—although I confess I might have said something stronger. I hung up the phone.

"What was that all about?" my girlfriend said.

"Ah, it's just the bomber messing with my head," I said.

Two minutes later, T-Bomb is standing in my girlfriend's doorway. He's breathing heavy, like he just ran up a couple flights of stairs—and at his size, this wasn't something he did just for the fun of it.

"Rob, Rob, get downstairs," he says. "The Chiefs are about to draft you. You got a call."

I just stared at him. And I thought to myself, "There's no way T-Bomb ran up a flight of stairs unless it was serious. He wouldn't run up a flight of stairs to see his mother." And it hit me: "Holy crap."

I ran downstairs and waited by the phone. When it finally

rang again, it was Marty Schottenheimer, the new coach of the Kansas City Chiefs. "Rob," he said, "I tried calling you before, but you weren't in and I got your roommate. I hope you don't mind, but we drafted you."

Did I mind? Did I mind? Oh, man!

"No problem, sir," I said. "I don't mind at all." I felt I had to explain why I wasn't by the phone, so I told him something about being outside saving a bunch of schoolchildren or something. He laughed, congratulated me, and hung up.

Three hundred thirty-five college football players were picked in the NFL draft on April 23–24, 1989. I was the 255th person chosen. Did that matter to me? Not a chance! I felt like I had just won the lottery.

I was ecstatic. I called my parents. I called my agent. And I called Ron Waller, the scout who worked with me a few weeks earlier. I got him at home in Delaware. He remembered me.

"Mr. Waller," I said, "I don't know what you said to the Chiefs, but thank you. You made my dream come true."

A few years later, Mr. Waller told my agent that in all his years as a scout, nobody had ever called him to thank him after the draft. But then again, he probably never had to sell somebody with such limited talents, so I felt it was the right thing to do.

Somehow, I was now a professional football player. My dream had come true. Now the question was: How long would it last?

CHAPTER FIVE

* * *

The NFL—
Dreams Do Come True

MY SOLDIER'S LIFE HAS TAKEN ME TO SOME FAIRLY exotic places—if you consider a tent in Afghanistan or a bunk in the U.S. embassy compound in Baghdad "exotic." I certainly do, because, truth be told, I wasn't exactly a world traveler as a kid or even as a young adult. I was a Jersey guy whose idea of a fabulous getaway was a car trip to Florida with parents and siblings.

In fact, even though I went "away" to college, I really didn't. Holy Cross was my home away from home. So after getting out of college, I was a twenty-two-year-old who really had never been away from home in his life.

Then, in the spring of 1989, I got on a plane bound for Kansas City to work out at a minicamp for rookies.

What do you wear to minicamp? That was the question. All

my years of Catholic school education gave me the answer: a suit and tie, of course. I was an adult now. I had to look the part, right?

When I got off the plane in Kansas City, there was a bunch of other young guys in the airport—my new teammates, all of them drafted ahead of me. They were wearing T-shirts, chains, and baseball caps. When I arrived in a suit, I swear, I think they thought I was from the FBI or something.

I started introducing myself, and it's pretty clear none of these guys had ever heard my name. Either that or they thought my name was "Rob Who." But I knew some of their names. The Chiefs' top pick that year, for instance. Derrick Thomas of the University of Alabama was the best linebacker in the class of 1989 and the fourth overall pick in the draft. But his football abilities were just part of his story. His father was an Air Force captain who was shot down and killed in Vietnam just before Christmas in 1972, when Derrick was just five years old. Ironically, the operation was code-named Linebacker 2. Derrick honored his father's memory by working with veterans' groups, and would go on to give a Memorial Day speech at the Vietnam Veterans Memorial on Memorial Day, 1993.

At the time, however, all I knew was that Derrick Thomas was a shoe-in to make the team, and he was a linebacker. That didn't bode well for me. I was the Chiefs' tenth pick that year and also a linebacker. So I figured I'd just work hard and enjoy the experience for however long it lasted.

The minicamp was really an orientation more than anything else, and for somebody like me, an absolute necessity. Never mind that I overdressed for camp or that the whole big-time experience of pro football was completely alien to this Holy Cross grad. The biggest change was getting used to the slow pace of life and the friendly demeanor of the people in Kansas City.

I mean, the people were nice. Really nice. The team took us as a group to see the Royals play the Yankees—my favorite baseball team. I was stunned as I looked at the crowd around me: first of all, people were buying glass bottles of beer. Glass bottles! They would never sell bottles in New York. If they did, they'd be used as murder weapons. And the people buying these bottles were so well dressed—the women were wearing high heels and dresses, and the guys, well, they looked like I did when I got off the plane from New Jersey. And these well-dressed, nice people walked and drove, like, well, like they weren't in a hurry. That was a change from life in northern New Jersey.

If I missed the frantic pace of the Northeast, I got all I asked for and more on the field. These guys were fast. The guys I played against in college didn't move like this. All I could think was, "Welcome to the big time, Rob."

As I mentioned before, I wasn't the biggest guy on the block. But I had worked hard on my speed and I did have a decent head on my shoulders, which helped me outthink guys who were faster and stronger and otherwise a lot more talented. Football isn't necessarily rocket science, but there's a good deal of information to remember, and more than one way to use your head as well as your body. "Work smarter and harder" was my motto. I studied the playbook and tried to play a thinking man's game of football. That didn't go unnoticed—throughout my NFL career, guys used to treat me like I was the brains of the operation. And all I could say was, "Look, if I'm the brains of this team, then we're in a lot of trouble."

I worked hard at minicamp, and I stayed in Kansas City for

an off-season weight-training program. I wasn't finished at Holy Cross yet, so I was flying back and forth all the time. I missed a lot of the senior-year stuff that goes on just before graduation—a bunch of my buddies went out to Cape Cod to celebrate, and everybody was saying good-bye to one another. In a small school like Holy Cross, you can't help but get close to your classmates and roommates, which is why to this day I'm still close to the people I met in college. I would have had a blast at all of the graduation rituals and parties, but I gladly gave them up for a chance to play in the NFL.

Besides, I wasn't exactly all alone out in Kansas City. Miraculously, two of my teammates from Holy Cross were also trying out for the team that year. Can you believe that? Three guys from the tiny little I-AA school of Holy Cross were trying out for the same NFL team.

Tom Kelleher and Gerry McCabe had played with me at Holy Cross a few years before and now they were both trying to make it in the NFL like me. Gerry graduated two years ahead of me and played briefly with the New England Patriots before signing with the Chiefs as a free-agent linebacker in the spring of 1989. Tom Kelleher, or TK, was drafted by the Miami Dolphins the year before me and had tried out for Don Shula's squad that year. Like Gerry, TK signed with the Chiefs the following off-season as a free agent in the hopes of making the squad as a fullback.

When Gerry was a senior at Holy Cross, I was a sophomore and I absolutely idolized him. I tried to emulate everything he did, from his workout regimen, to his game plan preparation, right down to how he wore his socks. I pulled them all the way up to my knees just like Gerry even though at that time it was "cool" to have them pushed down around your ankles. That didn't matter to me. As far as I could see, Gerry was the best player on our team, and if it was good enough for him, it was good enough for me.

TK was as equally tough and successful as Gerry. At Holy Cross, TK and I were always pitted against each other in practice. As a fullback, TK often found himself assigned to block me on running plays and I was usually trying to cover him as he ran his passing routes. The very nature of our two positions seemingly put us at odds with each other from day one. You would think we might come to dislike or even hate each other over the course of the three years we competed against each other at Holy Cross. But that was far from the case.

Although TK was a fierce competitor on the field, he never allowed that to affect how he treated people off the field. He was and is a compassionate and loyal friend who took me under his wing when I arrived in Kansas City. TK helped me find a place to live and showed me the ropes around the stadium and around town. More importantly, TK helped me develop my attitude as I took on the huge challenge that was an NFL training camp. TK knew that you can't leave life up to chance. You need to have a plan or you're destined for failure—again, not a bad lesson for a future soldier, never mind a linebacker. So we prepared our off-season workout plan, our nutrition plan, and our sleep plan. It's all about discipline, which is why so much of what I learned in football has come in handy in my military career.

There wasn't a single daily activity that TK didn't have a plan for. "If you don't know where you're going, any road will take you there," TK would say. His philosophy then and now was pretty simple: "You can't achieve a goal you haven't set for yourself."

Gerry and TK were incredible role models to me and anyone

else who played with them. They led by word and by deed. In doing so, they taught me that in order to be a success you have to follow two simple rules: (1) Set a clear goal for yourself; and (2) Dedicate yourself entirely to achieving that goal. Gerry went on to become a doctor and TK is the leader of a sales team for Westlaw, a legal research firm. Their success after football is no surprise to me, but not because they were good football players. Their success came because they set goals and they sacrificed in order to achieve those goals.

Today, a lot of kids find it hard to stay focused on a goal. So many things distract them from reaching their full potential. TK and Gerry showed at least one kid that when you know your priorities and set your goals accordingly, you can stay on track and achieve anything you want.

By the end of the summer of 1989, with the help of TK and Gerry, I knew what I wanted. Now, at the age of twenty-two, I just had to go out and get it.

WHILE I WAS training that summer, my agent was negotiating a contract for me. I gave him very simple instructions: "Brad," I said, "don't piss anybody off. I'm ready to sign anything they put in front of me. Just don't piss anybody off." He just laughed, although I wasn't kidding.

The longer I hung around Kansas City, the more I thought I might have a shot at making the team. I wasn't Derrick Thomas, but that came as no surprise to the coaching staff. I don't know what they were looking for in me, but what they saw, I think, was a guy who wasn't afraid to bust his butt and who loved having the chance to play football.

That's all I ever wanted to do, so I wasn't going to blow it because I didn't try hard enough. But I also knew that hard work and desire might not be enough in the NFL, this dreamworld where people got paid to play football. I was very aware that most draft picks don't make it through training camp, and that the average NFL career is less than five years. Not everybody, I have to say, seems to understand these cold, hard facts. My signing bonus was all of $7,500, which I was happy to have, but it wasn't going to set me up for life, or even for a season. I drove around in a little Nissan Stanza and shared a modest apartment with Gerry and TK.

One day, I saw that the only other guy drafted lower than me went out and bought two BMWs. I knew he was the only guy on the team making less money than me and I was just barely making more than the NFL minimum, which was $55,000 at the time.

I couldn't help but ask him about his cars. "Look," I said, "you're the only guy on the team making less money than me and I can't afford those two cars. How can you?"

"Hey, man," he said, "I'll make it up in my next contract. You'll see."

He never got a next contract.

I CAME HOME for a while in early summer, 1989, and every couple of days, my father would turn to me and say, "So, when does training camp start?" By the time he asked this for the hundredth time, my brothers and sisters would reply in unison, "July twentieth."

July 20—it was written on my calendar: the real start of this crazy experiment. I kept wondering if someone was going to tap me on the shoulder and say, "Sorry. There has been a mistake. You weren't supposed to be drafted. You're going to have to leave," but they never did and July 20 finally arrived.

I didn't wear a suit to training camp, you'll be relieved to know. But I did bring my desire, which I hoped would prevail over my lack of size. I thought if I worked hard, caught a little luck, and used my head, I might be able to pull this thing off. As I arrived at training camp on the campus of Liberty University in Missouri on a sweltering day, I was on the verge of achieving what I had only dreamed of all my life. I had a shot at making an NFL team, but one thing was for sure—no one was going to give it to me. If I wanted this to happen, I was going to have to take it.

After about ten grueling days of the Midwest summer, Coach Schottenheimer gave an interview with a local newspaper about the state of his draft picks. He worked his way down, through the first-, second-, third-, fourth-, and fifth-round picks. Through the sixth, seventh, eighth, and ninth picks. Then he got to the tenth pick. It was pretty amazing to me he even remembered he had a tenth pick, never mind who it was.

"Rob's a smart enough guy," he said. "He's got a real good grasp of the defense." So far, so good, I thought. I read on. "But he's overthinking out there. He has to relax and just play football."

Ouch. When I read this, I was shocked. I thought I was having a pretty good camp. I was working hard, and, I thought, very cleverly using my brain to compensate for all the lack of pounds and talent. But now the coach was saying, in so many words, that I stink. I thought to myself, "Damn, I'm gonna screw this up."

The following evening, as I got ready for a rare night

practice—it was too hot that day, even for sadistic football coaches—I had to come to grips with the very real possibility that I was blowing my one shot at the NFL. "This is it," I thought as I put on my pads. "You have one shot and one shot only to prove you can play. And if you don't go out there and leave it all on the field, you will have no one to blame but yourself. You will also have the rest of your life to kick yourself if you don't let loose out there."

That was it. I was finally where I needed to be mentally in order to reach my potential. I was "in the zone," as they say. That practice, I was flying all over the field from the first whistle to the last drill. Thank God we didn't practice in the afternoon, or I might have collapsed in the heat, but I don't think even that would have stopped me.

At the end of the practice, Coach Schottenheimer had us do a full-contact, 100 percent live scrimmage. It was just like game time. You're not supposed to hold anything back and I didn't. "Just play football," I told myself. "Just play like you've been playing your whole life." And I did. I was having fun. I just cut loose. I followed my instincts, I was flying all over the field, I was making tackles, and I was thoroughly enjoying myself. I practically had a smile on my face while I was doing it.

At one point, Schottenheimer yelled over to me, "Good hit, McGovern." It was the first time he'd said my name since camp had begun, other than telling the newspaper guy that I was thinking too much. It was also the first time he'd singled me out for praise and I loved it. For once, I felt like I belonged in an NFL training camp. I started to believe that I really could play at this level.

As I walked off the practice field, I could honestly say with more than just hope that I believed I could play in the NFL. And if I could make the team and play for only one season, well, that would be enough for me.

I spent the rest of training camp, and the rest of my NFL career, playing football like I always did and having fun doing it. After that, every game was fun. I just kept reminding myself that I was being paid to play football, lift weights, and work out. What could be more fun than that? It felt like I was stealing money.

PLAYING AT HOLY Cross had its advantages. I wasn't beat up like the other guys who played at big-time programs, who basically played football while everybody else went to class. I never had a serious injury requiring me to undergo some type of reconstructive surgery. And, thankfully, as that first summer wore on, my body didn't break down.

Some of the linebackers from the bigger schools had a hard time as camp wore on. Old injuries were bothering them. They were getting nicked here and there and having to leave practice. Years of pounding had already taken a toll on their bodies—and they were in their early and midtwenties. I didn't have that problem.

The Chiefs had a rotten season the year before, which is why management brought in Coach Schottenheimer to turn things around. When I walked into that locker room, I was blown away by the talent: Mike Webster, one of the NFL's greatest centers; Ron Jaworski, a Super Bowl quarterback; Deron Cherry, a nine-time Pro Bowl pick and future Hall of Famer; Jack del Rio, a great linebacker; Christian Okoya, a running back who would go on to be the team's MVP that year; and, of course, number one pick, Derrick Thomas, another linebacker. I'm not kidding when I say that I felt like pinching myself, just to see if all this was real and that, yes, I was sharing a locker room with some of the greatest players in the NFL.

When I walked into that locker room, I wasn't just a kid and a rookie—I was a fan. I grew up watching Jaworski when he played for the Eagles. I idolized Mike Webster, who was with those great Pittsburgh Steeler teams of the 1970s. Just being in the locker room with these guys was a privilege. For me, all of this was a dream come true. My job was to savor every moment of it.

After a month of sweating through two-a-day drills in training camp, we started our preseason schedule. Our opening game was against the Minnesota Vikings in Memphis, Tennessee—the NFL was testing Memphis as a possible home for an expansion team. (Memphis got a team when the Houston Oilers moved there and became today's Tennessee Titans.) Knowing that the NFL was watching, the city threw parties for us, and come game time, something like sixty-five thousand screaming fans showed up at the Liberty Bowl not to root for one team or the other, but to show how much they loved football and deserved a team of their own.

Coming from my modest I-AA roots, I felt like I was at the Super Bowl.

I was assigned number 53, which was actually Mike Webster's number as well. At this point in preseason, teams have so many guys that they double up on numbers. I thought it was pretty cool to be sharing a number with a future Hall of Famer. If Mike had an opinion on sharing a number with me, he was gracious enough to keep it to himself.

The coaches told me I wouldn't see any action until the second half, so I just relaxed and soaked up the atmosphere. The closest I'd ever come to this big-time atmosphere was our annual game with Army at West Point. As great as those games were, though, they couldn't compare to this. The crowd noise was unbelievable, bodies were flying, and I mean flying, up and down the field, and the hits were big-time. This was the NFL.

At some point in the second quarter, one of our guys on special teams got hurt. "Rob, you're in," somebody yelled. For a second, I figured there was some other guy named Rob on the team. But no, they were calling for me. Holy crap!

We'd just scored, so I was part of the kickoff coverage team. It's funny how you can block out everything, including thousands of people and even your emotions, once you step out on that field. I was playing in front of more than sixty-five thousand screaming fans but it felt like I was by myself.

The kicker put his foot into the ball. I took off downfield. I kept waiting to get hit, waiting for some other eager special-team rookie to show off for his coach by trying to plant me on my back. But nobody picked me up. It seemed like nobody even noticed me as I ran down the field. I mean, nobody laid a finger on me. So I raced down the field and now there's nothing between me and the guy who's about to catch the ball. *Pow!* I drilled him on the fifteen-yard line. It was incredible. It was my first play in the National Football League, and I made the tackle.

I was sky-high. I came running off the field, getting high fives and screaming and jumping up and down. And then I heard the public-address announcer: "On the tackle, number fifty-three." I listened for my name.

"Mike Webster." Huh?

Mike Webster! Damn! No, it's me! It's Rob McGovern, the other number 53!

Over on the sideline, I caught the real Mike Webster's eye. He had a huge smile on his face. "Thanks, Rob," he said, "I always wanted to make a big tackle on special teams." Yeah, well, I guess being mistaken for one of the NFL's greatest players wasn't such a bad thing after all.

Webster and some other veterans, like Jack del Rio, made a point of helping out the younger guys. It wasn't something they had to do, it certainly wasn't something they would be expected to do, but they did it anyway. Mike often stayed after workouts to help me practice long-snapping the ball to the punter. In the off-season, del Rio invited me to play golf with him and have dinner with his family. When I tried to thank him, he just shook it off and said, "Just make sure you do this for somebody else when it's your turn."

THAT'S THE KIND of class I saw in the NFL. Yes, I saw the arrogant players, too. But it's sad that most sports fans know more about the jerks than they do about the good guys in sports. They're out there, but they don't call attention to themselves. They just do their jobs and help out nobodies like me.

That's not to say that the locker room was *Mister Rogers' Neighborhood*. It was more like the atmosphere in some of the barracks I've been in. After all, we were all football players, all relatively young guys—even the oldest guys were younger than I am at the moment of this writing—thirty-nine—and so we acted the part on occasion. The older guys put me through all the usual rookie hazing, just like you've seen in the football movies. I had to sing the Holy Cross fight song at mealtime, and as I am sure you can imagine, it wasn't pretty.

On the last night of training camp, the veterans made rookies put on a rookie show and then we had to drink with the veterans until they said we could leave. The highlight of the night for the veterans was when they made each rookie sit in a chair and tilt his head back while holding his mouth wide open. The veterans then proceeded to pour all sorts of alcohol down our throats. I don't even know what most of it was, except that some of it burned my cheeks as it ran down the side of my face. It is safe to say that whatever it was, it wasn't a finely aged Pinot Noir.

The only way to obtain a reprieve from this onslaught was to drink until you puked or passed out. I don't remember which I did. Probably both.

SO FAR, I'D made every cut, but now came the moment of truth: final cuts before the start of the regular season. Guys like me were always on the bubble—it could go either way, and for reasons that didn't always have a lot to do with talent. If the coach wanted to go with one less linebacker, well, that might not be good for me, regardless of how I did in preseason. Guys have made teams simply because the guys in front of them got hurt. It's not the best way to make a team, but that's football.

If I was going to have a chance, I knew I'd have to overcome one guy: Bill Cowher, the young and newly hired defensive coordinator and linebacker coach for the Chiefs. Cowher was a great coach, as he proved by winning the Super Bowl in 2006. A better sign of his genius, however, was his opinion of me: he didn't want me on his team. He didn't say it in so many words, but I could tell. He wasn't a fan, although he wasn't a critic, either. It's just that he liked his linebackers big and I was small. I mean, Bill

Cowher wanted linebackers who looked like linebackers, not somebody who looked like he skipped dessert at the training table.

I didn't fit the linebacker profile. I remember hanging out in a bar and living the life of a young, single guy and I'd tell somebody, "Well, I'm in the NFL. I play for the Chiefs." And the person on the other end of this conversation—generally of the female persuasion—would say something like, "Oh, are you the kicker?"

I clearly wasn't Bill Cowher's idea of a linebacker. He wasn't about to risk his reputation with some overachieving, undersized kid from Holy Cross. If he wanted to see heartwarming football stories, he'd go to the movies. He was the Lou Grant of the NFL—the kind of guy who'd tell a linebacker, "Hey, you're small but feisty." And you'd smile and proudly reply, "Yes, I am." And he'd look back at you and say, "I hate small but feisty."

Coach Schottenheimer, on the other hand, was a guy who'd played backup linebacker for the Buffalo Bills and he'd played a lot of special teams, too. I can't prove this, but I could picture him saying to Coach Cowher, "C'mon, let's give this McGovern kid a break. Yeah, he's small, but ever since he stopped thinking too much, he's been all right. Let's give him a chance because somebody gave me a chance once."

I doubt that they ever actually had a conversation like that, but I do know that during one of the later preseason games, Cowher approached me on the sidelines and said, "All right, Mc-Govern, Coach Schottenherimer wants you in the game. He wants you to play." Again, you don't have to be a genius to figure out what Cowher was really thinking: "Look, McGovern, I think you're a sorry excuse for a football player, and if I had my way you'd be teaching history or hosting a game show. But the boss says you have to play. So you are going to play."

And I played. I even started the third preseason game, although I didn't find out that I was starting until five minutes before kickoff. I figured Coach Cowher was trying to give me just enough rope so I could hang myself and he'd be rid of me. Who could blame him?

So I knew what I had to do. I realized that I wasn't the second coming of Lawrence Taylor, but I was determined to win this little battle. I wasn't going to hang myself with that rope he gave me. Vince Lombardi once said that "desire is a fire and nothing stokes that fire better than hate." Of course, the hate Lombardi was talking about was the football kind, not the kind that drives people to fly airplanes into buildings. Not the hate that tries to stamp out freedom, the hate that drives our enemies.

Football hate forces you to excel despite yourself. It's actually positive, as opposed to the other kind of hate, which is the most negative force in the world.

In any case, I was determined to show Bill Cowher that he had it wrong: I belonged on this team.

THE START OF the season was only a few days away: time for the final cut. Make-or-break day for lots of guys like me. We finished practice and went to the locker room to change. Every one of us knew that the coach would be sending his messenger out very shortly—football's grim reaper. He was nicknamed the Turk. If you saw him walking in your direction, you hoped he was not coming for you. Sort of like being in battle and hoping that the bullet doesn't have your name on it.

When he passed you by, you felt great—sorry for the other guy, but relieved all the same. If he tapped you on the shoulder and said those terrifying words—"Coach wants to see you. Bring your playbook"—well, you knew and everybody else knew it was all over.

As I changed into street clothes and waited for Dr. Death, my training camp flashed before my eyes. I did okay, I kept telling myself. The waiting was horrible.

In the end, the Apocalypse passed me by. There was no tap on the shoulder. There was no knock on my door. Nobody asked me for my playbook.

That's how you find out that some dreams do come true. That's how you find out that you're in the NFL, for real.

I WAS LIKE a pig in slop. I was a kid in a candy store. I was a football player in the NFL. It doesn't get any better than that.

Two rookie linebackers made it through training camp: future Hall of Famer Derrick Thomas, and me, Rob McGovern, future captain in the U.S. Army. It's the last time you'll see those two names in the same sentence. Thomas was a star from game one. I was a backup and a special-teams guy, which meant I was fighting for a job every time I stepped out on the field.

I knew I was extremely expendable. So just like in training camp, I had to show the coaches that I belonged at this level, despite my shortcomings.

Still, I had a great time on special teams during preseason. When we opened the season against the Denver Broncos in Denver, I was named that game's special-teams captain. This meant that I would have to walk out to the fifty-yard line for the coin toss without tripping over my own feet. Given how excited I was, this wasn't going to be easy.

Waiting for us out at midfield were Denver's captains, which included some guy named John Elway, who was only one of the greatest quarterbacks in the history of the game. Being the quiet, reserved type that I was, as I walked with the other two captains out to midfield, I was saying over and over again: "Fuck John Elway. He sucks. We'll kick his ass." My cocaptains agreed.

We got to midfield, and there he was, with those perfect teeth and that look of leadership and greatness on his face. I went right up to him and shook his hand. Me, Rob McGovern, shaking hands at midfield with one of the greatest quarterbacks who ever played the game.

And then the big moment came. I spoke: "Hi, Mr. Elway. How are you? It's nice to meet you."

I was pathetic. I practically asked him to sign my elbow pads. Yeah, I was tough. Yeah, I was gonna kick his ass. Yeah, yeah, yeah—the minute I looked at this guy, I became a kid again. A fan. A guy who loved football and who'd gotten lucky enough to play it for a living. I ran off the field saying to myself, "Rob, you crumbled like a house on stilts in a hurricane." I didn't even look at my other cocaptains. I couldn't imagine what they were thinking.

Nice to meet you, Mr. Elway. I shook my head. Yeah, I was pathetic.

I'll tell you this, though—I wasn't lying.

I played a lot early in the season because one of our starters, Dino Hackett, had hurt his ankle in the opener against Denver. I played the second half at inside linebacker against the Broncos. I didn't get a chance to say hello again to Mr. Elway, although I tried. I also started our second game, against the Raiders and

Marcus Allen. Now there's another guy whose name you won't see in the same sentence as mine. But whether or not we belonged on the same field, it didn't matter. What did matter was that my job was to tackle Marcus Allen whenever he ran to my side.

From studying our game plan and scouting reports, I had been able to figure out a few things about the Raiders' offense that might be helpful to me during the game. I noticed in particular something that tipped me off to when Marcus Allen was about to get the ball and in which direction he would be heading.

If Allen lined up to the left of his fullback and his stance was slightly farther away from the line of scrimmage than his fullback, he was getting the ball and running to our right side. If he was lined up slightly closer to the line of scrimmage than his fullback, the fullback was getting the ball and Allen was going to lead-block for him on the side where he was lined up. If he lined up directly behind the fullback, it was a pass.

It seemed pretty simple and it worked about 80 percent of the time. Before each play, all I had to do was take note of which side Allen was on and whether his stance was further from or closer to the line of scrimmage than that of the fullback. With that knowledge, I could anticipate the direction of the play before the snap, and I could also figure out who would likely try to block me. That enabled me to foil their block and make the tackle. It worked. I led the team in tackles that game.

I came away from the Raiders' game feeling pretty good about myself. It was only the second game of my NFL career and I had already figured out how to think *and* have fun on the football field. But there was one problem: although I played a lot, which was good, that also meant I was on a lot of the game film, which was bad.

The following week we were playing the San Diego Chargers. They played a very simple brand of football: they flattened people. It was football as designed by George Patton or U. S. Grant—the merciless application of overwhelming force.

The Chargers' staff no doubt took one look at the film of me against the Raiders and said, "Look at that little guy playing inside linebacker. Here's what we're going to do: we're going to take the ball and run right at him all day long."

Which they did. Over and over again. I felt like my jersey was made of Velcro, because I'd hit that guard and try to shed him, like I'm supposed to, but he just stuck to me. I couldn't get him off of me. My job as a linebacker is to hit and shed, hit and shed (and don't try to say that five times fast). But San Diego threw these beasts at me on every play. I'd hit them and hit them, but yet there they were, still in my face. Eventually I figured out that if I couldn't get these guys off me, I would battle them to a draw. A tie may not be a great result in warfare, but in the trenches of football, a tie can be a victory if you're smart.

If I fought a blocker to a stalemate, I'd fill up the hole so the running back would be forced to find another place to run. That actually worked out okay, but it was really tough. When the game was over, I dragged my aching body into the locker room and personally massaged Dino Hackett's bad ankle back to health because if he didn't get better soon, I was going to get killed out there.

Hackett got better, and I went back to special teams, which was just fine with me. I'm not saying Bill Cowher was right about me, but that San Diego game reminded me that I wasn't in Worcester anymore—these linemen and running backs were big and fast and they left their calling cards all over my body.

Special teams were brutal in their own way, but it wasn't like I was on the field for every defensive down. The premium was on speed, which actually played to a strength of mine. I felt like I was getting faster. I guess there was a reason for that—I was losing weight. Most of us would think of that as a good thing, but not when you're an undersized linebacker in the NFL. The scale was dipping down to 215 pounds. For a linebacker, that's like being a six-foot center in the NBA and facing Yao Ming.

I did my best to fill up on junk food, but whatever else that stuff is doing to American waistlines, it didn't do anything for me.

I was 215 pounds when I was a college freshman. I was 215 pounds four years later, as a rookie in the NFL. Every now and again, I'd manage to hit 220 or even 225, but it never lasted. I couldn't keep the weight on. I knew this was going to be a problem if I expected any kind of sustained NFL career.

While I was in college, a guy I knew suggested I take steroids to get bigger and faster. It was tempting, because I was small even for a Division I-AA linebacker. I tried to get bigger, but nothing worked—maybe steroids were the answer. If I could put on another twenty or thirty pounds, I wouldn't have to worry about being considered "too small" for my position. That would have relieved a lot of stress.

I knew players who used steroids—not that they admitted it to me. But they were pretty easy to spot in a locker room. I mean, these guys were huge, too huge for their body frame. They also seemed just a little too edgy, a little too aggressive, even for football players. We called these guys "roid heads."

Regardless of how I felt about these guys, there was no question that they became bigger, stronger, faster, and better football players after one or two cycles of injections. Pretty good players became very good players. It was undeniable. Why should I keep struggling with my weight when other people were loading up the easy way? Especially when some of those guys were offensive linemen, the guys I was supposed to do battle with. They were 300 pounds, and I was 215. I'm no math major, but those numbers don't add up. It didn't seem fair.

There's no question that my football career, in college and the NFL, would have been easier if I had taken those steroids when they were offered. Who knows? Instead of being a career backup or a special-teams guy, I might have become a star, if only I could have added twenty or thirty pounds of muscle.

But at what cost? What would it say about me if I started taking drugs just to get ahead? Frankly, I'd always considered drug users as losers. I didn't have a lot of patience for the excuses people gave for screwing up their lives with drugs. Drug users took the easy way out, at least in my opinion.

Athletes who used drugs weren't just losers—they were cheaters. They couldn't get the job done with their natural talents, so they turned to drugs. Their cheating gave them an unfair advantage over those of us who were smaller but clean. What makes sports so appealing to people like me and most fans is the idea of a level playing field—if you're going to succeed as a professional athlete, you have to do it with hard work and God-given talent. It's a merit-based system.

But steroids changed that equation. If you didn't take them— if you didn't cheat—you were at a disadvantage. The playing field wasn't even anymore. It was tilted in favor of the cheaters.

The steroid scandal in baseball has played out in front of all of us. All these supposedly great home-run hitters got bigger before our eyes, but nobody said a word until it was too late. Now all their home runs are being called into question. Is it fair to compare these guys to guys like Willie Mays, Hank Aaron, and Babe Ruth?

I decided I hated steroids and wouldn't use them, regardless of the consequences for my career. I chose not to cheat, and I chose not to risk my own health. It was no secret then, and certainly is no secret now, that steroids are incredibly dangerous and even life-threatening drugs.

Only an idiot, I believe, would put this crap in his or her body. You could make an argument that twenty years ago or so, people took steroids without fully understanding the consequences. But that is no longer the case. Arguably, athletes like Lyle Alzado, the onetime Oakland Raider, died prematurely as a result of steroids. There is no sticking our heads in the sand anymore.

LIFE AS A rookie in the NFL—check that, life as a disposable rookie in the NFL—is not for the faint of heart. You're one big mistake away from unemployment, which, for most guys, means an abrupt entry into something called "the real world." Most players haven't had a whole lot of experience with reality. They've been praised and coddled since they first put on a pair of shoulder pads, held out as superior people because of their ability to catch or throw a football, flatten other big guys at the line of scrimmage, or chase down and tackle some two-legged deer with a football cradled in his arms.

Pressure? In real-world terms, maybe not. Football isn't life and death. It isn't war. It can't make the world safer from fanatics. It is pretty meaningless when compared with what's going on in the Middle East right now.

It's a game. It's just a game. But for players who've known nothing else, and who know nothing else, the pressure is intense. Basically, we're auditioning for a job every week in front of eighty thousand people in the stands and millions watching on television. Yeah, that's pressure.

Midway through my rookie year, I started developing severe stomach pains, especially at night. I figured I was hungry—any excuse to grab a snack and get my weight up. But then I'd eat, and the pain would get worse. Something was wrong.

A visit to the team doctor confirmed my unprofessional diagnosis. Yes, something was wrong—I had an ulcer.

"How the hell did that happen?" I asked the doc.

"Don't worry so much," he replied. This was back in the dark ages of medicine, when ulcers were thought to be purely a by-product of stress. Nowadays, the medicine men say ulcers are caused by bacteria.

I assured the doctor politely that being worried was an occupational hazard. So when he told me not to stress so much, I replied, "Easy for you to say, doc. Somebody's trying to fire me every day." Regardless of how I got an ulcer, that's exactly how I felt and how I lived.

As the season wore on, though, I felt a little more confident of my status on the team. I played every game and I even managed to score two points in a game against the Dallas Cowboys. It was the first year for Troy Aikman and Jimmy Johnson, a season that could best be described as a "learning experience." That's a nice way of saying they lost every game except one. And the low point of that low season had to be the game against us. Dallas was in punt formation, and we were looking to block the kick. I was supposed to get through the line and charge the Dallas punter, Mike Saxon.

The ball was snapped, I shed a blocker and now it was just me bearing down on Saxon. He very calmly took a step forward and punted the ball. Right into my face mask. The ball bounced away from me and kept rolling. Saxon tried to chase it down, but the ball went through the end zone before he could catch up with it. That's a safety, and I got credit for two points. (We won, 36–28.) You could look it up. If, for some reason, you wanted to.

If you ask Aikman or Johnson today what was the worst moment of that 1–15 season, they'd probably say it was the game against the Chiefs, when some little guy from Holy Cross put his face in front of a punt and got two points out of it. Of course, they also have Super Bowl rings and I don't. So that should make them feel a little better.

We finished the season at 8–7–1, a big improvement on the year before. What I found amazing, though, is the support we got from the Kansas City community when we got off to a 3–5 start. For a few weeks, it looked like the Chiefs were heading for a second straight dismal season. The fans, however, never got down on us. At one point early on, I was standing in a hotel lobby in Kansas City waiting for somebody—I think I was wearing something that indicated I played for the Chiefs. Maybe it was a shirt that said NO, I'M NOT A KICKER WITH THE CHIEFS. In any case, some pleasant guy came up to me and asked if I was with the Chiefs. Coming from New Jersey, I have to admit I wasn't sure how to answer that question. I mean, I just didn't feel like being berated by some season ticket holder, or having an armchair coach tell me what kinds of plays we ought to be running and how we ought to trade for John Elway and Lawrence Taylor and Barry Sanders. Or just having some guy say, "You guys suck," and hoping I'll take a swing at him and he'll have a nice lawsuit on his hands.

I decided to tell the truth, and simply replied, "Yes, I play for the Chiefs." "Okay," I thought, "here it comes."

"You guys are trying really hard out there," the guy said.

Now I knew this guy was up to no good. I mean, he was setting me up big-time. I was waiting for the comments like, "You guys try really hard, and yet you suck. Have you considered another profession—farming, perhaps?" So I braced myself for the blast I knew was coming and continued the conversation by saying "Yeah, we're trying."

"Yeah," he said, "you guys aren't doing so great." See—I saw this one coming. Then he politely said, "So keep on trying, because it's gonna pay off." The guy smiled and walked away.

I had to shake my head. What planet was I on? I mean, did some guy just walk up to me and say something nice? Well, Toto, I guess we really were in Kansas City after all.

Playing in a place like Kansas City seemed a little like playing in a college atmosphere. No tabloid sportswriters were looking to fire the coach after a few bad games, no bigmouthed radio hosts pretended to know more about football than the general manager, Carl Peterson. Fans came to Arrowhead Stadium, our home field, from four or five neighboring states—you'd see their Winnebagos in the stadium parking lot on Friday. This was totally different from the Meadowlands near my hometown in New Jersey, where tailgating was a day-of-game event. In Kansas City, fans made a weekend out of a home game. It was fantastic.

Management was great, too. The Chiefs' GM was and still is Carl Peterson, a great guy and a huge supporter of the military. Many years after I left Kansas City, in 2005, Mr. Peterson invited me back to Arrowhead Stadium to flip the coin before a game. It was a way not of paying tribute to me, but of thanking all our troops for their service overseas. It was an incredibly kind gesture, and it was especially nice that the Chiefs' venerable owner, Lamar Hunt, invited me to sit in his box and watch the game.

My family came out to see me play a couple of times and they loved the atmosphere, too. But they couldn't make every game, and when they couldn't, they made a deal with a local bar I used to hang out in called Finnegan's. The owner had a satellite dish, and he agreed to put on the Chiefs' games for my family and friends.

The man who set the tone in Kansas City, I think, was Mr. Hunt, one of the great gentlemen in professional football. I remember seeing him on the playing field once during a game and I noticed something peculiar about his appearance. I didn't want to stare, but finally I figured it out: the frame of Mr. Hunt's eyeglasses was broken and was being held together with Scotch tape. All right, I figured, maybe they had just broken and he didn't have an extra pair. But when I saw him with the same pair a few weeks later, well, I fell in love with the guy. Here was a man worth a gazillion dollars, and he's walking around with a pair of glasses held together with Scotch tape. You have to love a guy like that.

With the season over, I cleaned out my locker and reminded myself that there was no guarantee I'd ever return. I wound up leading the team in special-teams tackles and I played in every game, but still, I knew I was expendable—there would be a new crop of rookies in 1990. What I did in 1989 wouldn't matter when training camp opened in July.

I had been given an opportunity few guys ever get: I played a season in the NFL. I didn't get hurt, I didn't embarrass myself, I played for a great coach and I was a part of a great organization. What more could I ask?

"Okay, God," I thought. "If this is it, that's great. Thank You for the opportunity." I meant every word of it.

MOST FANS FOLLOW football from opening day in September to the Super Bowl in late January or early February. Football players—or players like me, in any case—don't have the luxury of walking away from the game for a few months once the season's over.

Just like most people don't appreciate all the work that soldiers do when they're not on the front lines, football fans don't realize how much work goes on away from the playing field—especially if you're a marginal guy like myself.

So I left my apartment in Kansas City around the holidays and returned home after the season, but I knew I'd be in New Jersey only for a few weeks. The Chiefs had an off-season workout program beginning March 1, and if you're a guy like me, you have to be there. The big stars could blow it off, but for the rest of us, well, they took attendance.

During that brief period between the end of the season and the beginning of off-season lifting and training, I had a chance to think about where all of this might lead, and how it might end. I knew there was no guarantee I would make the team in 1990, and that thought led me to think about a Plan B. What would

I do if the Chiefs cut me? Maybe somebody else would pick me up. But maybe not. Then what?

I still had this idea that I'd make a decent lawyer, because I knew I liked to talk and I loved competition. So I called a long-time family friend, Jerry Breslin, who had a law practice in Hackensack, near the Meadowlands. I asked him if he'd consider letting me hang around the office, carry his bags, or make coffee—whatever he needed. I'd get a taste of law, and he'd have a gofer. He was kind enough to accept these terms, and kinder still to let me sit in on a few trials. I loved it—the strategy decisions, the give-and-take, and the competitive spirit of the courtroom. I think it's fair to say I was one of very few NFL players who worked as a paralegal during the off-season, but I'm glad I did. I got a glimpse of life after football, and I liked what I saw.

When I returned to Kansas City for off-season training, I took the law school admission test. I actually didn't mind the lifting and the drills, and I remember thinking, "You know, my job is to stay in shape. How good is that?" But I also knew that sooner or later, this fantasy life would come to an end. I had to prepare for that, otherwise I'd be like some guys I'd already met—guys who spent their whole lives playing football, never thinking it would end. And when it did, they had no plan, and even worse, no other interests. That wasn't going to happen to me.

As my second training camp opened, I felt I had a little more breathing room than I had had the year before. But then I got a look at the competition—man, we had some studs out of the draft that year. And the Chiefs were definitely a team on the rise—a play-off contender, not just another .500 team. I was going to have to bust my butt even more than I did the year before.

We played our preseason opener in Berlin as part of the NFL's effort to build a fan base in Europe. It was a pretty exciting time to be in Berlin for reasons that had nothing to do with football. The wall had fallen, communism had collapsed, the Soviets were about to go out of business, and all of Eastern Europe was on the verge of a new beginning. It was fabulous to be there to see it all, if only for a few days. We took a bus tour as a team one day, and as we drove from west to east, the entire character of the city changed. It was like moving from a color movie to black-and-white. The East German communists and their Soviet masters had built a lifeless, colorless city that just didn't work. The buildings were drab piles of concrete, and the cars were all little Russian-made things that didn't look very safe. If you wanted to see the difference between capitalism and communism, Berlin was the place to be.

We also saw a bombed-out church that had never been repaired or torn down after World War II. I asked some of the locals about it. They told me it was left as a reminder to future generations of what Germany had brought on herself. That struck me as very impressive.

We played the Rams at Olympic Stadium, which also had a great history—it's where Jesse Owens won four gold medals during the 1936 Olympics and Hitler refused to shake his hand because he was black. If you think that kind of irrational intolerance belongs to another age, you haven't been following the news from the Middle East lately. Everything I've read about the Nazis and the fascists convinces me that our new enemies are using the same ideological playbook.

In any case, while Berlin was memorable, the game was not, aside from the fact that my family flew over to watch me, and that I made three or four tackles. I was more impressed by all the history around me. The game finished up at about ten o'clock at night and we were due to leave our hotel for the airport at six o'clock the following morning.

Being young, the players decided there was no point in going to bed. We'd stay up until six and then sleep on the plane ride home.

My brother Mike and I went with some of my teammates to a couple of bars, had some drinks, and then headed back to our hotels—I wasn't staying with Mike because I traveled with the team. I got back to my room a little before six, sat on the edge of my bed, turned on the TV, and . . . the next thing I knew it was eight o'clock. The plane was scheduled to leave at eight-twenty.

I grabbed my bags, flew down the hallway, raced across the lobby, grabbed a cabdriver who didn't speak English, somehow indicated that I needed to get to the airport, and then realized I didn't have any money. We must have broken a few traffic laws on the way to the airport but we got there with a few minutes to spare. I dragged the poor cabbie with me as I ran through the terminal so I could pay him somehow before I left. But first I checked at the Pan Am counter to see if the plane had left. It hadn't. Good.

I was standing near a huge window overlooking the runway. The woman behind the counter pointed toward the window. "Look, there they are now." I could see a Pan Am plane slowly getting into position for takeoff.

I was like Dustin Hoffman in *The Graduate*. I pressed my face against the window and yelled, "Nooooooo!" Too late.

I got some cash, paid the cabbie, thanked him for his help, and then I booked myself on a flight to Kansas City via Frankfurt and LaGuardia in New York. I must have been a pretty pathetic sight—and I must have smelled even worse. I had barely slept, hadn't showered, shaved, combed my hair, or even brushed my teeth. On top of that, as I was grabbing my stuff in the hotel room, I cut my finger on my razor and could only find some toilet paper to help stop the bleeding. And there I was standing alone in the airport in Germany trying to make my way home. As my dad would say in a moment like this, "You look like something shot at and hit." Well, I managed to get on my plane to begin my journey home.

As I boarded the flight, I saw that the cheerleaders for the Rams were on my flight. Wow! This is every thirteen-year-old boy's fantasy—and mine, too. Looking and smelling like I did, however, you can only imagine what the Rams cheerleaders thought of me. It didn't matter, though. I was asleep before we even got in the air.

Flying home with the Rams cheerleaders was the opportunity of a lifetime . . . and I slept the entire flight. I probably drooled all over myself while I was at it. That was just the kind of day I was having. It seemed like everything that could go wrong did go wrong. I guess I should just be happy a safe didn't fall on my head.

When I finally made it back to Kansas City, I explained what happened to Coach Schottenheimer, who seemed amused by the whole thing. "But still, Rob," he said, "I have to fine you a thousand dollars for missing the team plane." At the time, we were getting paid $500 a week during training camp—our real salaries didn't kick in until the regular season. So for my first two paychecks for the preseason, the total read: $000. If I have a family one day, I'll show my kids those pay stubs. "See, kids, you have it lucky," I'll say. "Daddy used to play in the NFL and they didn't even pay him."

Of course, I won't tell them that I would have played for free.

TRAINING CAMP WAS a lot less stressful the second time around. I did fine, and not only made the team as a backup linebacker and special-teams maniac, but I was getting sent in to play on goal-line stands and short-yardage situations, getting into four-point stands and going toe-to-toe with guys who weighed a hundred pounds more than me.

Now, a casual fan might wonder why a skinny linebacker would be sent in to face guys with biceps as big as the average thigh. Not a bad question. Maybe Bill Cowher figured if he couldn't cut me, he could at least kill me.

Even though we had a hell of a team that year, we didn't really hit our stride until after midseason, when we started on a decent winning streak. The most memorable game in that stretch came against our archrivals from the old days of the AFL, the Raiders. Their star running back was Bo Jackson, and everywhere Bo went in those days, the media followed. He was a two-sport wonder, playing baseball for the Kansas City Royals and then, once the season was over, jumping in as the Raiders' featured back. It was mind-boggling how this gifted athlete moved from being a star in one sport to being a star in another—just like that. One week he's hitting baseballs, the next week he's hitting a hole in the line.

At one point in the game, the Raiders were on our two-yard line, so we put in our goal-line defense—including me. About a thousand cameramen ran to the back of the end zone hoping to get a picture of Bo scoring a touchdown. I lined up on the outside of the line on the right, and I was thinking one thought only: "Oh my God. I'm gonna get run over by Bo Jackson."

Bo weighed 222 pounds, so at least it would be a fair fight.

Behind me, the cameras were snapping away just before the ball was snapped. I've seen pictures of the scene: you see this row of rear ends all pretty much in a straight line, until you get to the end, where my butt is about two feet lower than everybody else's.

They called the play, the ball was snapped, and Bo ran to the other side and got his touchdown. I had to figure the Raiders were afraid of me.

At around week ten, just as we were getting our act together, Coach Schottenheimer pulled me aside.

"Rob, we have to cut you," he said.

It turned out one of our defensive backs had hurt a hamstring and we needed to sign a new one. We only had so many roster slots, so something had to give. And it was me. So I was cut, but thankfully just for two games. But that's what life is like for most of us in the NFL. Yes, you're well paid and you're making a living at something you love. But ultimately, you're just a pawn. If somebody goes down—it doesn't matter if you're a defensive guy and the injured guy is on offense, or special teams—you might be the odd man out if they have to sign somebody new.

Getting cut is basically getting fired. And that stinks, no matter what you do for a living.

It happened again a couple of weeks later. Same thing: they needed to make a roster move, and I was the guy who moved—off the team. I was annoyed the first time it happened, but when it happened again, I hit the ceiling. I flew home to New Jersey and told my family that I wasn't going back. The hell with them.

"They're treating me like a yo-yo," I whined to my mom,

who, let me tell you, was having none of it. She and my sister Patti were listening to me bitch and moan until Mom decided she couldn't take it anymore.

"How stupid is the son I raised?" she asked. This question was considered for a moment. How stupid? Well, what are the choices: Very? Extremely? Stunningly? Shockingly?

She didn't wait for a reply. "Listen to yourself, will you? You're in the National Football League. This is just a bump in the road. You've gotta get over it. You've gotta go back there and play. And when the season ends, people aren't going to ask you about the games you missed. They'll ask you about the games you played."

It was hard to argue with that logic. So I flew back to Kansas City and finished out a terrific season for the team. We made the play-offs with an 11–5 record. I got a chance to play in a play-off game against Dan Marino and the Miami Dolphins. I went on to play for two more seasons and change. Thanks to my mother, my career didn't end after a year and a half.

How stupid is the son she raised? Not stupid enough to throw away an NFL career.

SO WE'RE IN the play-offs and in Miami, which is not such a bad thing in the winter, especially with Kansas City buried under about seventeen feet of snow. As we worked out at Vero Beach, Florida, in the days before the game, I noticed a pattern: I was starting to sink lower and lower on the depth charts. When you're on the second punt team one day and the fifteenth the next day, it's not hard to figure out that you might be in a little trouble, playing-time-wise.

Rather than wait for bad news, I decided to ask Coach Schottenheimer if I should be reading anything into the fact that the ball boy was seeing more action than I was.

"Coach," I said, "is there anything I need to know about this weekend? I've got family flying down here to see the game, but if they shouldn't make the trip, I'd like to tell them in advance."

Schottenheimer really was a decent guy. He didn't avoid the question. "Rob, I was going to tell you after practice today," he said. "We're making a move. You're going to get cut for the game. You can be on the sidelines, but you won't be playing."

It was great that the coach didn't play games with me. But still, I came away from this exchange with two words in my mind: this sucks.

And it did.

Then again, I was in Florida in the wintertime. I was going to be on the sidelines for an NFL play-off game—a pretty good thing. Fine. I'd have a blast. So I hooked up with the third-string quarterback, who was also cut for the game, and we went out drinking one night before practice. We didn't get hammered, but we had our share of woe-is-me drinks.

We were pretty hungover at practice the next morning. Yes, we were cut, but we still showed up at practice. We're professionals, after all.

You know, come to think of it, I was more than hungover. I reeked. My eyes were Kansas City Chief red. My head felt like they'd used me as a tackling dummy.

In this condition, I spotted the boss, Coach Schottenhiemer. "Hey, Rob," he said—from a distance, thankfully. "Change of plans. You're playing this week."

"Oh, great, sir. That's terrific. Thank you so much."

You wouldn't have a barf bag on you anywhere, would you, Coach?

Luckily the game wasn't for a couple of days, so that throbbing in my brain would be gone by game time. Not that it mattered. Even though I was told to dress for the game, I wasn't listed on the depth chart. And since I really hadn't practiced, I didn't know the plays. All this meant was that I'd get a chance to sit on the sidelines in a helmet and full pads. I decided not to bring along a lounge chair. That would have been tacky.

What an atmosphere! The NFL knows how to hype a play-off game. They bring out stars to sing the National Anthem, the crowds are crazier than usual, all the big network commentators are on hand—everything is big-time hype. And I'm enjoying the heck out of the experience. I've got a sideline seat, and it's a great game. It's a close, defensive game, but you could see Dan Marino and our guy, Steve DeBerg, trying to figure out a way to break through.

I can't say I watched every play—I mean, there were a lot of distractions: the cheerleaders, the cool videos on the scoreboard, the cheerleaders. So you might say my head wasn't entirely in the game when I heard some loud conversation and then noticed the players in front of me moving to one side or the other—a sea of grungy football players parting. Who was performing this miracle? None other than Bill Cowher, our defensive coach. "Rob, get in the game." Percy Snow, a linebacker who was a top draft pick that year, had gotten hurt. Who knew?

I didn't know where my helmet was. Thank God it happened to be nearby. I grabbed it and ran onto the field. Let's see—it's a play-off game. Check. We're the guys in white. Check. We're playing the Miami Dolphins. Check. Their quarterback is some guy named Dan Marino. Uh oh, that's not good.

While I'm running out onto the field and my name is being announced to a collective yawn from the fans, some coach for the Dolphins is watching very carefully from a booth upstairs. He's monitoring our substitutions—and we're doing the same for theirs. So at that very moment, they were sending word down to the Miami bench: New linebacker in the game. If they were really good, they were saying: New, underweight linebacker in the game, possibly still suffering from the effects of a hangover and may puke in his helmet because this is his first NFL play-off game and he didn't think he would actually be on the field. So let's see what he's got.

I doubt they got that specific, but you never know. Scouting is a big part of pro football.

I was a standout from the moment I set foot on the field because I was the only guy on defense whose uniform was immaculate. Not a stain to be seen. It wasn't hard for Dan Marino to figure out that he had somebody new to pick on.

I lined up at inside linebacker. Marino started calling signals. And, as God is my witness, the guy looked right into my eyes. I mean, he looked right at me. And I felt a chill go down my spine. Oh my God—one of the greatest quarterbacks in the history of the National Football League is about to make a fool out of me.

I got that thought out of my system. Marino was still calling signals. If they come right at me, I thought, they'll try one of two plays. They'll run the fullback, Tony Paige, at me to throw the lead block for the tailback and hope to spring him. Or they'll run the tight end, Ferrell Edmunds, down the middle of the field, and

I'll have to run with him and cover him the whole way. Okay. Got it. It's one or the other. I was ready. Now the ball's snapped. The fullback is coming right at me. It's a run! I hit Tony Paige hard. Nice work. Except that it was a fake, and I bit on it. I turned around and saw the tight end, Ferrell Edmunds, ten yards behind me and running downfield with the football. Marino had thrown a quick pass over the middle while I was biting on the fake.

I chased Edmunds down and tackled him, along with a couple of defensive backs, but not before he gained forty yards. It was a huge play in a tight play-off game. I got up off the pile and all I could think was, "Damn, this game is on national television."

When we got back in the huddle, Chris Martin, the outside linebacker, apologized to me.

"What are you sorry for?" I said. I was the guy who screwed up. But Martin reminded me that he was supposed to jam the tight end—hit him as he was coming off the line to throw him off his pattern. He didn't do it. "I missed the jam," he said. That was a classy thing to say to me. I felt a little better—not a lot better, just a little.

I played the rest of the game. Miami kicked a late field goal to go ahead, and we marched back and had a field-goal try of our own, but it fell short by about a foot.

I was mad. The game ends, the crowd is going nuts, the Dolphins are celebrating, and I'm on the sidelines, by myself, and looking very pissed off. I'm shaking my head and snarling and in general looking like a guy whose team just lost by a point in the play-offs. Then I look up and see myself on the Jumbotron. Some cameraman's focused on my face, and I notice a little ABC logo in the corner of the picture. That's when I realized that a couple of million households are watching me. That's entertainment!

Why would ABC be showing my face? I couldn't figure that one out. "Just act normal," I said to myself. "Just be cool. Don't think about the fact that millions of people are looking at you for some reason you can't figure out." The director eventually got tired of looking at me, but it seemed like minutes went by until I disappeared from that Jumbotron. Still, I couldn't figure out why ABC was interested in showing me—a backup linebacker. Weeks later, I found out that when I went for that fake and Marino completed the pass to Edmunds, Dan Dierdorf, the ABC announcer working the game, gave me a once-over. "Rob McGovern on Ferrell Edmunds—that's a total mismatch," he said. So I got all the blame. I was the goat, eh? Thanks, Dan.

In our meeting the day after, both Schottenheimer and Cowher told me that Martin missed the jam, that it wasn't my fault that Edmunds made a big gain on the play. I felt a little bit better.

They released me a few weeks later.

CHAPTER SIX

★ ★ ★

The Real World—
A Disposable Linebacker Finally Grows Up

I GREW UP ABOUT TWELVE MILES FROM THE MEADOW-
lands sports complex, home of the Giants and the Jets. I'm old
enough to remember when the area was just a big swamp with
great views of the Manhattan skyline. During the early 1970s,
New Jersey got the idea to build a football stadium, a track, and
an arena in the middle of this muck. A lot of New Yorkers
laughed when the state offered this swamp to the New York Giants as their new home. But the joke was on them when the Giants, and then the Jets, packed up and moved to this brand-new
facility near my home.

Over the years, New Jersey's top high school football teams
got a chance to play at Giants Stadium. My brothers played in the
state championships there. But when my turn came, for whatever

reason, we didn't get a chance to play on the big stage. I had to settle for another swamp, otherwise known as Bergen Catholic's home field.

So when I was looking for a new team to catch on with as a free agent in early 1991, at age twenty-four, I was pretty excited to get a call from the Jets. They were a hometown team, and they played in my backyard. If my family or friends wanted to see me play, they could almost walk to the games—almost.

After living in an apartment near Kansas City where my closest neighbors were cows, and I'm not kidding about that, I was pretty happy about the idea of home cooking and old friends. Plus, I'd finally get a chance to play at Giants Stadium.

But the Jets weren't the only team desperate enough to be inquiring about my services. The Pittsburgh Steelers called, too. That's right—the Steelers, coached by the legendary Chuck Knoll, then the winners of four Super Bowls, one of the NFL's great old franchises. Oh, how the mighty had fallen—the Steelers of 1991 were not the Steelers of the 1970s. They needed some help in the linebacking department, which was a pretty sad thought considering how great their defense was during the glory years.

My heart was with the Jets. But after two years in the NFL, I knew that very few people could afford to make decisions with their hearts—and I wasn't one of them. If I picked the wrong team for the wrong reasons, I had no illusions about what would follow.

No matter what the coach thought of me as a person, I could be out of work and out of the league in a minute. That's life in the NFL. If I had one advantage over some of the other guys I met along the way, I guess it was my realistic perspective: I knew how expendable I was. I realized that I lived in a fantasy world that wouldn't last forever—I considered myself lucky that it had lasted this long. Some other guys took football for granted, which is fine if you're a star, but even a star fades and then disappears.

I remember having a conversation with one of my teammates who had reported to camp late after holding out for more money. I didn't think he was right, but one day in the locker room, he explained why he'd done it. "After football," he said, "I'm pumping gas. I don't know how to do anything but play football, and I know that won't last. I have three kids, and I want to send them to college. I've got about four more years to make some money, and then I'm at the gas station. So if I can get another five hundred thousand now, I gotta do it. Because I don't have anything else after football."

No wonder most guys don't think about the future. The idea of life after football is almost as scary as thinking about death, except that my faith assures me there is life after death. For a lot of guys, there is no life after football.

In the end, I decided I had a better chance of keeping my football dream alive a little longer by going to Pittsburgh. The Steelers seemed to value speed more than the Jets did. They were looking for a linebacker who could think. So I told them I took the Law School Admission Test and was planning to be a lawyer someday. Heck, if I thought it would work, I'd show up at camp carrying *War and Peace* and wearing half-rim glasses. I was trying everything to convince them I was their man.

There were a couple of other arguments in favor of the Steelers. They might not play in my backyard, but Pittsburgh wasn't as far as Kansas City. The McGovern clan and friends wouldn't have to get on an airplane to watch me play. Plus, hey, they were the Steelers! Terry Bradshaw, Mean Joe Green, Jack Lambert, and Lynn Swann! Sure, they were gone, but the aura was still there. You could smell it in the locker room. At least, I think that's what I smelled.

There was another reason why you couldn't walk into the Steelers' locker room without thinking of all those great players—the place hadn't changed a bit since they'd left. By the 1990s, lots of teams were getting new stadiums or, at a minimum, updating their facilities to accommodate the more refined tastes of the modern professional football player. In other words, they were getting bigger Jacuzzis.

But in Pittsburgh, it's like they decided not to touch a thing in honor of the legend of Terry Bradshaw and Company. Tradition is fine, but that doesn't mean you can't get a new carpet every now and then.

If you dared to suggest that perhaps the Steelers could invest in a new Universal weight system, some old-timer was sure to growl. "It was good enough for Jack Lambert," he'd say. "Do you think you're better than Jack Lambert, kid?" The correct answer to this question was, "No, sir. I meant no disrespect to Mr. Lambert. I will be happy to use the same equipment he used twenty years ago, and I promise not to complain about his karma, which clings to this equipment like cellophane to leftovers."

Actually, it was pretty cool to be in the same locker room that Jack Lambert once used. I grew up idolizing Lambert and the other great linebackers of that era—Dick Butkus of the Bears, Willie Lanier of the Chiefs, and Mike Curtis of the Colts. When I got to the Steelers, I taped a picture of Lambert inside my locker, to remind me of the kind of player I'd like to be. Yeah, some football players are just overgrown fans, or, in my case, barely grown.

I knew Lambert's number was 58, and I also knew that I was not only unworthy to wear Jack Lambert's number, but it wasn't even available. It had been retired. So I asked for number 56, which, when you think about it, looks like number 58 if the sun is right and you're looking at it from up in the nosebleed sections.

Well, I got a kick out of it anyway. It hit me the most every time I walked into the locker room on game day. I would see a Pittsburgh Steelers jersey hanging in my locker with my name on it. I mean, legends wore that jersey. It meant something to me to be a Pittsburgh Steeler.

SIGNING AS A free agent with the Steelers didn't assure me of a job. It just meant I had a chance to earn one in training camp. But by now, I knew the drill: bust my butt, and maybe I'll have a shot. But if the numbers don't add up, well, they'd say, "It's been great knowing you. Here is a bus ticket to New Jersey."

Being on a new team also meant I didn't know a soul. Who would have predicted that I'd wind up with another guy from New Jersey as my training-camp roommate?

Dan Walsh was a running back out of Montclair State in New Jersey's Essex County, about fifteen miles or so from my house in Bergen County. He approached me on the field one day during the minicamp practices held in early spring after the college draft. He had just signed with the team as a free agent from the Philadelphia Eagles.

I had no idea why this guy was so interested in talking to me, but I figured I would hear him out. As I listened to him quietly, it became apparent that his primary objective was to tell me how great I was. I quickly realized that he thought he was talking to Merrill Hoge, our star running back out of Idaho State. I looked a little like Merrill, and Dan wasn't the first person to make this mistake.

I decided to let Dan go on and on about how great he thought I was—it was a refreshing change from what I usually heard from the coaches. Finally, though, I couldn't take it anymore. Dan was laying it on so thick I just had to stop him. "Listen, man: I am not Merrill Hoge and you can stop kissing my ass."

It tells you something about Dan that he didn't get upset at all. He laughed, and so did I. We wound up talking—or I wound up listening—for half an hour or so as we stood there on the field. Dan is a great communicator. He could talk a dog off a meat truck. By the time his monologue was over, I agreed to be his roommate for the summer and to find an apartment for us to live in as well.

I remember walking off the field and thinking, "I just said I'd live with a guy I didn't even know twenty minutes ago. I must be an idiot." As it turned out, it was one of the best decisions I ever made.

Dan Walsh is a real American success story. It was a miracle that a guy like Dan even made it to an NFL training camp. Not too many Division III players show up on the scouting radar screens. I got along with him right away because he busted his butt like nobody else in camp and it became pretty clear that we shared the same attitude toward the NFL.

At night, after working all morning, lifting all afternoon, and finishing it all off with a late-afternoon run, we'd go back to our apartment, make a couple of milk shakes—both of us were size-challenged—and watch the movie *Patton* for the hundredth time.

Dan would turn to me and say, "Rob, does anybody have a better life than us?" That was exactly my attitude: we were getting paid to work out, drink milk shakes, and watch a great war movie.

Dan and I were getting paid to do something we would have done for free. We loved playing football and we appreciated the incredible opportunity we had been given by the Pittsburgh Steelers. No, nobody had it better than us that summer.

America has its flaws, and so does football, but where else in the world can two guys like Dan Walsh and Rob McGovern follow ridiculous dreams—and see them through to fruition? I'd never say that I joined the Army to make the world safe for football. But I believe we as a nation are trying to make the world safe for other young men and women to follow their dreams, however unlikely.

But let's not forget that our troops, and our cops, firefighters, and other first responders, have been given the responsibility of making our country safe from those who would take away those dreams, and replace them with their dreary, fascist ideology.

DAN FOLLOWED HIS dream that summer and played great in the preseason. But because the Steelers' roster of running backs contained names like Hoge and Barry Foster, he wound up getting cut while I was lucky enough to make the team. But Dan decided to stay in Pittsburgh and coach running backs for a local Division III football team, so we kept the apartment together.

While I played for the Steelers, Dan coached running backs at Washington and Jefferson College just outside of Pittsburgh. They were young kids who had dreams of making the NFL like Dan used to have during his days at Montclair State. Dan made them better football players by teaching them to run, catch, and block. But he also taught them something much more important. Dan taught them the value and meaning of words like *dedication* and *sacrifice*. Dan came from a very modest upbringing and he has worked for everything he has in life. He taught those young kids the same lessons he learned early on about personal determination and resolve in the face of overwhelming odds.

Years later, Dan moved back to the New York area, got a job as a foreign-currency trader on Wall Street, and started making big-time money. His accomplishments haven't surprised me in the least—he was one of those guys who knew what he wanted and was willing to work hard to achieve it. If the objective is out of reach, they're strong and smart enough to recognize that and find another goal. Dan wanted to be an All Pro football player, but it didn't happen. So he put his talents to other uses and became a success. To me, that's the beauty of sports in general and football in particular: the games we play really do teach us life lessons. They train you to be a winner, no matter what life throws your way. You learn to work through disappointment and you learn what it takes to overcome challenges. It didn't work out for Dan in the NFL. But it worked out for him in real life. He remains one of my closest friends, and he is the reason I remember that year in Pittsburgh with such affection.

SAD AS IT sounds, I started feeling beat up that season in Pittsburgh. I'd been in the NFL for all of three years. I never had a serious injury, and I wasn't a starter, but even so—the pounding at training camp, at practice, and in games starts to take a toll pretty quickly. Playing on Astroturf in Kansas City and

Pittsburgh definitely didn't help—the rugs we used to play on were hard and unforgiving, a lot like the game itself. Today's artificial turf is a tremendous improvement over what I played on. I just don't know what took so long.

I am not alone in feeling this way. Few football players are ever 100 percent healthy, whether they're playing on grass, turf, or a feather pillow. You get a nick there, you get a bump here, and it all begins to add up. My hips and knees bothered me, but not enough to keep me from playing. I'd have to be pretty beat up to tell a coach I couldn't play. Luckily, it never came to that, although it could have. But I did nearly get myself killed one day on the practice field, thanks to a pretty competitive teammate named Greg Lloyd.

Greg was a star outside linebacker—a legit NFL standout. He was also not the nicest guy I'd ever met, a quality that no doubt helped him in his quest to punish offensive linemen for being, well, offensive lineman. Suffice it to say, he wasn't the sort of guy you'd invite over to your house for dinner. The word in camp was that Greg Lloyd didn't respect you unless you killed a grizzly bear. In front of him. With your bare hands. Since I did not meet these qualifications, he probably didn't think much of me. So I wisely kept my distance.

One day, the linebackers were getting loose for practice in the way we always do: we were slamming into one another. It wasn't serious hitting—just a little light contact. Most of us didn't bother to buckle our chin straps because it was not an all-out contact drill. We were just getting loosened up before practice really began.

As I prepared to participate in this little ritual, I fired out of my stance and rammed into the torso across from me. It belonged to Greg Lloyd. Unfortunately for Greg, my helmet "accidentally" made contact with his jaw. Unfortunately for me, he hadn't buckled his chin strap.

Greg's helmet went flying. He stumbled back and forth for a moment. He looked stunned. I knew then what it's like to take aim at a grizzly bear, fire, and then realize you've only wounded him and now you have a very angry grizzly bear.

It was a terrible thing to watch. He slowly gathered himself, put his helmet back on, and—oh, no—he then buckled the chin strap. "Okay, McGovern," he said, "I guess you want to play today." *Click.* The chin strap was put into place.

The next sound I heard was that of my own chin strap being buckled to my helmet. I mean, what was I going to do? Beg for mercy? No, I couldn't do that. I had to die with some dignity, I thought. I also considered trying to prepare my last will and testament, but there wasn't enough time for that, either. Instead, I just turned to the guy next to me and said, "Tell my family I love them."

Over the next three hours, Greg Lloyd made my life miserable and painful. This was football's answer to the pain and suffering of the military's basic training. Every chance he had to hit me, he did. Even if we were just playing chess, he'd have found a way to clobber me. I walked off the practice field that day feeling like a very old man, but lucky to be alive.

I also understood what made Greg Lloyd a great player. He didn't need some mishap during warm-ups to get him motivated to practice each day. He was a great linebacker for the Steelers because he came ready to perform and play hard every single day. He played hard during games and sometimes he played even harder during practice. He also put in the time in the weight room and the training room to make sure he was strong enough and healthy enough to play week in and week out. His athletic ability wasn't a result of good genes or the product of privilege. Greg Lloyd earned his success because he was the epitome of giving 100 percent all day and every day.

That day, Greg Lloyd taught me that there is no substitute for hard work and preparation. Again, not a bad lesson for a future soldier to learn. He also taught me that you can't just "turn it on" during the game. You have to breathe it, eat it, and sleep it.

Being the best at what you do has to be more important to you than partying or chasing girls or hanging out with your buddies. It has to be worth sacrificing the comforts and pleasures of an undirected life and replacing them with long hours of sweat and tears. In football, it also helps to be one tough character.

THE NFL GAVE me some great opportunities to give something back to the community. In Pittsburgh, I was involved in a terrific service program called Project Bundle Up. We were each matched with an underprivileged kid from the city, where we took the kids to stores to buy them warm clothing for winter. For me, it was almost like being back in Worcester, because this was the kind of stuff we'd done at Holy Cross all the time. Pittsburgh loved the Steelers, and it felt right to be giving a little back to some people who needed a helping hand.

The Steelers ran a bunch of programs in the community, and I have to credit the Rooney family for this commitment. It's not as though the Steelers needed to reach out to the community to sell tickets. The place was filled to capacity every week, and we weren't a particularly good team that year. But these projects weren't about outreach. They were about service.

On the field, I tried to be of service as best I could, but we had a tough year. The aura of the past might still linger in the locker room, but at times, it was overwhelmed by the stench of the present. We won our last two games to salvage a bit of pride, and even with a record of 7–9, we actually were in play-off contention until the very end of the season.

If nothing else, I made it onto the stat sheet for one category again. In our game against the Cincinnati Bengals, I was lined up at midfield as part of our kickoff return team. The Bengals surprised us with an onside kick—believe me, if the coaches saw this one coming, I wouldn't have been out there. The ball came directly to me, which probably was part of the Bengals' plan. You know what they had to be saying in the huddle: "See that little linebacker over there, the guy who wears number fifty-six because he thinks it looks like number fifty-eight? Yeah, let's kick it in his direction. He can't catch a cold. He won't know what to do, and we'll get the ball back."

I was the most surprised guy in the stadium, except for my coaches. But I managed to fall on the ball, which foiled Cincinnati's well-thought-out plan. I got credit for, of all things, a kickoff return. You can put it in the record books, one return for zero yards. That's right, I was now officially an NFL kickoff return man. Well, at least the yardage part seemed accurate.

When the season was over, Chuck Knoll announced that after twenty-three years, he was packing it in. Some people have claimed that my play for the Steelers was the last straw. Coach Knoll just couldn't take watching me butcher the profession he loved so much. But that can't be proven—at least I hope it can't anyway.

As his replacement, the Steelers hired a guy I knew a little bit: Bill Cowher, defensive coordinator of the Kansas City Chiefs and definitely not the president of the Rob McGovern Fan Club. (That was my mom's job, anyway.) Just in case I didn't get the point, when Cowher was hired, one of the first things he announced was that he planned to move the recent number one draft pick from the University of Florida, Hughie Richardson, from outside linebacker to inside linebacker—my position. Great.

Within a matter of days, I was a former member of the Pittsburgh Steelers.

As a Plan B free agent, I once again had to come to terms with the possibility that nobody was interested in me. On the other hand, desperate people do desperate things, especially in the National Football League. I couldn't rule out the possibility that some desperate team might make the mistake of believing I could slow their drift toward oblivion.

The phone finally rang. The call was from the New England Patriots. They weren't exactly desperate, but they also weren't the same team that got their clocks cleaned in the Super Bowl in 1985 by the Chicago Bears. The Patriots' coach, Dick McPherson, was a great guy who liked his linebackers lean and mobile. I was hopeful I could fit that bill.

The Patriots put me through something I hadn't faced before: an actual job interview. Usually, you do the lifting thing and you show how agile you are and then you run for forty yards as fast as you can and then some guy with a stopwatch basically puts in a good word, or the opposite. With New England, I did all of that, but I was also asked to sit down with Coach McPherson and his staff in his office. The coach sat behind a desk, like any other management guy conducting an interview, and his staff stood in a semicircle behind him.

"Holy mackerel," I thought, "this is a job interview. I never did one of these before." They fired off questions about game situations, about my "thought process" as a linebacker, and, like Mr. Waller, they tried to find out what made me tick. I was pretty impressed, and I guess I made an impression, too, because they signed me. Again, all that meant was that I had a chance to compete for a job. No guarantees.

Hooking up with the Patriots was a nice fit for me because of my Holy Cross roots. My sister Betsy still lived in the Boston area, my brother Bill was coaching in the area, and I had plenty of friends in and around Massachusetts. Foxboro Stadium wasn't a bad drive from New Jersey for my family, either. I was looking forward to playing in New England and for Coach McPherson, who struck me as one of the nicest guys I'd met in football.

I had a pretty good training camp, I thought, and I played pretty well in our four preseason games. Not exactly highlight-reel stuff, but good, solid workaday linebacking and special-teams play. I wasn't threatening any starter's job, but I made a pretty convincing case for journeyman Rob McGovern, in my welcome role as backup to the stars.

The morning after our last preseason game, the phone rang way too early. Nobody calls with good news at that hour—especially on the day when my team was making its last cuts before the regular season. "No way I'm answering that phone," I said to myself. I sat on the edge of my bed and listened to somebody leaving a message for me at this ungodly hour.

"Hey, Rob, it's so-and-so"—I don't remember his name, but

I knew he was from player personnel. "Could you come in this morning? We need to talk to you." Then came the phrase I dreaded hearing. "And bring your playbook."

I was a goner.

More than a decade has passed since that moment, but I still remember sitting there on the edge of my bed, feeling like somebody had just put a stake through my heart. I was prepared, I thought, for this moment. I knew that nothing in the NFL was a given—to make room for me with the Chiefs, for example, they'd cut Jack del Rio, a terrific linebacker. That wasn't fair, but neither is the NFL when it comes to the numbers. I guess they felt that del Rio's days as a starting linebacker were over, but he was too expensive to keep around as a backup. I was cheaper. I got the job. Del Rio got fired. Talk about injustice.

Now I was getting fired. As much as I thought I was prepared for anything, I really wasn't. I thought I had played well enough to make the team. But my opinion didn't matter. In the papers the next day, McPherson talked about the team's final cuts. He said the two toughest cuts he had to make were Marvin Allen, who was a four-year veteran with the Patriots, and me.

"They're legitimate NFL players," McPherson said. "They can play, but they're gone. I do believe both of them will be playing somewhere."

That was nice of him to say, but I couldn't count on his recommendation. Nobody was going to hire me because Dick McPherson said I was a legitimate NFL player.

I packed my bags and went home to New Jersey. My agent called to remind me to stay in shape. "Hang in there," he said. "You never know when somebody's gonna sprain an ankle."

I don't have the temperament to sit by a phone and wait—

that's how I missed Marty Schottenheimer's call on draft day back in 1989. So I went to work for my father's trucking company, loading and unloading trucks. Not a bad way to stay in shape, but not what I wanted to be doing. I started filling out law-school applications and I even interviewed for a job selling insurance with Liberty Mutual.

I was trying my best to keep busy and be proactive about my future, but I was a mess. All those brave words about being prepared for a sudden end to my dream, all those plans I thought I had in place, all that talk about being grateful for the opportunity I'd been given—they just seemed like words that didn't mean a thing.

At the age of twenty-six, I wasn't ready for life after football. I was no different from those other guys who thought their football careers would never end. I thought I had a plan, but I found out that even a great plan isn't enough if you don't have the will to act on it.

Every year, dozens of players go through this torture—guys like me who are on the bubble, good enough to play in the NFL but, at the same time, not good enough. They're the guys who get cut in late August, guys who believe, like I did, that they have the talent to make it somewhere. They wait for somebody to get hurt. They wait for a coach to be fired and a new one brought in—a new guy who might want some new players. Tough luck for the other guys. Good luck for you.

That is just the way it is when you're hanging on to your dreams with only your fingertips. It's hard to let go. Harder than I ever thought it would be. I wanted to get back into the game, somehow, some way. I tried to remember that I was supposed to be happy that I'd even gotten a chance to play. I knew I should be thinking about all those guys, like my buddy Dan Walsh, who would've sacrificed everything to play one season, or even one game.

I kept lifting, I kept running, I kept doing drills, and I kept telling myself that I still had a chance. Some days I believed it. Other days I didn't.

Weeks went by. I avoided watching any games on TV, although when I did, I'd make a point of singling out some poor linebacker who made a bad play. "Hey, I can play as bad as that guy," I'd say. This is not necessarily the best way to maintain one's confidence.

The phone rang on December 2, 1991. The Patriots needed a linebacker quick (a quick linebacker would've been good, too), and I fit the job description. Except that they wanted me to play outside linebacker, even though I'd played inside linebacker my whole life. Outside linebacker was one of the toughest positions there is and far more difficult than inside linebacker. You have to be strong enough to line up directly over an offensive tackle and pound him into the ground, agile enough to keep pace with a shifty running back, quick enough to corral a scrambling quarterback, and fast enough to run with a wide receiver all over the field.

Simply put, you had to be an outstanding defensive football player with absolutely no weaknesses. That wasn't me, but I didn't care if they didn't care. So I signed a contract for the rest of the season—just four games—and on December 6, I was on the field for our game against the Colts.

As miserable as I had been from September to December, the Patriots were, in their own way, just as bad off. They were having a terrible season. They'd won just two games and lost ten. They were going nowhere and they knew it. But for me, those four games might as well have been the Super Bowl. They were a chance to get back, to earn a shot at being invited to next year's training camp, to impress the coaches enough to bring me back in the summer.

My personal highlight came in our last game of the season in Foxboro on December 27 against the Dolphins. In the first quarter, I hit Dolphin kickoff return man Barry Parmalee, causing him to fumble. Our kicker, Charlie Baumann, recovered. The turnover led to a twenty-five-yard field goal by Charlie a few plays later and a 13–3 lead early in the game. I finished the game with three special-teams tackles.

Although I played only the last four games for the Patriots, I finished the season tied for sixth in special-teams tackles, ahead of nine guys who had played all year on special teams for the Patriots—not bad.

For my teammates, this rotten season couldn't end soon enough. We lost all four games I played, finishing 2–14. When it was over, predictably, Dick McPherson was fired. In his place, the Patriots announced with great fanfare that they had convinced a coach to come out of retirement to lead them to new glories: Bill Parcells.

AS I MENTIONED before, the McGovern family had this wonderful connection to the Parcells family through Dougie Parcells. You couldn't play a sport in Oradell and not know Dougie. As the head of the town's recreation department, he was more powerful—and popular—than the mayor. He was also beloved for the way he truly enjoyed kids and watching them grow.

In fact, he even joined in on my educational development a few times. I once asked him if I could be a ball boy at a Little League baseball game in town for some older kids. I was probably eight or nine at the time.

"Sure," he said. "But you first have to spell the word *penguin*."

I was stumped. I ran home, got the correct spelling from my mom, ran back to the field, and recited it back to Dougie. I was allowed to serve as ball boy for the Little League game and to this day I know how to spell *penguin* without batting an eye or running home to ask my mom.

Even though I knew Dougie's brother Bill would have a slightly tougher test for me with the Patriots, I was still hopeful I'd be invited back to the Patriots' training camp in 1993. I was right, but again, the invitation came with no assurances. I'd get a chance to fight for a job—that's it. I decided to spend the offseason in New England, but not necessarily to be closer to the Patriots' gym. My short but involuntary retirement in the fall of 1992 had given me pause—well, more than just a pause.

I realized that I had to get ready, really and truly ready, for a day when I'd turn in my playbook for the last time, and nobody would be calling me to help salvage their losing season.

I'D ALWAYS BEEN interested in politics, so I thought it might be fun and worthwhile to see what government was like on the inside. While I was working as a volunteer with a local DARE antidrug program in Massachusetts, I mentioned to some of the staff that I'd like to get involved in government one day. Somebody suggested that I look into becoming an intern for a state senator in the Massachusetts legislature.

"You know," I said, "I like that idea. Do you know any Republicans I can work for?"

"Honey," a very amused young woman said, "this is Massachusetts. We had a Republican once, but I think he's in a museum somewhere."

Oh, right. Massachusetts.

The contacts in DARE hooked me up with a Democratic state senator named William Keating, who turned out to be a great guy and a man of conviction. He was also kind enough to allow a Republican on his staff.

I spent the summer in Senator Keating's office as his all-purpose coffeemaker. Somebody once said I had to be the only NFL player who worked in a politician's office during the off-season. I agreed. The others had dignity. I, apparently, had none.

My only contribution to the public good came when the senator asked me to look into a disturbing report that a new drug—methamphetamine, known by its street name of "ice"—was making its way into the cities and towns of Massachusetts. Neither one of us had heard of it. The senator asked me to find out everything I could about the drug and prepare a report for him. I did, and the report got some attention, but it did nothing to slow the popularity of this now-common and highly addictive drug.

Years later, I'd find myself prosecuting people in New York for selling it. Like any other drug, this one has ruined and ended countless lives—and yet there are some who think, inexplicably, that drugs should be legal.

My work with Senator Keating and my status with the Patriots came together that summer when I planned and coordinated an event to raise funds for a boy in Senator Keating's district named Anthony Ando, who had polycystic kidney disease and hepatic fibrosis. I rounded up some of my teammates for an autograph session to help raise money for the child's medical treatment.

The night before the event, I was working out in the Patriots' gym and in walked our number one draft pick, Drew Bledsoe. I didn't know him from Adam, although I knew full well that he was our top pick and the guy everybody thought would lead the Patriots to better days. I introduced myself while he was on the treadmill and asked him if he'd help me out with this autographing session. He never missed a beat. "Sure, Rob, I'd be glad to come."

I'll never forget that. Drew's gone on to have a pretty good NFL career, which is great, but for me, he's an All Pro for a more important reason. He had no obligation to me—he didn't even know me—but he felt a larger obligation to his community. A lot of NFL players feel the way Drew does and they act on it every day. These real heroes should be praised for their efforts and we should all try to remember these good guys out there when we're reading about all the jerks who give pro athletes a bad name.

AROUND ORADELL, THEY used to call Bill Parcells's father "Chubby." It had to be some kind of guys' joke, because Bill's father, whose real name was Charles, was anything but chubby. He was tall and thin, and had the posture of a five-star general. He was a graduate of Georgetown Law School and worked for years for the Federal Bureau of Investigation.

My dad and Mr. Parcells became friends when I was a boy as the two men tried to raise their growing families in a little suburban sanctuary called Oradell. I saw the affection myself when I caddied for them at Hackensack Golf Course. That's where their relationship started, and it's where I think they had the most fun together. Again, the power of sports.

My dad was several years younger than Mr. Parcells, and he grew to admire and respect him. He often sought Mr. Parcells's guidance in all aspects of life—from work, to his personal life, to raising a growing family. They had more than golf in common, but golf was their enduring bond.

I remember carrying their bags one day on the thirteenth fairway. Off in the distance we saw some guy heading in our direction. It was Coach Bill Parcells, who at the time was defensive coordinator for the Giants. I was pretty much struck dumb with awe—I mean, there I was, a high school freshman with dreams of playing in the NFL, and I'm saying hello to the defensive coordinator for the New York Giants. Life is good!

A few years earlier, my brother Jack and his Holy Cross team played against the Air Force Academy, then coached by none other than Bill Parcells. My father flew out to Colorado to see the game. He showed up in Parcells's office unannounced just before game time. He told somebody he was a friend of the coach's dad—I'm sure they'd heard that one before.

But sure enough, Parcells invited my dad into his office and chatted with him for about half an hour—this is on game day. They were interrupted by a secretary who told Parcells that the Holy Cross athletic director, Ron Perry, needed to speak with him. The secretary introduced Mr. Perry to Coach Parcells, and then motioned to my father: "Oh, that's Mr. McGovern. He's here to give Coach Parcells all of Holy Cross's plays."

My dad and Coach Parcells laughed. Mr. Perry, I hear, didn't.

Football fans will not be surprised to learn that Bill Parcells isn't what you'd call a warm and fuzzy guy. Day one of Camp Parcells was as grueling as any day I've ever spent in a training camp. We weren't there to get to know one another and swap addresses for our Christmas-card list. We were there to lift and to run and to lift and run some more.

And at the end of the first day—the very first day—Parcells cut a guy who had been with the team the year before and was a starter. He was an offensive lineman and he looked a little out of shape. An easy victim, but one that got our attention big-time. That was Coach Parcells's style—he'd find a veteran, usually a journeyman, and he'd cut him right away. That was his message to the rest of us: get in shape, do it my way, or hit the road. It worked.

Not long afterward, we were doing a blitz drill with Drew Bledsoe taking snaps. Bledsoe, of course, was the stud of training camp—the guy who would turn around this sad sack of a team, with a little help from Coach Parcells.

The point of the blitz drill was to teach the offense how to recognize the blitz and how to stop it. Pretty important stuff, if you'd like your quarterback to survive the season. So we're doing this drill, and one of our cornerbacks blitzes, but the wide receiver doesn't pick him up. The cornerback had a free shot at the quarterback.

In a real game, Drew Bledsoe would have been leveled by the cornerback. He would have had no chance to react, to protect himself, because he'd never have seen him coming—at full speed and untouched by human hands. We'd be picking him up off the field with a stretcher.

Coach Parcells blows his whistle and stops practice. He walks out on the field and walks up to the wide receiver who missed his assignment. Every one of us was quiet.

Parcells got in the cornerback's face and let loose. "Listen," he said in the loudest voice I'd ever heard, "I can go down to any bus stop in Providence"—we were training in Rhode Island at the time—"and find a hundred guys who can run as fast as you. But I can't get somebody who throws the ball like him!" He pointed to Beldsoe. "So don't ever miss your block again!"

More silence. Dead silence. And we're all thinking, "Oh, that's a good point, coach, sir. Yes, we'll make a mental note of that, sir. Don't miss your blocks. Very good, sir."

I never was on the receiving end of that kind of blast. Coach Parcells was a little nicer to me. When I'd make a mistake, he'd come up to me, and in the most pleasant, cordial way he could, he'd look me in the eye and say, very slowly and very quietly: "You do that again and you're cut." And then he'd walk away.

If that didn't make you pay attention, well, you were an idiot and of no use anyway except maybe as a tackling dummy.

None of this would surprise most football fans, who've seen the icy glare of Bill Parcells on television. He's an intimidating guy. But I also saw another side of the guy, thanks to my family connection. Every now and again, he'd come up to me on the field or in the locker room and ask about my dad, or one of my brothers. But it wasn't just personal stuff—he'd tell me what I needed to work on, what needed improvement, and what I was doing right. That's good coaching, but it's not the kind people think of when they picture Bill Parcells.

One day in camp, Coach Parcells saw me talking to Mickey Corcoran, an older gentleman who was a legendary coach at

River Dell High School in Oradell. River Dell was the public high school located only a few miles away from Bergen Catholic, my alma mater. I had a lot of friends from grammar school and from around town who went to River Dell, so I was very familiar with their athletic programs.

I never had the opportunity to play for Coach Corcoran but I wish I had. He was a legend in town and probably the only man who was held in higher esteem than Dougie Parcells. Like everyone who knew him, Bill Parcells had a special place in his heart for Coach Corcoran. I think the connection I already had to Parcells was made a little stronger when he saw me talking to Coach Corcoran. He came over and chatted with us for a while, and again asked me about my parents and family. It was a nice break from the usual training routine.

A FEW WEEKS later, Coach Parcells sat me down in his office and had a little heart-to-heart with me. Being from the same town, knowing that our families knew each other, and out of deference to Coach Corcoran, I think he felt he needed to tell me what he was really thinking.

"You know, Rob," he said, "you're never going to the Pro Bowl." Yeah, well, like I said, he wasn't a warm and fuzzy guy. I remember thinking, "No kidding, coach. But can't you let me down easy?"

"You've got a good head on your shoulders. You're a smart guy and you have a bright future ahead of you. But you need to be thinking about a future after football. You need to be thinking about the long haul. You're doing all you can with your limited size, fooling them with smoke and mirrors out there. But you need to be thinking about your life after football."

I cringed as I sat there and listened to him. I knew all about life after football, enough to know I wasn't ready for it. I didn't want to hear this from anybody. It was like talking about your own mortality to an insurance agent. "You know, Rob, you're going to die someday. Have you thought about term insurance?" But by the same token, no coach had ever been so honest with me. It wasn't easy to hear, but I also knew the guy was being straight with me. He was telling me the truth, whether I wanted to hear it or not.

I guess he read the expression on my face, because he softened the blow just a bit. "Don't worry," he said. "You've got every shot of making this team. But you need to know now that you're not going to the Pro Bowl, and that you're not going to be playing for ten years."

When time did run out for me, Bill Parcells wrote a letter of recommendation for my law school application and, even later, wrote a letter to the Manhattan D.A.'s office when I applied for a job there. So maybe he's not warm and fuzzy, but he's a hell of a guy.

WE PLAYED THE Cleveland Browns in Toronto in our next-to-last preseason game. It was hard for me to get a read on how I was doing, but there's no question that Parcells's little talk helped my attitude. Sure, it only confirmed what I knew already, but in a way, it made me more prepared for what might happen.

The Browns's coach was a former assistant to Parcells, Bill Belichick. The two of them had made their reputations with the New York Giants, and continued to be friends after they went their separate ways. After the game, we hopped on a plane and flew back home. One last preseason game. One last hurdle.

The next morning in the locker room, I got a tap on the shoulder. It was Al Groh, our defensive coordinator. "Hey, Coach wants to you see," he said.

Then those rotten words, again. "Bring your playbook."

I turned to whoever was standing next to me and I shook his hand and said good-bye. "Nice knowing you," I said. "I'm getting my head chopped off. See you around."

I walked down a hall toward Coach Parcells's office with Groh, who turned to me and said, "Don't worry—it's not as bad as you think."

"How could it not be as bad as I think," I said. "I'm getting cut. There's no other option."

Coach Parcells was at his desk when I walked in. "You have a half an hour to get on a plane," he said. "Pack your bags. You're going to Cleveland."

I was prepared to be cut. I wasn't prepared to be . . . traded? Traded? What the hell was this all about?

Coach Parcells looked at me and gave me one of his "Why are you still standing there? Get moving!" looks. I took the hint, bolted from the room, and made the flight.

I couldn't help wondering why the hell he didn't trade me the day before, when both teams were still in Toronto. I could have just jumped on the plane back to Cleveland with the Browns.

The real question was why did Coach Parcells trade me at all? I have a theory: I think he's a bigger softie than he wants to admit.

I think he knew he had to cut me, but he just couldn't do it. He thought about his dad and my dad, Dougie, Mickey Corcoran, and he just couldn't do it. So, I think, he called his buddy Coach Belichick and said, "Listen, Bill, if I cut this guy, Coach Corcoran's gonna be mad at me, a lot of people are gonna give me grief if I cut him. So do me a favor. Take him off my hands, and if you have to cut him after a week, you cut him."

That's my theory, and until somebody proves otherwise, I'm sticking to it.

I finished up training camp as a member of the Cleveland Browns, and got a chance to play in Municipal Stadium, one of the NFL's great old venues. I was immediately impressed by the difference between the two friends and coaches. When Coach Parcells entered a room, you knew it. Sometimes when Coach Belichick came into the room, we didn't even notice. Somebody would have to get us to shut up so the coach could speak.

We played the Rams in our final tune-up game, and I played about a quarter and a half. When we reviewed the game film as a team the next day, Coach Belichick said some nice things about my play. I was amazed he even knew who I was—which is another reason I suspect something else was going on here. When the film session was finished, the lights came on and, literally at that moment, somebody tapped me on the shoulder. "Coach wants to see you," the voice said. "Bring your playbook."

He was nice about it, gracious even. "I talked to Coach Parcells about you," he said, which sort of confirmed my theory about the trade. "You've done a great job in camp, and I'd love to have you on the team. But I can't do it." That morning, I read that the Giants had released Pepper Johnson, an All Pro linebacker who played for those great Parcells-coached teams. His availability made me even more expendable than ever. Belichick was up front about that. "Pepper's available, and we want him."

So I was the odd man out. But to his credit—and I'm sure Coach Parcells had something to do with this—Coach Belichick didn't just dismiss me with some platitudes about my alleged abilities. He encouraged me to think about the future—a future without football. Wearing what looked to be the world's oldest and dirtiest Cleveland Browns sweatshirt, his hair a mess, he peered at me from across a huge desk in his office.

He spoke softly and plainly. "You've got a lot going for you" he said in almost a whisper of a voice. I strained to hear him as he patted my ego on the head. "I can tell that you are going to be a success after football. I just think it may be time for you to focus on what that future might be. It is time for you to start focusing on the rest of your life."

That is when it hit me. It was really over, I thought. I stood up, shook his hand, packed my bags, and went home to New Jersey. This time, there would be no midseason calls. This time, there would be no waiting around, no checking the papers to see if some linebacker somewhere had sprained an ankle. It was over and I was beginning to accept it.

I'D BEEN ACCEPTED at Fordham University's law school for September, but I deferred my admission because I was in training camp and I had this idea that I'd be playing football in the fall of 1993. Now it was late August, school started in a week, and I was back home and out of work at the age of twenty-six. I had to do something to keep my focus off football—even though I knew it was over, there was that small voice telling me that maybe I'd get a call. That small voice was amplified by my agent, who reminded me that linebackers sprain ankles all the time. If I couldn't throw myself into law school, I knew I'd spend way too much time debating with myself about whether or not that call would come.

Fordham graciously allowed me to start right away. A week after leaving training camp, a week after my last NFL game, I was a full-time law student. At first glance, it seemed as though I had my act together, that at long last I understood the deal—my football career was over, I was grateful for the opportunity, and now I was getting on with my life. And I was, sort of. But when I wasn't studying case law and old Supreme Court arguments, I was lifting. I was running. I was staying in shape.

And believe it or not, I did get a phone call. Not from the NFL, but from the Toronto Argonauts in the Canadian Football League. It was January 1994, and I'd just finished my first semester. The CFL plays in spring and summer, so it wasn't as if I would be joining Toronto in midseason.

It was a tempting offer. I had to have a long talk with myself, because this really was the moment. I thought I'd put football behind me when I left Coach Belichick's office—but I hadn't, really. How could I? Football had been a part of my life since I was a kid. Football *was* my life. It was the greatest thing I ever did, and I loved every minute of it. I consider myself, even now, a football player. You don't walk away from that so easily or so quickly. Law school was great, but it wasn't football.

I told my agent I needed to think about it for a couple of days. If I dropped out of law school and played for a couple of years— if I was lucky—where would I be? Going back to law school, preparing for life after football, doing what I already was doing. Except that it would be three years later, and I'd be nearly thirty.

I'd never gotten badly hurt over the years. I broke my fair share of bones and my body ached, but it wasn't anything that bad. I saw firsthand what football does to strong bodies—it wasn't pretty. "You've had a good career," my father told me. "You still have a life to live. You're still in one piece, and you're not like these guys who can hardly walk. You can enjoy golfing. You can have fun playing basketball. You haven't mortgaged the rest of your life to play football for a few years."

My father never told me what I should do. He just offered an opinion—and said that he and my mother were proud of me no matter what I decided.

I called my agent. "I appreciate the offer, Brad," I said, "but no thanks. I'm going to stay in law school."

It really, really was over. I was no longer a football player. I was going to be a lawyer.

WHAT I LIKE about the law is that there is a beginning, a middle, and an end. That used to be true of war, too, but not anymore. Who can really say when the War on Terror really began? Was it 9/11? Was it the attacks on the U.S.S. *Cole* in 2000, or on our embassies in East Africa in 1998? Was it when our Marines were attacked in Beirut in 1983?

Are we in the middle of our War on Terror, or is this just the beginning? And how will we know that it's over? You can be damn sure there will be no surrender ceremony when our enemies are defeated. A beginning, a middle, and an end—it works in law, and even in football, but not in the War on Terror.

The competitive nature of law also appealed to me as a natural, although somewhat more polite, extension of the life I led as a football player. After a year at Fordham University Law School, I knew I wanted to be a trial attorney, as opposed to a contracts lawyer or some other kind of practitioner who mainly writes briefs. I wanted to be in the thick of the fight in the courtroom. I wanted to go after bad guys—even though work as a lowly assistant prosecutor didn't pay very much. That's why I signed up in the Army Reserves, too. But there was more to it than that.

As a football player, I had always wanted to make sure I was good enough to look my older brothers in the eye, and the only way I could do that was by being as good as they were. Now, in this new phase of my life, I found myself drawn to government and current events. But who was I to offer opinions about why we should intervene in Kosovo or Bosnia or Somalia or why we should change our trade policy toward China? What credentials did I have? How could I look somebody in the eye and say, "Yes, we ought to send troops"?

I always respected my father for being a Marine. I always wanted to feel that, like him, I had done my part. I didn't want anybody to say to me, "Hey, McGovern, when did you ever do anything for your community, or your country?" I'd have no response for such a challenge, and I hated that feeling. I felt everyone should serve their country in the military for at least a few years or donate some part of their life to their nation or community. I also felt I needed to earn the right to speak about things I believed in strongly.

While I was on semester break from law school in the mid-nineties, I flew down to Florida to see my brother Jim, a pro golfer who was playing in a PGA event, the Honda Classic. Jim, I should point out, was one of very few guys on the PGA Tour who lived in the Northeast—in New Jersey—during the winter with his wife, Lauren, and their four children. Almost everybody else, no matter where they were born, lived in the sun belt so they could work on their game all year round. Not Jim. He came home to Jersey when the Tour was off to be close to his family and friends.

While I was walking the course and following Jim, I ran into an old friend of the family, Ed Merrigan. Ed had moved to Florida, was practicing law, and like me was playing a little hooky on the golf course. We walked together, and as we did, Ed told me about his years in the Reserves as a JAG officer.

By the time Jim finished his round, I was ready to sign up. I don't think Ed was trying to recruit me, but whether that was his intention or not, something he said appealed to my yearning to do something else with my life, something of service, something more rewarding than taking endless depositions about cases that just weren't very exciting.

I joined in December of 1997 and was assigned to the 77th Regional Support Command based in Albany, New York. I had just turned thirty-one and had recently joined a law firm. My dad thought I was crazy. In fact, the words my father used were the following: "What, are you crazy or something? You're a thirty-one-year-old lawyer. You shouldn't be running around playing soldier. You'll get yourself hurt."

My mom, on the other hand, made no such objection. As my

father was expressing his surprise and shock, I could see my mother just over his shoulder. She looked at me and nodded with approval. That was all I needed.

In a way, my dad's concern about my age was well founded. When I was sworn in, I had to sign a waiver basically agreeing with the Army that I was so ancient that if I got hurt, it was my own damn fault and not the U.S. government's. That was a nice dose of reality, even though I knew I wasn't signing up to be a combat soldier. I knew I was too old for that, and besides, I knew I'd be terrible as a real soldier. I had never even held a gun, much less fired one. And I could get lost in a phone booth. Instead, I hoped to bring whatever intelligence and talent I might have as a lawyer and a prosecutor to the service of my country.

My plan was to serve eight quiet years in the Reserves, which is the standard hitch. I did my monthly drill and my two weeks over the summer. I enjoyed the routine, not only because I was serving my country, but because, frankly, I felt like I was part of a team again. I always enjoyed the team environment, and enjoyed team sports. Being in the Reserves reminded me how much I enjoy working cooperatively with people whose talents I respect and admire—and working together toward a common goal.

ONE OF MY law professors was a noted defense lawyer named Ron Fischetti, who got me going by telling me, more than once, that he couldn't wait to get me in court one day—at this point, it was pretty clear that I was destined to be a prosecutor, and not a defense attorney. My personality and demeanor just seemed to fit the role of a prosecutor. Fischetti's cool approach made him an excellent defense lawyer. "I'll rip you apart when we meet in court," he said—he was kidding, I think.

In keeping with my personality and interest, I did an internship with the U.S. attorney's office in Brooklyn, where I worked with a well-known prosecutor named Laura Ward—she was an assistant U.S. attorney who was part of the team that prosecuted mob boss John Gotti.

I got a chance to listen to some of the wiretaps the feds had on Gotti. Every now and then, Gotti or one of his thugs mentioned Laura Ward by name, and then called her a word I have no intention of repeating. It was a little chilling to hear his voice talking about her in that way, but she got a kick out of it. "John Gotti has a very special name for me," she'd say. She was a fearless prosecutor and a role model.

Although Laura Ward could have made millions of dollars by becoming a partner in a Manhattan law firm, she has dedicated her life to government service. Service that has required her to put in long hours away from home, in return for a government salary and death threats from some of the world's most dangerous and violent criminals. She is everything honorable a lawyer can be. Today, she is still serving her community and putting criminals behind bars as a New York Supreme Court judge in Manhattan. As she was back then, she is still a noble government servant and a role model for all Americans who want to do something worthwhile with their life.

After graduation, instead of following my heart and my instincts by getting a job as a prosecutor, I took a position with a law firm in Newark. The money was ridiculously better than what I would have made as a prosecutor, and I couldn't resist.

But the law I was practicing wasn't exactly the *Law &
Order*-type stuff I had been thinking about and expecting in a
legal career. It was all about who crashed into whom on what
highway. If there was a car accident anywhere in the state of New
Jersey, well, my firm was going to be involved in the lawsuit.

After about two years of this boredom, I took a deposition
from a seventy-year-old woman whose husband had been killed
in a car accident. I was representing the company that made the
car her husband was driving when he was killed. My job was to
question her about the accident in ways that would limit or
minimize my client's liability. It was awful. The widow cried,
understandably, as she relived the tragedy. And there I was, trying to figure out how to get my client off the hook.

I went home that night wondering what I was doing with my
life. There was none of the exhilaration and satisfaction I was
looking for. I was disgusted with myself.

"If I have to do this job for the rest of my life," I thought, "I'll
kill myself."

AT THAT MOMENT I made a life-changing decision. I decided,
finally, to follow my heart. With letters of recommendation
from Coach Parcells and Dick McPherson, my first coach in
New England, I landed a job with the Manhattan District Attorney's Office in late 1999, when I was thirty-three years old. I
was assigned to the Special Narcotics Unit, which had jurisdiction in all five boroughs although it was based in Manhattan.
Within three weeks, I was in a courtroom, prosecuting two guys
charged with drug crimes. I convicted both guys after a one-
week trial.

"This," I thought, "is the greatest thing since sliced bread." I hadn't felt that way since leaving the NFL.

As a narcotics prosecutor, I worked closely with undercover police officers who were the frontline soldiers in the war on drugs. Along with fellow prosecutors like Tom Schellhammer, Lou Peral, and Jon Shapiro, I saw firsthand what drugs do to human beings and to neighborhoods, just as I'd seen firsthand what steroids did to desperate athletes. And I'm as adamant about street drugs as I am about steroids—they're junk, and they're for losers.

Worse, those losers don't just ruin their own lives. They also ruin the lives of innocent people—and sometimes end them. Junkies steal, maim, and kill for their habit. And yet there are powerful voices in America demanding that we legalize this crap. Do they think that if heroin were legal and more available, addicts wouldn't clobber some kid over the head with a brick so they could steal her iPod and sell it for more drugs? I don't understand this reasoning.

I can say firsthand that drugs like heroin, crack cocaine, and methamphetamines are some of the most destructive forces our society has ever seen and their legalization will only serve to increase their destructive impact on the lives of thousands of Americans all over our country.

Anyone who lives in a drug-infested neighborhood knows that illegal narcotics rob the individual addicts' ability to reason and exercise sound judgment. These drugs quickly and mercilessly steal a person's self-control, discipline, and work ethic, replacing them with an unrelenting, unnatural, and insatiable desire that can only be temporarily satisfied by the next hit, snort, or injection. Illegal drugs also corrupt, control, and eventually destroy any community in which they are able to take root.

Alcohol abuse, although harmful in its own right, does not have nearly the devastating effect on entire communities as the presence of illegal narcotics. This is because as the addict's self-control gives way to his narcotic obsession, his respect for the law, his fellowman, and his own dignity are lost in the haze. What remains of the user and his community are the shriveled and faded likenesses of a person and place that many once welcomed but can now hardly recognize.

Who took that dignity away from that person? Who destroyed that community? It was your local drug dealer—that's who. And it is for that reason I consider drug dealers to be some of the most despicable and immoral figures our society has ever had to deal with. They are despicable because they prey on human weakness and despair for the sake of profit. They are immoral because they descend on decent communities and leave only devastation and lawlessness in their wake.

I truly believe that drug dealers must be purged from every corner of our society and punished with the harshest of sentences because they, themselves, impose the harshest of sentences on their unsuspecting victims, who now face a life devoid of hopes, of dreams, and of true happiness. In this regard, they are the same as the child pornographer and the pedophile.

A drug addict who breaks into a little old lady's apartment to steal some money does so only to feed his habit. But the drug dealer selling drugs on the sidewalk just outside her apartment is a far greater threat because he is trying to steal her community. So treat the addicts and help them to break their addiction. But don't legalize the source of their misery—and ours. The price is just too high.

I LOVED BEING a prosecutor. I loved winning cases, and I hated losing. Regardless of the outcomes, though, I felt useful and satisfied. I believed I was doing my part for society by putting away people who were threats to society.

That's how I felt on the morning of September 11, 2001, the day we all became aware of another, deadlier kind of threat.

Chapter Seven

* * *

Afghanistan—
Cultures May Collide but Malalay
Will Always Be My Friend

BAGRAM AIR BASE IS TWENTY-FIVE MILES NORTH OF Kabul. It is seven miles southeast of the city of Chārikār. And it is a million miles from home.

It's hard to believe that we were actually at a crossroads of history. Not far from this dusty, treeless, hardscrabble collection of tents and hangars were the remains of Greek columns and other reminders of the conquest of Alexander the Great. Surrounding the base were the Hindu Kush Mountains and the Kyber Pass, which had proven so formidable to the British in the nineteenth century. And within the base's wire were structures built by the Soviets a quarter of a century earlier.

Alexander, the British, and the Soviets had invaded Afghanistan as conquerors. The United States came in self-defense and to liberate an oppressed population. And on November 4, 2002, I landed in Bagram to do my small part for the liberation of a people I knew very little about, except for the fact that they had recently lived under the draconian control of the Taliban.

Along with Captains Geier Martin and Eric Dodson, I was assigned to the Combined Joint Task Force 180, under the command of a three-star general named Dan K. McNeill, a soft-spoken, friendly, but decisive man who was in charge of all military forces in Afghanistan. You might wonder what the heck a lawyer does in a combat zone. As a JAG officer assigned to Lieutenant General McNeill's staff, my job was to advise him on legal aspects of combat operations—rules of engagement, treatment and interrogation of prisoners, the use of weapons systems, the confiscation of enemy weapons, and the legal issues involved in designating enemy combatants international terrorists. I was also lucky enough to be involved in the planning of a series of humanitarian aid projects, helping lay the groundwork for building an Afghan national army, and working with some of the most dedicated and patriotic Americans you'd ever have the chance to meet.

Bagram Air Base, located in the most forbidding and desolate place I'd ever seen, was my new home and our main launching pad in the campaign against the Taliban and Al-Qaeda. Only a year had passed since U.S. forces arrived after the attacks of 9/11, so Bagram still had the look and feel of a makeshift encampment. When it was dry, the place was a dust bowl. When it was wet, we sank into mud. Underneath that soil in some parts of the base were thousands of land mines left behind by the Soviets. Most of the mines were being cleared by special demining machines, but some of the work was done by old-fashioned sappers with the 10th Mountain Division and other coalition units. It was dangerous work, which didn't proceed without incident. Explosions were as much a part of the base's background noise as the thud of helicopter blades. When I went for a jog around the airfield, I knew not to stray from the designated path—there were mines lurking under the ground to our right and left. During these runs, I'd pass a little mud house located just beyond the wire. Unbelievably, the house was occupied, even though the yard was a minefield. Signs were posted warning people to stay away. But this guy continued to live there. I asked an interpreter why somebody in that situation didn't just move. "It's Allah's will," the interpreter said.

The guy never moved, and he never got hurt, either. But around Afghanistan, land mines killed or maimed civilians all the time. Kids with missing legs were a common and awful sight in the countryside.

About seven thousand coalition troops lived at Bagram in endless rows of tents. Even the centerpiece of the base, our Joint Operations Center, or JOC, was housed in a huge tent. Outside the JOC, the base looked like a Civil War encampment. Inside the JOC, it looked like the bridge of the starship *Enterprise*.

Sitting in rows of desks, JOC personnel monitored combat operations around the country with computers, huge video screens, secure Internet lines, satellite radios, and all the other technology that is essential to modern warfare.

Moving in and out of the JOC was like moving in and out of the twenty-first century. Outside the wire was another world, one that made our spartan living conditions seem like a five-star hotel. The long-suffering Afghan people who lived near the base were friendly, nomadic people who lacked most of the things we associate with modern life. But even the poorest Afghan seemed to own an AK-47 assault rifle.

If you took the weapons away, as well as the occasional car and the more common bicycle, you felt like you'd been transported back to biblical times. I used to think that if John the Baptist walked up to me and said, "Hello, Rob," I would probably just say hello back and think nothing of it. It was astonishing to witness, and you couldn't help but notice that the people seemed content with their lives and happy to see us. Still, the contrasts were both startling and, in a way, comforting: picture a Black Hawk helicopter flying over the most isolated village you can imagine, and think about the American soldiers inside that chopper and the Afghan people looking up at them. You couldn't imagine a greater contrast. And yet that's all it was, a contrast—not a clash. They accepted us, and we accepted them.

MY WORK AT the Joint Operations Center put me in touch with troops from America and from other members of our coalition who were not only fighting the terrorist enemy but were also rebuilding Afghanistan. My commander, General McNeill, dispatched what we called Provisional Reconstruction Teams, or PRT teams, made up of soldiers who were trained not only to kill but to interact with civilians and civil leaders.

Since Vietnam, cynics routinely sneer at the notion of winning over the "hearts and minds" of civilian populations in a war setting. But believe me, that kind of effort is not only imperative, it's the right thing to do, and it works. It works by educating the Afghan people who don't know why we're there and it exposes the lies being put out by our enemies. This honest and open communication directly with the Afghan people helps to build strong and lasting relations between our soldiers and the local population. This leads to greater trust and understanding, which is essential to accomplishing our mission.

The troops who work on the PRTs are, in my opinion, the unheralded heroes in our effort to win over the Afghan people. These troops are generally dispatched to remote villages and isolated regions, which makes them extremely vulnerable to enemy attack. In their interactions with village elders, they try as best as possible to respond to the needs of the people, and they coordinate with us back in the JOC to best direct our humanitarian and reconstruction aid. In Afghanistan, we are not just seeking out and killing the terrorists who have declared themselves our enemy. We also are trying to create a bond with a people who have known little else but war and oppression for decades.

I'd occasionally be dispatched to Kabul for one assignment or another. Life there was a little more familiar to a twenty-first-century American, but there was no mistaking Kabul for New York City. Our mission in Afghanistan and throughout the world is not to turn Afghans or Iraqis into images of ourselves. It is merely to liberate them by expelling a totalitarian regime, and allow them to live their lives as they see fit, with the universal freedoms we believe they are entitled to as human beings.

Anytime I jumped into a convoy heading to Kabul, we usually stopped by a market area known to us as Chicken Street. Like a lot of roads in Kabul, it's more like an alley than a street and it's lined with merchants selling all kinds of stuff, from food to trinkets. Our troops often bought things like linens, silks, and even Persian rugs to send home to friends and family.

The kids who lived around the market area loved to see us,

which was interesting to observe. If they were being told at home that Americans and Westerners were evil, they certainly wouldn't have been approaching us with smiles and hugs. But they were. A lot of them spoke English, so as we got out of our vehicles, we'd be surrounded by kids who said they wanted to be our bodyguards. It was hilarious. We were the ones carrying the M-16s. But they wanted to be our bodyguards. We all got a kick out of it.

During one of these visits, an adorable ten-year-old girl named Malalay asked to be my bodyguard. I couldn't resist. Malalay was a thin, brown-haired girl with a beautiful smile that made you warm to her immediately. She seemed like a really smart kid with a lot of energy who was completely intrigued about Americans and unafraid to approach and talk to me. If the Taliban were still in power, she'd be doomed to life as a second-class citizen, or worse. She'd be barred from school, from playing any part in society other than as a mother and wife, unable to leave her husband's property without first concealing herself in a blue burka that covered her from head to toe. But under the new government of President Hamid Karzai, she was free to lead a very different kind of life if that's what she chose.

Every time I went to Chicken Street, I made sure Malalay was my bodyguard. As we walked up and down the street, she would ask me all kinds of questions about my family and my life back in America. On one of these trips, I asked Malalay why she had learned to speak English. "I want to be friends with the Americans," she said. "I want to be friends with them for the rest of my life."

Hopefully, she will be. That's why we're there.

About eight months later, when it was time for me to leave Afghanistan, I paid one last visit to Chicken Street, mainly to say good-bye to Malalay. But, for the first time, I couldn't find her. I walked up and down Chicken Street, moving through the throngs of people carrying on the daily routine of Afghan commerce, but I couldn't locate her. I was pretty disappointed. As I started to get back into my vehicle to leave, I saw her. She was at the back of a gaggle of boys who were pressed up against the passenger-side door where I was sitting. They were all waving good-bye.

I rolled down my window, sort of shooed away the boys, and cleared a path for her. She ran up to me, I said good-bye to my friend and bodyguard, and thanked her for her "protection" during my stay in her country. I told her "America will always be your friend." She thanked me back and smiled one last time before turning to run back to her friends across the street. I turned to the driver and said, "We can go now." As we pulled away, I looked back to see her waving at our departing vehicles. I never saw her again.

I was and still am touched by her affection and friendliness. I'm convinced that her actions spoke for the feelings of so many people in Afghanistan. They want to be friends with Americans and they want that friendship to last for a long time. We have started something good and decent in this war-torn country and our continued presence there is necessary in order to ensure that the people retake control of their country from the warlords and terrorists who have used the Afghan people for their own hateful ends.

We entered Afghanistan to defend ourselves against the terrorist organization that launched the 9/11 attacks and the Taliban regime that harbored them. Only if we have the courage and resolve necessary to defeat the enemy in Afghanistan will we be able to leave that country as a free, safe, and peaceful nation whose people, like Malalay, will be our friends for a long, long time.

AS PART OF our staff work at the JOC under General McNeill, my fellow JAGs and I helped plan a series of combat operations throughout the country, and then monitored the battle's progress in real time from the JOC.

Some of these operations included not only U.S. forces, but units from Italy, Romania, and other allies. Units with names like Task Force Devil and Task Force Tiger were made up of soldiers from the 504th Parachute Infantry Regiment of the 82nd Airborne Division. They conducted combat operations in the southern and eastern border regions of Afghanistan with names like "Deliberate Strike," "Lightning Strike," and "Gazelle." Elite Special Forces units from Task Force 5 and Task Force 11 engaged the enemy in operations like "Fox Hunt," which was focused on Al-Qaeda and Taliban remnants hiding out in the Deh Rawod region of Afghanistan. These and countless other operations were tremendously successful in routing out and killing our enemies in Afghanistan.

I did not participate in these missions. My colleagues and I in the JOC helped to plan them, monitor them, and then advise General McNeill and his staff about issues like the rules of engagement as the operations progressed.

As troops engaged the enemy on the battlefield, my workplace consisted of a computer terminal inside the JOC command center. I was part of a team of officers and enlisted soldiers wearing headsets and sitting at rows of tables arranged in tiers like stadium bleachers. Computers lined the tables, and three large screens were arrayed in front of us. One screen displayed a map of Afghanistan. Another zoomed in on the exact area in which an operation was about to take place. The images on the third screen varied—sometimes they showed visuals from an un-manned aerial vehicle flying over the battlefield, giving us a real-time feed of an operation as it was taking place.

Seated in front of us was the chief of operations, or CHOPS, Lieutenant Colonel Joseph Grubich. He, like the rest of us, wore a headset. He was in constant communication with units in the field and with those of us in the JOC. As we monitored the bat-tle, my job was to provide the chief of operations with legal advice—an odd concept, I know, but a pretty important one in the kind of irregular war we're fighting in Afghanistan and Iraq. I was expected to know military law and our rules of engage-ment, and I had to be able to deliver my opinions in clear lan-guage as quickly and decisively as possible.

Of course, the world knows that a few U.S. soldiers—an in-credibly small number—have been accused of brutal crimes against Iraqi civilians. The charges, if true, are appalling. Sol-diers who are found guilty of murdering or abusing civilians are a disgrace to their uniform and their country.

Still, it speaks to our nation's commitment to the Geneva Conventions and the customary rules of war that JAGs have such tremendous influence over battles taking place hundreds of miles away. Not every soldier is perfect, as we have discovered. But I believe the U.S. Army has safeguards in place to ensure that we follow the rules of warfare, even if our opponents do not.

Basically, as JAGs, we were there to reduce civilian exposure to our battle plans. If I believed that a particular tactic or weap-ons system we were using violated the rules of engagement (ROE) or, worse, would amount to a war crime, I was duty bound to tell the chief of operations. He could then take a different course of action against an enemy target. If necessary, he could even call off the mission entirely.

For example, if we were pursuing a clearly identified enemy force during a combat engagement, I might hear the chief's voice on my headset: "Okay, JAG, what is my ROE?" Talk about pressure—I mean, playing football was nothing compared to this. If I said, "Okay, sir, fire them up," the enemy would be destroyed by an air strike. If the people were not able to be clearly identified as the enemy and there was a chance we might endanger innocent Afghans, we would hold our fire. That's because the U.S. military doesn't operate like the Wild Wild West. We don't just roll into town and shoot at everything and everyone we see. It was my job to make sure of that, in part to limit the possibilities of civilian casualties.

Early on in my tour, I was on the JOC floor monitoring an operation when a helicopter got hit by enemy fire and went down. It wasn't a crash—it was more of a hard landing—and we got word that all the troops on board were alive but banged up. That was the good news. The bad news was that they'd gone down in a very hostile area, and they needed medical attention and evacuation.

As the JAG on duty that night, I was asked the big question. "What's my ROE for a medevac LZ?" In other words, the chief needed to know what the rules were if the troops or the medical evacuation team saw people in the landing zone area who might—or might not—be the enemy. Did they have to wait for the enemy to fire at them or could they shoot first?

"You can fire 'em up," I said. I thought to myself that it would suck at that moment to be anything but a U.S. soldier in that area, because we were prepared to fire on anybody who wasn't wearing our uniform. But by the same token, this was a combat area, there were wounded troops on the ground, and our job was to get them out of there safe and sound.

The evacuation was a success. No shots were fired.

On another occasion, a JAG named Major Jeff Bovarnick was on duty in the JOC. Major Bovarnick, or Major B, was from Boston, and he served as the chief of operational law in Afghanistan. He was a tireless and dedicated soldier whose only character flaw, that this Yankee fan could detect, was that he loved the Red Sox. Major B spent hours in the JOC responding to questions and providing advice to General McNeill. This one particular night, a forward operating base came under a rocket attack from terrorists who were then spotted fleeing in a red pickup truck. They were making a dash for the Pakistani border.

Our troops regrouped and were now in hot pursuit of the pickup truck using two Apache helicopters equipped with surface-to-ground missiles. In the JOC, Major Bovarnick followed this chase in real time. As the vehicle sped closer and closer to safety on the Pakistani border, a voice came over the headsets of everyone in the JOC. "We've got him, but he's getting close to the Pakistani border. Can we engage?"

The CHOPS looked at Major Bovarnick. This was his call to make. "Do they have positive identification that these are the same guys who just fired at them?" Major B asked the CHOPS over the radio, or "net." The answer came back: "Affirmative." Major B continued, "Have they lost visual contact with the vehicle since the engagement began?" The reply: "Negative." That was all the information he needed. Major B looked at the CHOPS and said calmly, "You can fire 'em up." The red pickup truck was no more.

The key to this engagement was that our troops were in hot pursuit of the enemy, and they had positive identification of the individuals who had just attacked them. In this situation, they were completely authorized to use deadly force. The terrorists had been spotted in a red pickup truck, and the troops had the truck in their sights the entire time. If they had lost the truck at any point, or if the truck wasn't the same color, or if they were unsure of the color to begin with, Major Bovarnick would have advised them to break off the engagement so as not to risk the loss of innocent human life.

WE'RE ENGAGED IN a highly irregular war against an enemy that is indistinguishable from civilians in terms of dress and vehicles. We have to be extremely careful in situations where civilians might be in peril. Major Bovarnick had to make a split-second decision that would affect who lived and who died. He made every possible effort to ensure that we used lethal force only when it was absolutely necessary and that when we did so it was in a careful and measured manner. That's because we value innocent human life and we try to do everything possible to protect it. Our enemies, however, have no such scruples. But, I guess, that is exactly why they are our enemies.

The stress in the JOC was nothing like the pressure combat soldiers have to deal with on a daily basis, but making these instant decisions still requires discipline, knowledge, and preparation. When the chief of operations wants to know if we can engage the enemy in real time, you don't have time to say, "Well, sir, that's a good question. Can I get back to you?" You have to know the answer and you have to know it now.

And you know the answer by drilling, by practicing all kinds of battlefield scenarios with commanders and soldiers, and by studying battle plans before they are implemented. It is tremendously important work because JAGs have to make instant judgments that might or might not put our troops in further danger. I was always worried that some decision I made would needlessly cause a soldier to hesitate on the battlefield, leaving him defenseless and in harm's way. I never wanted my advice to a soldier to result in basically taking his weapon out of his hands.

Part of my duties as a JAG involved briefing troops on the rules of engagement before they went on a mission. During these briefings, which could be held anywhere from the back of a building or in a gym, I'd give them the rules and then go over any common or potentially troublesome factual scenarios they might encounter, but I'd end every briefing with the same instructions. "There is no way to predict every possible scenario that could occur on the battlefield. So, if you remember only one thing I say to you today, remember this. You never lose your inherent right to self-defense. If you think you're in danger, you can fire."

I always went out of my way to stress this last point to the soldiers before they left on a mission because I didn't want anybody holding back out there. This was combat, not contract negotiations, and I wanted them to know that they could be as aggressive as they needed to be if they or their buddies were in danger.

RARELY DID A day go by without some reminder of how brutal and merciless the Taliban had been during their despotic rule over the Afghan people. Most Americans are familiar with the more notable stories. The criminal destruction of an image of Buddha carved into a mountainside; the repression of women and girls; the ban on kite flying. These stories told us a great deal about the character of our enemy, but there was so much more.

On May 12, 2003, I was at my station in the JOC when I received a report that some of our troops had uncovered a mass grave in the northern part of the country. I forwarded the specifics to Central Command in Florida. A war-crimes investigation team was dispatched to the site, where they found the remains of hundreds of ethnic Tajiks murdered in cold blood near their homes. The grave site and evidence eventually were turned over to the UN for further investigation. For me, it was yet another reminder of the character of our adversary and the plight of the people who fell under the Taliban's rule.

Land mines, as I mentioned before, were a plague that shattered the lives of so many Afghan civilians, especially children. The Soviets planted them during their long occupation, but, in fairness, they carefully designated minefields and accounted for where they had been placed. During the civil war that followed the Soviet withdrawal, however, the Taliban dug up the mines and placed them indiscriminately throughout the countryside. Nobody knew where they were now, including the Taliban.

That resulted in a daily catastrophe—men, women, and children blown apart while walking through a field, or playing outside, or planting crops. At Bagram, we became grimly accustomed to hearing explosions from outside the base. The routine was generally the same: a loud explosion, followed minutes later by horrified civilians racing toward the base and holding a tarp containing a body or a still-living civilian with bloody stumps where his or her legs used to be.

Our combat hospital at Bagram developed the expertise and facilities to save some of these victims, and pretty soon we were swamped with casualties from all over the country, many of them children who were carried by their parents or other family members from their homes to safe houses operated by our Special Forces. If the medics there could repair the wound, they did so. If not, we got the call. And sometimes the wounds were horrible, more horrible, in fact, than the loss of limbs. One medevac mission brought us a young boy of no more than seven or eight whose face was shattered when a mine exploded in front of him. He'd lost an eye, the bones in his face were shattered, and he'd been burned on his torso and arms.

The boy was placed in the care of Major Karl Temple, a maxillofacial surgeon assigned to the combat support hospital at Bagram. Dr. Temple faced a difficult medical problem: how to reconstruct the boy's face without using prosthetic plates. He knew the boy probably would never get the follow-up surgery that plates would require as his body grew and changed. But he was also determined to do all he could to restore this boy's appearance. I couldn't tell you how he did it, but he did. The boy left our hospital with a repaired face and a glass eye. He suffered a terrible wound and literally was scarred for life. But Dr. Karl Temple, a U.S. Army surgeon, gave him a second chance at a normal life.

For more conventional victims of mines, if that's the right term, we were limited to simply repairing wounds, amputating mangled limbs, and then sending these people on their way. This left the medical staff and all of us stationed at Bagram extremely frustrated. These people needed prosthetics, but we didn't have any to provide. Then we learned of an amazing Italian doctor in Kabul, Alberto Cairo, who'd gained fame for his work in building prosthetics and rehabilitating the victims of land mines, particularly children. Dr. Cairo made thousands of prosthetic devices during his fifteen years in the city as a member of the Red Cross. His work was so respected—and necessary—that the Taliban actually left him alone.

He could do what we couldn't—he could follow up, he could rehabilitate, he could fit victims with new legs and arms. We needed to see him. I joined several other officers, including Major Elizabeth Baker, a nurse at the hospital in Bagram, for a trip to Kabul to see Dr. Cairo and discuss ways we could work together to help the victims of this horrible legacy of war.

In his midforties, with a slight goatee, graying hair, and glasses, Dr. Cairo greeted us warmly and immediately agreed to take on this additional workload. Until this point, most of his patients had been from the Kabul area, but we received land mine victims from all over the country. Still, he didn't hesitate. Thanks to this remarkable man, and to our own medical personnel like Dr. Temple and Major Baker—along with many others— these innocent victims of Taliban cruelty are now getting the help they need.

I came to know and work with a number of extraordinary, selfless medical personnel at the air base. Their stories and their work have not received very much publicity, but make no mistake about it—they represent all that we are doing right in that country, and for all the right reasons.

I worked with Major Baker on a project called the Cooperative Medical Assistance (CMA) Program. It was modeled on a similar program run by U.S. forces in Central and South America in the 1980s and 1990s that became commonly known as "tailgate medicine." In Afghanistan, our program dispatched medical personnel into the countryside to visit villages and other population centers. As they rolled into town, they literally dropped the tailgate down on their vehicles and set up a makeshift pharmacy and first-aid station. These medical professionals would then attend to all comers before leaving for the next town. Each team consisted of about ten to thirty health-care providers along with security teams serving as protection. For those inclined to see this as an exercise in American cultural imperialism in Afghanistan, let me point out that these teams worked with local medical personnel and practitioners of folk medicine. We weren't looking to impose our cures and our medicine. We just wanted to help people heal.

Major Baker, Colonel Chris Post, and Lieutenant Colonel Donna Hershey were just three of the people who helped turn this plan into positive action by figuring out ways to earn the trust of the people and to help our medical staff and Afghan medical personnel better understand one another and work toward the common good.

MIDWAY THROUGH MY tour, I and the other JAGs attached to the XVIII Airborne Corps received word that we'd be getting a new boss—Colonel Malinda Dunn, who would replace Colonel Dave Hayden and become the Staff Judge Advocate for CJTF 180 in Afghanistan. In civilian language, that meant she would be the top lawyer in Afghanistan. For the JAGs in my unit, all of them male, that news was greeted with some trepidation—not because they didn't want to work for a female superior officer, but because they might have to clean up their language and pay more attention to personal hygiene.

But any concerns that may have been raised by Colonel Dunn's impending arrival were completely unfounded, as we soon found out that she could drop an f-bomb with the best of them. Colonel Dunn had heard it all before and we soon realized that she was one great leader, too.

Colonel Dunn's father had been stationed at the U.S. Embassy in, believe it or not, Kabul in the mid-1970s. After she arrived, we'd occasionally travel together on convoys into Kabul, where she'd point out some building along the way and say, matter-of-factly, "Oh, there's where my high school prom was." Or we'd pass some nondescript bit of countryside and she'd tell us about the picnic lunches she once had there with her dad and friends.

She was the first female to hold the title of Staff Judge Advocate in the 82nd Airborne Division and the XVIII Airborne Corps, and she went on to become the first active-duty female general in the JAG corps, a title she currently holds. I loved working for her, because she was decisive, clear in her orders, and would back up her junior officers when things got hairy. You couldn't ask for anything more.

AMERICANS CONTINUE TO hear debates about whether or not women should be in combat. I've got news for people on both sides of the issue: the debate is over. Women are already there. Although they may still be barred from frontline infantry duty, that doesn't mean they're not in combat every day in Iraq and Afghanistan. In my view, I can't imagine the military without the talents and patriotism of the women soldiers I've met at home and overseas. Women are an integral part of our fighting force, and, frankly, we couldn't do what we do without them.

FOR SEVERAL MONTHS, I served as the legal adviser to a group that met once a week to plan and finance humanitarian assistance and reconstruction projects throughout Afghanistan. The amount of time and money put into this facet of our presence was truly breathtaking. And yet few people in America even know it is taking place—and that it is succeeding.

While I was in Afghanistan, the two people most responsible for conceiving, planning, and carrying out these projects were not celebrity humanitarians like Angelina Jolie or Brad Pitt—they were a couple of Army captains named Wayne Mingo and William David "Doc" Meredith.

These two civil affairs officers worked seven days a week for a year planning, coordinating, and implementing hundreds of humanitarian assistance projects throughout the country. Some of these projects were relatively straightforward, like making repairs to schools and medical facilities. Other projects, however, were so complex even Donald Trump would have to tip his hat to the organizational skills, determination, and sheer talent of Captains Mingo and Meredith.

Typically, the two of them would scour requests for assistance from units in the field as well as from local Afghan officials. Because they had access to all the pertinent information—and knew about the needs of various regions from firsthand fieldwork—they were able to evaluate the need and importance of all these requests for assistance. Again, because they took the time to learn from local civilian leaders and tribal elders, they knew the importance of dividing any aid as equitably as possible along tribal and regional lines.

After deciding where and how the assistance would be provided, Doc and Wayne presided over the equally complex task of contracting out the work. More often than not, they made sure that the contractors were local people who had shown an ability and a desire to do the work. This was yet another example of the two captains' sensitivity and authentic concern for the long-suffering Afghan people—and further proof that America's presence in the world is far more benign and far more progressive than our critics will ever acknowledge.

U.S. forces distributed approximately $14.3 million worth of humanitarian assistance from October 7, 2001—the day the coalition launched its campaign against the Taliban and Al-Qaeda—to October 30, 2002. Some were decidedly small-scale and ingenious, like handing out small backpacks filled with school supplies to local children, whose smiles were worth more than any Super Bowl victory.

Other projects ran the gamut from digging water wells and irrigation canals to the repair of 128 schools to a massive highway project called the Ring Road, which was designed to link Kabul and Kandahār to some outlying regions. The Ring Road project was considered so important in the new Afghanistan that President Hamid Karzai and U.S. Secretary of Defense Donald Rumsfeld regularly made personal inquiries about its progress.

The project was critical to reconstruction efforts because it would connect the major urban population centers of Afghanistan, which would, in turn, facilitate the flow of people and commerce throughout the countryside. As people and goods moved more freely from region to region, it would strengthen the country's economy and enable Afghanistan to eventually reenter the global trading community. But the project had another equally important objective. The Ring Road would foster greater contact and better communication between the various tribes and ethnic groups scattered around Afghanistan's rugged and difficult terrain. This second goal is an essential prerequisite to uniting the entire Afghan population under one national identity.

But that didn't mean the large urban population centers received all of our aid and attention. Half of all our humanitarian assistance projects during the first year in Afghanistan went to rural regions. As a result, we have enjoyed an incredible amount of cooperation and affection from the local population. We're winning their hearts and minds, you might say. The American soldiers who helped bring this assistance to villages and rural settlements were received with great warmth, and they left knowing they truly had a positive impact on the lives of a war-weary population.

Captain Wayne Mingo and Captain Doc Meredith were the architects of these projects that helped rebuild things like a food storage warehouse in the village of Deh Rawod, a hospital in Adi Ghar southeast of Kandahār, and a teacher training center in the Gardez region. With their hard work and dedication, these incredible Americans didn't just help repair and restore these buildings. Their efforts and sacrifice are helping a country and its people find their way back into the community of free nations. And when Afghanistan does get back on its feet again, America will have these great patriots to thank for it. But we need to give them and all their fellow soldiers the time and support they need to get the job done.

ULTIMATELY, WE KNEW that for all the great humanitarian work we were doing, we were not on a peacekeeping mission. We were fighting a war against vicious terrorists who did not recognize any of the legal or moral obligations of combatant armies.

So it became necessary to identify and maximize the use of all available equipment to ensure that while we were effectively engaging the enemy, at the same time we were also capable of adequately protecting our forces across the country. JAGs and paralegals all over Afghanistan and Uzbekistan, like Sergeant Christian Bono, Captain Kevin Brown, Captain Dave Blalock, Captain Rich Sudder, Captain Dan Froehlich, Captain Eric Young, Captain Sean McMahon, and Captain Darrin Grove, played major roles in the development of these critical "force protection" measures.

As a member of the Force Protection Working Group for CJTF 180, I was tasked with identifying available resources and equipment so that we could better protect the lives of coalition troops as well as local civilians. At the time, we were faced with two persistent problems—the vulnerability of our forward operating bases to rocket attacks, and the ease with which terrorists were able to disrupt convoy traffic with roadside bombs.

After researching our available options, I recommended that we obtain several antimortar tracking systems that would enable us to follow the paths of incoming rockets and pinpoint their launch sites. That way, our troops could quickly and accurately return fire and destroy the threat to our forces. To combat the rash of roadside explosions and car bombs, I suggested we obtain newly available handheld explosive detectors and a vehicle X-ray machine.

This huge X-ray machine allowed our forces located at our base in Karshi-Kanabad in Uzbekistan to X-ray any non-American vehicles seeking entry into the base. The handheld explosive detectors were distributed to military police units assigned to base security at Bagram and other locations around Afghanistan so that they could screen vehicles before permitting them access to some of our most sensitive sites. Thankfully, these rather minor equipment upgrades served to dramatically reduce the vulnerability of our bases and troops to attacks by suicide car bombers.

On a similar note, Major Bovarnick helped take dangerous weapons out of the hands of terrorists without ever firing a shot. One day, Major B asked me to see if I could identify any congressionally appropriated funds that would enable us to implement a "cash for weapons" program similar to those used by the mayors and police departments of some of our biggest cities back home. The difference, of course, was the kind of weaponry Major B was talking about wasn't the Saturday Night Specials and zip guns our big cities are used to, but Russian-made rockets.

Major B received a report that some less than reputable characters were trying to sell thirty-four Thermobaric heat-seeking rockets on the streets of Kabul. The rumors proved to be true and the decision was made to have a "strawman" make the transaction. So some Special Forces soldiers contacted an Afghan middleman they'd dealt with in the past and enlisted his assistance in making the purchase. The meeting was arranged, the day came, the plan worked, and the sale went off without a hitch. Those weapons could have been used to kill Americans or innocent Afghan civilians. Thankfully, Major Bovarnick ensured that they were taken out of commission.

Developing force protection measures and confiscating deadly weapons certainly don't equal the accomplishments real combat troops are making every day on the battlefields of Iraq and Afghanistan. When I volunteered for active duty, I knew I could never be that kind of soldier. I may have played pro football but I was not as hard-core as the incredible men and women of our armed forces who are fighting the enemy every day. But I did know that I could use what talents God gave me to help our combat troops fight and defeat that enemy. My job as a JAG may not have been glamorous, but I felt like I was doing my part for my country, no matter how small my role.

AS LAWYERS, JAGS were often called in when our troops had to negotiate with local civilians or leaders who had a gripe with us. As much as our efforts were appreciated by the average civilian in Afghanistan, it ought to be obvious that sometimes conflicts arose. For example, Captain Grier Martin from Raleigh, North Carolina, was our claims officer in Afghanistan. That meant he had to meet with every disgruntled Afghan civilian who had a beef with the U.S. Army. This was good training for Grier, I guess, because he's now serving as a representative to the North Carolina state legislature. I'm sure he's still busy responding to complaints, only this time they are from voters in his district.

One time in particular, Grier and another JAG, Captain

Patricia Cika, met with and helped an Afghan civilian whose home had been damaged when our forces blew up a cache of captured weapons they'd found in a nearby cave. The incident took place in a remote mountain village called Kohe Sofi. The rugged area was so mountainous that our chopper pilot had a hard time locating the place and then finding a spot flat enough for him to land. After we finally touched down, we walked about two miles along the cliffs and jagged edges of a mountainous ravine until we reached the village.

Wouldn't you know it, the guy's home sat on the very top of the mountain. So we lugged ourselves all the way to the top, and when we arrived, still panting from our climb, Grier and Patricia offered our apologies and gave the villager a sum of money that would help him fix the damage to his one-room mud-and-stone hut with dirt floors and a thatched roof.

As I observed the spectacular view from the top of this mountain and tried to catch my breath, I couldn't figure out how this nice Afghan man who looked like he was eight hundred years old could even manage to build a hut on this incredibly steep perch, much less climb up and down this mountainside to get to it day after day.

To the eyes of an American like myself, or anybody else from the developed world, these villagers lived in conditions we'd invariably describe as primitive and impoverished. But as soldiers trained to respect the local populace, Grier and Patricia knew it wasn't our mission, and shouldn't be, to turn rural Afghans into Western-style consumers. Their traditions were centuries old. They lived on land their ancestors had lived on. Just like us, they loved their religion and their children. And just like us, they wished only for peace. A peace that we are helping to restore. A peace they rightly deserve.

ON ANOTHER OCCASION, I was the lead negotiator on what should loosely be called a real-estate transaction between the Army and some local Afghans from a village on the border with Pakistan. We had a firebase in the area that was constantly coming under attack from terrorists inside Pakistan, which meant that the troops there were caught in both a real and a diplomatic cross fire. Pakistan was a vital ally in the War on Terror, but certain ideological communities in that Islamic nation would have loved to overthrow the government, kill as many leaders as possible, and install an unfriendly fundamentalist government in Islamabad. So we had to be careful in any engagements near the border and we had to ensure that we respected Pakistani sovereignty.

The only problem was, the terrorists knew that, too, and took full advantage. The rules of engagement were for us, not for them. They didn't have JAGs advising them about matters of operational law.

The decision was made to pull back from Fire Base Lwara, so called because it was located near the border town of Lwara. Our troops had a far more appropriate nickname for the base, and they plastered it on a sign near the entrance to the compound. The sign read EL ALAMO.

By pulling back from El Alamo, the Army would reduce the troops' exposure to attack and avoid the possibility of any international incidents. A new firebase would be located a few miles farther inland, far enough from the border that our troops wouldn't be sitting ducks for terrorists taking aim at them from the relative safety of the mountains in Pakistan. Our attitude was simple: "All right, guys, if you want to come after us, you are going to have to come into our playground now."

Upon arrival, my job was to arrange the transfer of the old firebase to the Afghans who lived in the nearby village. Needless to say, this was pretty tricky since it wasn't our property to begin with. In fact, it had been a military base during the Soviet occupation, but because of its strategic location, we wanted to make sure it didn't fall into the hands of terrorists as soon as we pulled out. So I flew into the village on a CH-47 Chinook helicopter and met with the village elder, Dr. Ahmed Sha Wazir.

The word *wazir* is used to describe a tribal chief or elder and is a title reserved only for the most respected members of a tribe. Before I met with the *wazir*, I met first with the local Special Forces commander, Major Nester A. Saddler. Major Saddler informed me that the *wazir* had been very helpful to him and his men in identifying and going after elements of Al-Qaeda in the area. The *wazir* had always supported the American presence in the region and had repeatedly alerted Major Saddler of potential threats to U.S. forces operating in the area.

Receiving this kind of support in this particular area was no small feat. Since the village of Lwara was located so close to the tribal region bordering both Afghanistan and Pakistan called Waziristan, the *wazir* took quite a risk associating so openly with American forces. This lawless region is thought to house many supporters of the Taliban and Al-Qaeda and is where some even suspect Osama bin Laden has found refuge for the past few years. So, as you can see, taking such a pro-U.S. stance in this volatile area carries with it a very real health risk. But the *wazir*'s support for our mission was unwavering, constant, and true.

After meeting with Major Saddler, I met with some more troops assigned to Major Saddler's Special Forces Operational Detachment Alpha Team. These are the guys who try to blend in with the community to show them that we're all on the same team. They're well trained in the art of war, no question about that, but they're equally well trained in the art of peace. One day they're firing at the enemy, the next day they're providing medical assistance to a local kid with a broken leg. They know that to be successful in the kind of war we're fighting today, we need the support of the local civilians.

Their unanimous support for the *wazir* and their heartfelt gratitude to him for his assistance spoke volumes about the propriety of transferring this isolated yet critical crossroads outpost to this man.

I approached the *wazir* and greeted him with the traditional blessing: *"As salam aleykum."* His first words to me were *"Aleykum salam.* I love America!" He was a fairly young-looking man, in his early forties. It seemed remarkable to me that he possessed such a senior position in the community, but his emotion and enthusiasm soon convinced me of what the others had known for some time. He was on our side. I listened to him reiterate the phrase *I love America!* several times as he thanked me and outlined his plans to convert the compound into a medical facility.

I came to believe in this man's sincerity and his solidarity with our shared goal to rid that country of outlaw warlords and foreign terrorists. This meeting convinced me, more than ever before, that our mission in Afghanistan had to succeed because the people there, the truly good and peace-loving people of that country, needed us and were counting on us. We can't let them down simply because some people think it is taking longer than expected.

As I said good-bye, the *wazir* expressed his desire to continue to provide assistance to our forces in that area and I told him how much I appreciated his support. Then I did something I wouldn't normally do. I pulled close to him and assured him that we were in this thing together and that the United States would not let his people down.

I don't know why I felt it was necessary to make this extra promise to him, but I did anyway. I guess I made it because I really think it's true. I feel we are bound to the Afghan people, and their fate is now, partly, our fate. I also believe we have the ability and the resources to ensure that their future and ours can be one of promise, peace, and friendship. I only hope the voices today calling for withdrawal and complaining about cost don't jeopardize the future of an entire nation of people for the sake of expediency. If this happens, we will have turned our back on our loyal friends in Lwara and on the ideals we hold so dear.

IT SEEMED AT the time that I was in constant contact with civilians and with the countryside beyond the borders of our base in Bagram. Again, unlike the old stereotype of the ugly American, we were trained to respect the customs of the local population not simply because we wanted their support, but because it was right. As I had done with the *wazir,* whenever I approached a village elder to begin a negotiation or a simple exchange of views, I put my right hand over my heart and said *"salam"* or *"salam aleykum."* They would reply by saying *"aleykum salam."* I didn't speak the local language, but the elders invariably appreciated my greeting and my respect for their culture and customs.

Showing sensitivity helped soften the sharper edges of this astonishing cultural encounter. My life could not be more different from that of the villagers I met. I often had to remind myself that many of the people I dealt with had never seen a helicopter before. The sight of American soldiers dressed in helmets and body armor getting out of a chopper must have been as astonishing to them as the villagers' appearance and lives were to me. It was critical that we showed them the respect we knew they deserved. Anything less would have been wrong and could have been disastrous for all concerned.

Before going out on missions, Captain Eric Dodson and I often filled the cargo pockets on our pants with candy. Sometimes, when we weren't entirely sure where we were landing and what kind of reception might be in store, we'd get out of the chopper and deploy in defensive positions amounting to a semicircle around the helicopter, just in case the enemy was lurking nearby.

Several times while we were deployed in this defensive posture, some local kids would run up and just stare at us while we tried to focus on the horizons for anything that looked unfriendly or out of place. With the noise of the chopper blades and the sight of smiles from the local kids, it was a pretty surreal and confusing scene. But on at least one occasion, I motioned one of the kids over and handed him a bunch of little sugar bunnies that the kids back home eat around Easter time. I seem to remember that these candies are called Peeps. Somebody had sent them to me, and I wasn't going to eat them myself.

Well, this kid's face just lit up, and he ran back to his friends with the sugar bunnies in his hand. I think they weren't sure what they were, but at least the gesture helped break the tension.

The Taliban had banned the taking of photographs as an offense against Allah. As a result, a lot of young Afghan kids had never seen themselves in a photo. Those strictures were removed when the Taliban was overthrown, so I made it a point of carrying around a little digital camera when I went to a village. I'd snap a picture and then show the kids the image on the screen. It was like I was holding a handful of seeds in Trafalgar Square in London. The kids were like the pigeons that call that historic square home, circling around me, trying to get a glimpse of their image.

Some of them, I later learned from the interpreter, not only had never seen their pictures, they'd never even seen their own reflection because they did not own a mirror.

It was at times like these, when I was out in the isolated villages of Afghanistan, that I really formulated most of my thoughts on our mission and our purpose. It was in these forgotten locations that I came to firmly believe our presence in Afghanistan was not only just but necessary. The support we received from the tribal elders and local villagers in Lwara and Kohe Sofi demonstrated to me that the Afghan people—as formally uneducated and as physically isolated as they may be—are smart enough to know that their physical and political isolation is not sufficient to protect them from men who seek to destroy their free will. They realize that our presence is serving a greater good. A good that will one day make them free and safe.

The children I came to know in Afghanistan taught me that children are the same no matter what the culture, no matter what the religion, no matter what the language. Children want to laugh and play in Afghanistan the same way kids want to laugh and play in America. For that reason, I know that Afghanistan is capable of sustaining a true democracy, and one day, if we stand by their side, I am confident Afghanistan will grow to become a dependable and reliable friend of America.

Democracy is not the sacred prize of a gifted few, nor do its blessings belong only to a selected race or faith. When I looked in the faces of those children and saw them laugh and smile, I knew for sure that those children were entitled to the same freedom and democracy as American kids. And it is up to us to help them achieve it. No matter how long it takes.

I RETURNED TO duty in the JOC at Bagram on the evening of March 22, 2003, standing by as troops in the field launched a major operation against an enemy stronghold. I was drinking coffee and monitoring my station while others scurried back and forth on the JOC floor carrying messages and making changes to the battle plan that was unfolding before us. I wasn't particularly stressed that evening because I was now getting familiar with this type of operation. I'd been in on the early planning, so I felt prepared for any contingencies that might come up concerning the rules of engagement or any other facets of operational law.

As usual, I sat in the bleachers with my headset on, sipping a cup of coffee. I was talking with the deputy staff judge advocate, Lieutenant Colonel Bob Cotell, while my eyes were moving periodically from my computer screen to the three large video monitors in front of us. So far, so good: no problems.

Then, out of nowhere, we heard an unbelievable report out of Kuwait, where our troops had recently begun pouring over the border into Iraq. According to these scattered reports coming in to us in Bagram, one of our own guys in Kuwait attacked his fellow soldiers while they slept in their tents. There were casualties, including some fatalities.

Every soldier in the JOC that night was a veteran of sorts. I wasn't a combat soldier, but I certainly had seen and heard enough by then to at least qualify as someone who was hard to rattle.

This news from Kuwait, however, was something we weren't prepared for. I felt like somebody had punched me in the gut. We all sat at our stations, silent, almost paralyzed by the shock. How the hell could this have happened?

We switched one of the large video screens in front of us to a live news feed from one of the cable news stations. And that's how we learned the shocking details about the case: a soldier in the famous 101st Airborne Division had attacked his comrades with grenades and small-arms fire. He wounded more than a dozen troops. Two were dead. The soldier suspected in the attack, Sergeant Hasan Karim Akbar, was a thirty-one-year-old American who had converted to Islam.

The attack was as well planned as any ambush. Just before dawn, with the troops asleep in their tents and awaiting their chance to push into Iraq, Akbar turned off an electricity generator, rolled grenades into three command tents, and then, with panic and surprise achieved, he opened fire with his M-4 assault rifle.

For what seemed like an eternity after we heard the report, nobody in the JOC said a word. All activity came to a halt. Every man and woman in that tent was stunned. Then the chief of operations snapped us out of our funk. "Hey, people, let's get back to work. We're fighting our own war here, remember!" With those words, the JOC sprang back to life as soldiers returned to their duties monitoring the operation that was under way in southern Afghanistan. As the familiar buzz of activity and noise returned to the JOC floor, it seemed to carry with it a new, more somber tone. Not only had we recently opened a new front in the global War on Terrorism in Iraq, but the attack on the 1st Brigade of the 101st Airborne Division reminded us that this war was like no other. In this war, the enemy was hard to see and could even come from our own ranks. The threat seemed more amorphous and shadowy then ever and even harder to define. The only thing we did know for certain was that we were heading into uncharted waters.

ABOUT THREE MONTHS after Sergeant Akbar's attack, I rotated back home to Fort Bragg, along with the rest of my unit, after serving eight months in Afghanistan. I left there proud of the work Americans were doing on behalf of the Afghan people, and proud to have done my small part to build trust and friendship between the United States and Afghanistan.

We landed back at Pope Air Force Base in Fayetteville, North Carolina, in June of 2003. My time as a mobilized reservist was about to come to an end. I was scheduled to be demobilized in the fall of 2003, and frankly, I was looking forward to returning to civilian life. I loved what I was doing for the Army and for my country, but it seemed like it was time to return to the D.A.'s office and to my life as a narcotics prosecutor.

The McGovern clan in 1972. My mother's favorite is in the lower left corner wearing the snazzy dark sports coat. Well, that is how I see it anyway.

Me with my mom and dad at my Holy Cross College graduation in May 1989. Howard and Terry McGovern are the most incredible and loving parents to all nine of their children and now they enjoy being grandparents to twenty-four grandchildren . . . and counting.

My grandfather, George Thomas McGovern (center), began G. T. McGovern Trucking, Inc., with only a horse and buggy at the age of fourteen in 1914. Over the next ninety years, his hard work and determination has anchored four generations of the McGovern family.

I am proud to be the next generation in my family to serve in the U.S. military. My father (left) was a U.S. Marine in the early 1950s and my maternal grandfather, Edward Markey (above, third from right), served as a sergeant with the 107th Infantry Regiment in the 1920s and 1930s.

After serving in the army, my grandfather (right) became a police officer in West New York, New Jersey, before going on to be the "poor master" for the social welfare department.

At Holy Cross I tried to follow in the footsteps of my brothers Jack and Bill who were stars on the Holy Cross football team. Here I am as #58, a number I would later wear for the Patriots. I was lucky enough to play with some pretty good teammates and friends such as Gerry Trietley (#60) and Dave Murphy (top left). (*Photograph courtesy of Holy Cross College*)

Playing for the Kansas City Chiefs with my good friend from Holy Cross, Tom Kelleher (#39), was a dream come true. During this preseason game in 1989, Tom and I are on the kickoff return team together. I'm the one running on the emblem of the Chief's helmet. Tom was a great athlete and an incredible motivator who took me under his wing in my rookie year and helped me reach my full potential.

In my second season with the Chiefs in 1990, we traveled to Berlin, Germany, to play an exhibition game against the Rams. During media day, I chatted with the Commissioner of the National Football League, Paul Taglibue. From the look on my face, I was probably telling him what I thought of his shirt.

In 1991, I played for the Pittsburgh Steelers and their legendary head coach, Chuck Noll. As a back up to starting linebackers, David Little and Hardy Nickerson, I could usually be found in this familiar position . . . sitting on the bench. (*Photograph courtesy of the Pittsburgh Steelers*)

After one season with the Steelers, I signed as a free agent with the New England Patriots (#58). By this time, I was officially known as a "journeyman." Here I am lined up for a punt return against the Indianapolis Colts on December 6, 1992, in Foxboro Stadium. (*Photograph courtesy of the New England Patriots*)

Dan Walsh and I met when we tried out together for the Pittsburgh Steelers in 1991. The bonds formed by athletes on playing fields across America are not that different from the ones formed by soldiers on battlefields around the world. The night before I deployed to Afghanistan in November 2002, Dan took off from work and flew to North Carolina to see me and say goodbye. He will always be my teammate and friend.

John O'Brien is my closest friend. We met as freshmen at Bergen Catholic High School. We went to school together, we played football together, and we trained together. My dream of playing in the National Football League would never have come true if it wasn't for John's influence in my life.

In 2000, I was sworn in by the legendary Robert Morgenthau as an assistant district attorney for New York County at 80 Centre Street in New York City. I was assigned to the Office of Special Narcotics for New York City where I spent most of my time and energy investigating violent drug organizations and their dealers. (*Photograph by Laura Badger*)

After witnessing the terrorist attack on the World Trade Center towers, I shook President Bush's hand during his visit to Ground Zero on September 14, 2001. It was an emotional moment I will never forget and it had a significant impact on my decision to go on full-time active military duty. (*Photograph by Edward Reed*)

Life at Fort Bragg regularly involved "airborne operations" where sometimes hundreds of paratroopers descended from the sky on a designated drop zone or DZ. I am standing with Captain John McCabe before one such jump at St. Mere Iglese DZ in 2005. John is a great prosecutor and was the first to obtain a conviction in the Abu Ghraib prison cases.

I met General Tommy Franks during his visit to Bagram Air Base in 2003. When he told me to always "treat them right," the "them" he was referring to were the enlisted soldiers. It is a lesson I have not forgotten.

Malalay (center) was a wonderful little girl who taught me that Afghanistan's future is a bright and hopeful one. She was also an excellent "body guard."

Dr. Cairo and his team of professionals in Kabul showed a special kind of compassion and devotion to the long-suffering people of Afghanistan. During our visit, Dr. Cairo (center, wearing white coat) introduced us to a young Afghan boy who was trying out his newly fitted prosthetic limbs after losing both his legs in a mine explosion.

One of our missions in Afghanistan was to help the new Afghan Government of Hamid Karzai establish the rule of law. In this photo, Major Jeff Bovarnick (second from left), Captain Erik Dodson (far right), and I are just leaving a meeting with the chief judge of the Supreme Court of the Islamic Transitional Government of Afghanistan. With us is the top Afghan Army JAG, General Gurat.

The prosecution team that convicted Sergeant Hasan Akbar of capital murder. From left to right: Criminal Investigation Division Special Agent David Maier, me, Special Agent Shawn Burke, Captain John Benson, Special Agent Angela Janysek, Special Agent Angela Birt, Special Agent in Charge Michael Graziano, Lead Prosecutor Lieutenant Colonel Michael Mulligan, and Chief Warrant Officer 3 Philip Kraemer.

The trial lasted for twenty-three days before Judge Stephen Henley at Fort Bragg, North Carolina. The military jury returned a unanimous verdict of guilty and a death sentence in April 2005. This sketch depicts my direct examination of Air Force Captain Mark Wisher who described the surprise attack that night in late March 2003. Sergeant Akbar looks on in silence. (*Photograph courtesy of The Associated Press*)

The real cost of war. Captain Christopher Seifert (above) and Major Gregory Stone (below) are two American heroes who were murdered by fellow American, Sergeant Hasan Akbar, on the eve of battle. The trial taught me that the war we are fighting in Iraq and Afghanistan is born out of the hate filled ideology of our enemies and not, as some would suggest, the materialistic motives of our leaders.

Here are three big reasons why I am a huge supporter of women in the military. Major Karin Tackaberry (left) is an outstanding prosecutor I worked with at Fort Bragg who has survived a fight with cancer and combat in Iraq. Brigadier General Dunn (second from left) was my boss in Afghanistan, Iraq, and Fort Bragg. This photo was taken at the promotion to Major of Kelly Hughes (third from left) in August 2006. Kelly is an incredible lawyer, a combat veteran, a sky diver, a martial arts expert, and . . . the love of my life.

Major Kelly Hughes did me the honor of becoming Major Kelly McGovern on November 10, 2006, at Hanscom Air Force Base Chapel in Massachusetts. (*Photograph by Charlotte Boccuzzi*)

The prosecution team from Task Force 134 assigned to try terrorists and insurgents in the Central Criminal Court of Iraq (CCCI). I could not have worked with a finer group of U.S. soldiers, sailors, airmen, and Marines. These brave men and women risked their lives every day to ensure that the people captured for attacking our troops paid for their crimes.

My morning commute to work at the CCCI. This bombed out former museum located in downtown Baghdad and outside the protected Green Zone was the only courthouse in Iraq with nationwide jurisdiction.

Trials or "investigative hearings," as they were officially termed, were conducted in the judge's chambers. Here I am using video teleconference equipment to prepare a witness for trial back at Fort Bragg. The Iraqi judge, Judge Fathal, who will hear the case is to my left.

During trial, my interpreter sat to my left and translated everything for me in real time. The defense attorney is sitting behind me and the two men in front of me are American contractors who maintained the video teleconference equipment and satellite link.

A little Iraqi girl I met in the courthouse. She symbolizes for me the hope and promise that is Iraq's future.

In August 2005, I traveled with the Iraqi Minister of Justice, Wakeel Hussein, as he inspected all Iraqi run prisons in the south. I am standing with the Minister of Justice (center) and the Iraqi Director of Prisons, General Juma (left), at the British Embassy compound in Basra. The British military detail responsible for the ministers' security required me to dress in civilian clothes during the trip.

The weather in Iraq was sometimes tough to endure. Here I am at FOB Danger in Tikrit during one of the many sandstorms.

I did a lot of traveling in Iraq by helicopter. It was on these trips that I saw Iraqi children run out of their homes to wave at our passing helicopter, giving me hope for our mission in Iraq.

Nothing beats coming home.

★   ★   ★

IN MID-JULY, HOWEVER, one of my superior officers in Afghanistan, Lieutenant Colonel Cotell, asked to speak with me. I'd worked side by side with him while we were overseas, and we'd been together when reports of Sergeant Akbar's attack on the 101st Airborne Division poured into the JOC that night in March.

Back at Fort Bragg, Colonel Cotell was chief of the Criminal Law Section for XVIII Airborne Corps, which made him the senior prosecutor at Bragg and my boss once again. It was great to work for him. He is a man of impeccable character and integrity and, like Brigadier General Dunn, a born leader. He has worn the uniform for his country for over fifteen years and served all over the world. He was stationed in Europe during the Cold War and did another overseas tour in South Korea in the early nineties. Just before we deployed to Afghanistan, he was handpicked to serve as the top military legal adviser to the U.S. and international law enforcement agencies working security for the Winter Olympics Games in Salt Lake City, Utah, in 2002.

In Afghanistan, he flawlessly handled some of the most high-profile and touchy legal matters the United States military was facing. He thoroughly and carefully approached highly sensitive issues without the benefit of previous experience. His advice was always thoughtful and well reasoned. His work ethic and willingness to take on challenges that others run from make him an indispensable asset in our fight against terrorism. Simply put, Lieutenant Colonel Bob Cotell is an American we can all be extremely proud of, and he is a guy I will respect and admire for the rest of my life.

It was late July 2003 when Colonel Cotell called me into his office. This wasn't an unusual request. He often called me in to discuss my open cases and any upcoming trials I might have. I always enjoyed speaking to him, as he was an experienced prosecutor with a wealth of knowledge on criminal law. He also provided regular doses of more practical knowledge to young lawyers still trying to figure out which table in the courtroom they were supposed to sit at during a trial. But this particular request seemed a little unusual because I was preparing to go to airborne parachute training at Fort Benning in Georgia. In preparation for this training, I had recently pushed off all of my cases until mid-September, when I would return from airborne school. I didn't think there were any hot issues we needed to discuss.

Colonel Cotell greeted me warmly as he stood by the open window that cooled his office—yes, he had an air conditioner, but it didn't get the job done. At forty-two, Colonel Cotell is a tall, lean, and handsome man with brown hair that is just beginning to show a little gray. He is quick with a smile and is even quicker on a four-mile run, as he often reminded me and other younger officers during our physical training sessions each morning.

But this day he didn't seem interested in talking about his speed or about airborne school or even his defective air-conditioning unit. After a few pleasantries, he offered me a seat and quickly steered the conversation to the heart of the matter.

"Rob," he said, "you're about to be demobilized. Now, you can ride out the next three months, if you want." He paused for a second. I noticed he had a sly look on his face. "Have you heard of the case against Sergeant Hasan Akbar?"

Of course I had. "Yes, sir." I said. "Everyone in the Army has.

That's the guy accused of trying to kill the members of his own unit in the 101st."

"That's right," he replied, like a teacher who had just asked a question with an obvious answer.

The prosecution of Sergeant Akbar had been transferred to our unit, the XVIII Airborne Corps, at Fort Bragg, from the 101st Airborne Division. So my unit would be given the task of investigating the evidence and presenting the case against the defendant.

As Colonel Cotell summarized the evidence in the case and where it stood, he got to the real reason he'd asked to speak with me. Prosecuting the Akbar case would take months of hard and often stressful work.

Not prosecuting the case, he added, was an easy ticket back to civilian life, to my old job with District Attorney Robert Morgenthau and, most likely, a much easier workload. Then he paused, leaned forward in his big leather-backed chair, and looked me straight in the eye. "So, I guess, you could decide to go back home and let your life return to normal," he said quietly.

"Or," he continued, "you can be the guy who prosecutes Sergeant Hasan Akbar."

"Where do I sign?" I said.

He broke out in a big smile. "I figured you'd say that," he said, extending his hand. "So I already told Colonel Dunn you'd take the job."

I'm sure she wasn't surprised.

This was incredible news. I had wanted to do something important for my country since I saw the towers collapse that horrible day in September 2001. I did all I could in Afghanistan and I was proud of my contribution as a reservist, however small and limited. But this case was different. This case would be like no other. I could think of no more serious crime a soldier could commit and I could think of no more important service I could offer to the families of the murdered soldiers than using my training and experience as a criminal prosecutor to bring Sergeant Akbar to justice. This case was the opportunity to do my part. Hell, it was the opportunity of a lifetime and I wasn't going to let it pass me by.

CHAPTER EIGHT

★ ★ ★

U.S. vs. Hasan Akbar—
The Enemy Within

OPERATION IRAQI FREEDOM WAS ONLY A FEW DAYS old on the night of March 22, 2003. Saddam's iron grip on the lives of his countrymen was about to be loosened forever as men and women from faraway nations overwhelmed the dictator's armed forces and gangs of thugs.

In Kuwait, a nation that knew all about the threat Saddam posed to the region and to the world, thousands of troops gathered near the Iraqi border awaiting their turn to strike a blow against Saddam's tyranny. They followed the progress of the first waves of the attack, and were preparing, each in his or her own way, to join that battle.

The American soldiers were all volunteers. Each man and each woman had made a conscious decision to become a frontline soldier in the defense of freedom. They knew it was not an idle choice, like deciding between a beach vacation or a few weeks in the mountains. Their decision to serve their country could lead them to a faraway place they knew little about, in the service of people whose language and customs were foreign to them.

And so they waited in Kuwait for orders to move into Iraq. Their overarching mission was to deliver the Iraqi people from oppression and cruelty in the name of certain universal freedoms. These freedoms are the fundamental human rights that Americans hold dear and that we believe are endowed to us not by governments but by our Creator.

On the night of March 22, 2003, Captain Christopher S. Seifert and Major Gregory L. Stone retired to their sleep tents in Camp Pennsylvania in Kuwait. As they lay down on the floor of their tents, they knew that the hour was fast approaching when they would cross the border into Iraq and join the push to topple Saddam. Captain Seifert went to his tent reluctantly—he had been working extraordinarily hard in recent days, so his immediate boss, Major Kyle Warren, had told him to get some sleep. Major Warren remained to go over some last-minute details about the upcoming movement into Iraq.

Captain Seifert and Major Stone were assigned to the Headquarters Detachment of the 1st Brigade Combat Team of the 101st Airborne Division. The 101st is one of the most storied units in modern American history. Most famously, men from the 101st landed behind enemy lines in the predawn hours of June 6, 1944—D-day. But the unit's conspicuous bravery on that night was just part of its legend, and all who joined the 101st were aware of the division's history and traditions. Each was expected to do his or her part to uphold the reputation of the 101st once the order was given to move out in support of the 3rd Infantry Division.

Major Stone and Captain Seifert upheld the division's tradition of courage and service. Major Stone was forty years old and from Idaho. His parents divorced when he was a young boy. Reared by his mother, he reestablished a warm relationship with his father as an adult. He was the divorced father of two preteen boys, Alex and Joshua. He planned to marry his new love, Tammie Eslinger, when he returned home after the war.

Captain Seifert was his parents' only child, delivered to them after twelve years of marriage. His parents had nearly despaired of having children until Christopher miraculously came into their lives. He was twenty-seven years old, married to his beautiful wife, Terri, and the proud father of Benjamin, who had been born only three months before his deployment to the Middle East.

Captain Stone and Major Seifert were surrounded by comrades with their own unique and often extraordinary life stories. Captain Greg Holden, asleep in a tent in the Kuwaiti desert, was a military intelligence officer with the legs of a dedicated runner. He regularly ran two miles in less than twelve minutes, a terrific pace. He was about to lead an infantry unit into combat, which he hoped might help him achieve his career goal—a place in Special Operations.

Captain Holden wasn't the only outstanding runner in camp that night. Captain Andras Marton was a marathon runner whose idea of a good time was running five miles every morning. He had enlisted as an infantryman, but was now a JAG serving on the brigade commander's staff.

In the tents of Camp Pennsylvania that night, U.S. soldiers

went to sleep knowing that they were about to face the enemy. They had no idea that the enemy was not across the border. The enemy was inside the camp, with a plan that had been long in the making. Tonight, he would execute it.

HUGE, STAND-ALONE GENERATOR lights, the kind you see on highways when workers are doing repairs at night, illuminated the camp during the hours of darkness. There was no reason to conceal Camp Pennsylvania in the dark—nobody expected the enemy to conduct a ground strike that far south of the border.

Shortly after midnight, the lights went out in the area where Captain Seifert, Major Stone, and their comrades were sleeping or burning the midnight oil in front of their computers. Major Kenneth Romaine, the brigade's executive officer, was among those still awake and working in his tent, which he shared with Colonel Ben Hodges, who was asleep in another part of the tent, and Sergeant Major Bart Womack, who was awake and sitting in front of a television. Major Romaine heard footsteps—somebody was walking near the entrance to his tent. He made a note of it, but went back to his work. Even though almost everybody was down for the night, it wasn't all that unusual to hear footsteps late at night. People came by to see him at all hours—he was, after all, the brigade's second in command.

He was staring at his computer screen when a huge spark erupted from underneath the table. It happened all the time—the combination of the desert heat and personal electronics gear often led to short circuits and other electrical problems.

Major Romaine had had experience with incendiary grenades as a platoon leader with the 3rd Infantry Division during Desert Storm. During that campaign, as his vehicle raced through the desert in pursuit of Iraqi forces, he'd dropped incendiaries on mounds of equipment that the enemy had left behind, making sure they wouldn't somehow wind up back in the enemy's hands. More than a dozen years later, back in Kuwait, Major Romaine quickly recognized that the spark in his tent wasn't the result of a computer malfunction. The spark came from a grenade.

They were under attack.

Both Major Romaine and Sergeant Major Womack reacted swiftly. They jumped to their feet immediately and yelled to Colonel Hodges, who was asleep in the back of the large tent. When the colonel didn't respond, Womack ran in his direction.

Romaine followed but boxes blocked his path. He was in the center of the tent when another grenade exploded. He would not remember details of the blast, only that he thought to himself, "An explosion has gone off. We're under attack." He was right, the grenade had just wounded the brigade commander and torn his tent apart.

As Romaine recovered from the blast, he reached for his pistol, made sure it was loaded, and moved toward the entrance of the tent. He expected the enemy to follow the grenade attack with a direct assault. He slowly moved to the entrance and peeled back the tarp that covered the opening. It was dark—the lights were out. He clutched his weapon with both hands, holding it out in front of him. Then he heard a sound to his right. He quickly wheeled around, his pistol level, and saw a flash. With that, a bullet hit his right pinkie, sliced through his left hand, came out his left wrist, and entered his left thigh.

Stunned, he fell back into the tent entryway. He pulled himself back up to one knee and tried to charge his pistol. It was locked in the open position. His weapon was damaged by the bullet that had just wounded him. It was no use. His wounds left him helpless. He couldn't grip his pistol firmly enough to get it to work. So he braced himself in the vestibule of the tent, fully expecting his assailant to move toward him to finish him off. He waited, wondering what he would do to defend himself.

But nobody came. The assailant moved on to the next tent, pulled the pin on another fragmentation grenade, paused, and then yelled into the tent, "We're under attack." Then he rolled the grenade into the second tent. The men inside heard the sickening sound of a grenade rolling across a hardwood floor. It exploded, filling the tent with smoke, shrapnel, and confusion.

Major Stone was hit. He took the brunt of the explosion. He lay on his side, propped up on his right elbow. He reached out to a friend, Captain Mark Wisher, and said the only words he could: "Help. Help. Help." Captain Wisher, also wounded, crawled over to his friend and held him in his arms, but he could do nothing. Major Stone's body had been riddled with shrapnel from the grenade—he suffered eighty-three separate wounds. Blood was pouring from his neck. He had lost a finger and a toe.

The assailant moved on to the next tent. An officer, Captain Ramon Rubalcaba, came charging out just as the assailant approached. "What the fuck?" the captain said, looking at this fellow U.S. soldier. "We're under attack," the assailant replied. Captain Rubalcaba pushed by him and raced toward the two tents that had just come under attack. The assailant moved closer to the tent the captain had just left. He pulled the pin on a grenade and rolled it into the tent. It exploded, sending shrapnel into the hand of Captain Seifert and others still inside the tent.

The sounds of explosions awakened Staff Sergeant David Michael Phillips of Bravo Company, 4th Battalion, 4th Brigade Combat Team, 101st Airborne Division. He was in a tent nearby. When he'd heard the first explosion, which wounded Colonel Hodges, he said to a buddy, "That was either a mortar round or a hand grenade." When he heard the explosion from Major Stone's tent, he revised his opinion. "That was a fucking hand grenade," he said.

Staff Sergeant Phillips usually slept with his boots on because the camp routinely received warnings of possible Scud missile attacks requiring him to run to a nearby bunker. He got tired of looking for his boots every time there was an alert. On this night, however, he'd decided to take his boots off for a change. He scrambled to find them and got them on in a hurry. Phillips put on his body armor and Kevlar helmet and had started racing to get outside the tent when he heard the explosion in Captain Seifert's tent, which was right next to his. Staff Sergeant Phillips hit the ground. A few seconds later, he heard a rifle shot. As he and his buddies raced out of their tent, not knowing what to expect, Staff Sergeant Phillips saw Captain Seifert lying on the ground, clearly in great pain. Phillips, a trained combat lifesaver, moved quickly to the captain's side.

"Where are you hit, sir?" he said.

"My back," the Captain said, trying to point to his lower back. The attacker had shot Captain Seifert in the back as he ran out of his tent.

Phillips went to work immediately as Captain Seifert groaned in pain. Sergeant Phillips calmly told him, "You're going to be okay. I'm trying to help you, sir." Somebody turned on a flashlight to help Phillips examine the captain and dress his wounds.

As other troops helped Phillips, he yelled, "Look for an exit wound." Generally, exit wounds from rifle fire are more traumatic than entrance wounds. But nobody could find an exit wound. Staff Sergeant Phillips dressed the entrance wound, and as he did, a major showed up with a litter. "He needs to go," Phillips said, gesturing to Captain Seifert. "He's been shot. He needs to go."

They carried Captain Seifert to a vehicle that would eventually take him to a helipad for medical evacuation. Major Romaine was already aboard the vehicle, also on a stretcher, his leg and hands dressed. Major Romaine saw his friend and realized he was badly hurt. "Come on, Chris," he said. "We're going to make it. We're going to be okay." The young captain only moaned.

ONCE THEY TOOK Captain Seifert away, Staff Sergeant Phillips went inside the tent where Chris Seifert had been. There were more victims inside, moaning and pleading for help. Both Captain Marton, the marathon runner, and Captain Holden, the sub-six-minute-miler, were bleeding profusely. The grenade had exploded directly between them, causing serious wounds to these great athletes' legs and thighs.

Staff Sergeant Phillips looked at the two and decided to treat Captain Holden first. Surrounded by battlefield chaos—the cries for help from other wounded soldiers, the confused shouts of troops trying to figure out what was going on—he methodically put a pressure dressing on Captain Holden's wound and tied it off. He grabbed another captain, Mike Sabatini, and asked him to help keep pressure on Captain's Holden's wound. "Just hang on to his thigh and don't let go of it," he said. The wound was serious.

Phillips then turned his attention to Captain Marton. "Where are you hit, sir?" he asked.

Marton was on the ground, in pain. He pointed to his left ankle, where there was a small puncture wound, but Phillips quickly realized Captain Marton had a more severe wound to his right thigh. As he dressed the wound, the staff sergeant looked over to Captain Holden. The captain's eyes were rolling back in his head. "I think he's going," Sabatini said.

"Just keep talking to him," Phillips said. "Just say something. Talk to him."

Staff Sergeant Phillips stabilized Captain Marton and returned to helping Captain Holden. Captain Holden's thigh was bleeding again. Phillips told Sabatini, "We have to elevate that leg." As Phillips and Sabatini went to pick up the captain's left leg to raise it, Holden's foot nearly fell off. He had been wounded badly in the ankle as well as the thigh.

Captain Holden screamed in pain. "What the hell are you doing?" he growled. Phillips was glad to hear it—the pain had brought the Captain out of shock. "Thank God," he thought. "You're back with us."

Staff Sergeant Phillips got both wounded men onto litters and that's when he remembered he had other duties in addition to being a combat lifesaver. He was a noncommissioned officer as well, and that meant he had to account for his soldiers. It's one of the first things we're taught to do in any crisis.

He left the tent, looked down at his boots, and realized he'd put them on the wrong feet. If something happened to him on this confusing, deadly night, he thought, he wanted his boots on the correct feet. He changed the boots around and went to find his men. During his search, he saw something he wasn't looking for—a discarded pull pin for a grenade, and a shell casing for a 5.56 round. They were lying in front of Colonel Hodges and Major Romaine's tent. The shell casing was for the same kind of round that U.S. soldiers were issued as ammunition for their M-16s and M-4 rifles.

The pull pin looked identical to one for a U.S.-issued M-67 fragmentation grenade. Phillips pointed the items out to Major Kyle Warren, who visually examined the pin and shell casing without moving them. Warren then told Phillips to stand guard over them. Phillips did just that—for the next eight hours.

WHEN MAJOR WARREN heard the explosions, he thought the camp had been hit by Iraqi Scud missiles. As an intelligence officer and the brigade S-2, he was responsible for identifying threats and protecting the camp from attack. When he heard the rifle shots, however, he knew something else was going on. He was concerned that there was some kind of coordinated enemy assault taking place. It seemed like the base had been infiltrated. He wanted to find out the threat being posed to the base and his troops. He had no idea of the size and location of the enemy force he thought was responsible for the attack. So he rounded up some troops to establish a security perimeter.

After securing the area, he reported to Colonel Hodges, who, although wounded, was still commanding the brigade's response to the assault. After being wounded by the grenade that exploded in his tent, Colonel Hodges made his way to the Tactical Operations Center (or TOC) that housed the brigade's command and control center. With his arm bandaged and in a sling, Colonel Hodges addressed his security officer and told him, "This may have been one of our own." The colonel had learned that the 2nd Battalion could not account for a soldier named Sergeant Akbar. The unit also reported that some ammo was missing.

Major Warren set out to secure the perimeter. He still wasn't sure who exactly was involved in the attack. He knew he had to be discreet, because he didn't want the attacker or attackers—whoever they were—to think that they were under suspicion. Major Warren wasn't ready to flush out anybody until he knew the nature of the threat and was sure his troops were ready.

As he continued his patrol, he saw a figure kneeling on the edge of a bunker. When he got closer, Warren saw the name Akbar on the soldier's helmet band.

He remained calm, holstering his weapon and casually asking the soldier what was going on. Operating more on instinct than with any plan in mind, he walked behind the kneeling soldier and began to address the next soldier in the bunker. Then Major Warren turned quickly and grabbed the soldier from behind by the shoulders. The soldier resisted. Major Warren tried to push him forward, but the soldier fought back. As the two men wrestled, Major Warren grabbed the soldier by the helmet, twisted it, and finally pushed him facedown to the ground and secured him. "Don't fucking move," Warren said. He asked the solider if he bombed the tents. The soldier said yes.

That soldier was Sergeant Hasan Akbar.

MAJOR STONE AND Captain Seifert died of their wounds. Major Romaine's hand is permanently deformed. Captain Holden and Captain Marton will never run again. Eleven others were wounded in the attack. Sergeant Akbar was accused of the murder of Major Stone and Captain Seifert and the attempted murder of sixteen of his comrades, including Major Romaine, Captain Holden, and Captain Marton.

As a member of the prosecution team assigned to the case, I shared the responsibility of holding Sergeant Akbar accountable for his actions on that night. The trial was held at Fort Bragg in North Carolina and lasted twenty-three days. The court-martial heard testimony from sixty witnesses and considered over two hundred pieces of physical evidence, including the murder weapons and dozens of photos from the crime scene. At the conclusion of the trial, Sergeant Akbar was unanimously convicted of the premeditated murders of Major Stone and Captain Seifert and the attempted murder of fifteen Army soldiers and one Air Force captain. He was sentenced to death on April 28, 2005.

AS OF THIS writing, Sergeant Akbar's case is on appeal, so there are limitations on what I can say about it. The narrative of that awful night in Kuwait should speak for itself. I can say, however, the prosecution of this case could not have been successful without the assistance of so many hardworking and dedicated people. Before the case was transferred from the 101st Airborne Division to the XVIII Airborne Corps, before Lieutenant Colonel Cotell called me into his office to ask me if I wanted to be on the case, before two other experienced prosecutors joined the team being assembled to prosecute Sergeant Akbar, the case was handled by two talented Army prosecutors for that historic division. They were Captain Harper Cook and Captain Micah Pharris.

These diligent Army officers conducted the initial investigation and made the difficult charging decisions that every prosecutor must make at the outset of a case. Captain Cook even personally traveled to Kuwait and Iraq during ongoing combat operations to interview witnesses and to identify potential evidence before it was lost or discarded in the confusion of war. Captain Pharris, who went forward during the initial assault into Iraq with the 101st, left his unit in northern Iraq just long enough to join Captain Cook for the Article 32 proceeding being held at Fort Knox in Kentucky in June of 2003.

An Article 32 proceeding is similar to a grand jury hearing and was the first major hurdle cleared in the prosecution of Sergeant Akbar. At such a hearing, the government offers evidence to an investigating officer who determines if the case should proceed to a court-martial. When the Akbar case was transferred to XVIII Airborne Corps shortly after the Article 32, I only needed to review their fine work and pick up where they left off.

This was a capital murder case and the first one in the U.S. military in many, many years. In fact, the last person to be executed in the military was an Army private first class named John Bennett. Private Bennett was convicted and sentenced to death on February 8, 1955, for the rape and attempted premeditated murder of an eleven-year-old Austrian girl. He was hanged on April 13, 1961, in Fort Leavenworth, Kansas. Although approximately 150 members of the U.S. military have been executed between 1916 and 1961 (sources can't agree on an exact number but it is probably somewhere between 135 and 170), there has not been a military execution since Private Bennett's sentence was carried out.

So as you can see, this was far too important a murder trial to leave in the hands of a former New York City drug prosecutor who had never even tried a murder case before. To bring Sergeant Akbar to justice for his crimes would require the talents and experience of more than just one person. A team needed to be assembled that could handle both the legal and moral challenges that come with prosecuting a high-profile, capital murder case.

Captain John Benson is as grumpy and grouchy a person as you are ever going to meet. I can say this about John because he is a good friend and I know that behind his gruff, crotchety demeanor beats the heart of an honest and loyal military prosecutor. I also know that deep down inside, John is really just a big old teddy bear. No one else works harder at his craft.

So it was no surprise when Colonel Dunn and Lieutenant Colonel Cotell decided John would join the prosecution team.

As the team was taking shape, so were our roles. I was assigned as the primary prosecutor on the case. That meant I would be responsible for handling the day-to-day challenges that came with preparing a capital murder case for trial. John continued to serve as a prosecutor for XVIII Airborne Corps while assisting me periodically with things like witness preparation and production of discovery to the defense. As the trial date grew closer, however, John dropped all his other responsibilities and joined me full-time. John and I traveled to Kentucky, Tennessee, Georgia, and Pennsylvania to locate and interview witnesses and identify evidence. We worked long hours, late at night and on weekends, conducting legal research and writing briefs.

John and I got along great and worked well together. We each brought different skill sets to the table, and when we disagreed over how to proceed, we always managed to find a compromise that resulted in a well-balanced and thorough work product. I was lucky to be working with such a talented attorney, whose expertise in criminal law and refusal to do anything less than his absolute best ensured that we left no stone unturned.

I wish I could tell you that I was the most important member of the prosecution team. Unfortunately, and it pains me to say this, I can't. Without a doubt, the most critical person to the success of the government's prosecution of Sergeant Akbar was Lieutenant Colonel Michael Mulligan. Lieutenant Colonel Mulligan is a forty-eight-year-old American who lived much of his childhood in Niagara, Canada, where his dad worked as a manager of a trucking company. Like any self-respecting young boy in Canada in the 1970s, Lieutenant Colonel Mulligan grew up to love and play the national sport of hockey. He ended up being a pretty good left wing for Oswego State College's hockey team in New York and he went on to play in the European professional hockey league for the Buchloe Bears in Bavaria, Germany, from 1981 to 1983.

After his hockey career, Lieutenant Colonel Mulligan enrolled in University of Tulsa Law School, graduated in 1988, and became an assistant district attorney in Tulsa County, where he was assigned to the Traffic and Misdemeanors Division. As a newly minted A.D.A., he prosecuted misdemeanor after misdemeanor cases before graduating to felonies. He made a name for himself among defense attorneys as a blunt but fair prosecutor.

In 1989, he traded in his A.D.A. badge for an Army uniform and was commissioned as a First Lieutenant in the United States Army. He soon found himself in the familiar role of prosecutor and in the equally familiar surroundings of Germany. What followed was a criminal law career that has few rivals.

As a First Lieutenant and later captain in Fulda, Germany, during the 1990s, he established himself as a lawyer to be reckoned with when he prosecuted the brutal murder of a U.S. soldier. On December 7, 1993, Sergeant Stephen Schap attacked a young Army specialist whom he believed was having an affair with his wife. Without saying a word, Schap approached the victim and began stabbing and slashing him with an eight-inch doubled-edged knife. Schap then repeatedly kicked the now-dangling head of his victim until he finally separated it from the body. Still not satisfied, Schap held up his victim's head, displaying his "prize" to some horrified onlookers.

Captain Mulligan successfully convicted this monster for his brutal crime. Sergeant Schap was sentenced to forty-five years in prison.

After being promoted to major and a supervisory role over younger prosecutors, Major Mulligan again climbed back into the ring to prosecute a high-profile case for the Army. This time he was in Texas and the charge was conspiracy to commit murder.

The defendant was a specialist named Jacqueline Billings, who was also the local "governor" for a notoriously violent street gang known as the Gangster Disciples. During the trial at Fort Hood, which was held before military judge Stephen Henley, Major Mulligan received repeated death threats from gang members and was assigned a personal security detail to protect him and his family. Regardless of the danger, Major Mulligan convicted Specialist Billings, or "Big Momma," as her gang members referred to her, of ordering her gang members to commit robberies and assaults in and around Killeen, Texas, and engaging in other organized criminal activity. She was sentenced to several decades behind bars.

Lieutenant Colonel Mike Mulligan, with his vast experience and unmatched expertise as a criminal prosecutor, was the ideal choice to lead the prosecution of Sergeant Akbar. This was the first case charging a soldier with killing his fellow comrades during wartime since the Vietnam War. This case also grabbed the media's attention because it was the Army's first capital murder case in a decade.

Images from the attack were flashed around the world—some even reaching me in the JOC in Bagram, Afghanistan, only minutes after the carnage occurred. The country was watching, so there was no room for error. This would require the best the Army had to offer and Lieutenant Colonel Michael Mulligan was the very best.

The team concept didn't stop there. Any prosecutor knows that no one can handle a case like this all alone. The newly assembled trial team was no different. We realized that our success or failure in the courtroom would depend, in large part, on the kind of help we would receive from enlisted paralegals, non-commissioned officers, and criminal investigators. This help was absolutely essential because there were over ten thousand documents and literally hundreds of pieces of physical evidence and photographs. We needed to scrutinize all of this evidence in order to identify leads and then we needed to run all of those leads down. Our investigation would require us to travel to many states and to bring witnesses in from all over the world to testify.

This monumental task proved to be surmountable only because the trial team could call upon the skills of some of the brightest and most enthusiastic young soldiers the Army has to offer. People like Staff Sergeant Burt Broussard, Master Sergeant

Diana Clark, Master Sergeant Deatric Alexander, Staff Sergeant Jennifer Green, Sergeant Xoel Torres, Sergeant Jarrod Kary, Staff Sergeant Donald Purchase, and Specialist Mangola Prifti were just some of the fantastic enlisted soldiers and NCOs who helped us ensure that our case was thoroughly and completely prepared for trial.

Special recognition must also be given to four outstanding officers, Major Karin Tackaberry, Captain Adam Kazin, Chief Warrant Officer Three Phillip Kraemer, and CID Special Agent Angela Janysek. These officers spent countless hours investigating leads, locating witnesses, conducting legal research, preparing evidence, and helping to comfort the families of the victims. Although these military professionals never had the chance to sit at the prosecution table during the trial, their help and assistance was essential in obtaining a conviction in this case.

The legendary head coach of the Penn State football team, Joe Paterno, once attributed his success to a simple technique: he tried to surround himself with people a lot smarter than he was. Lieutenant Colonel Mulligan had a similar philosophy. He told us, "There are no great prosecutors, just great prosecution teams." All my life, my parents, coaches, and teachers instilled in me the belief that a group of motivated people focused on the same worthwhile goal can accomplish far more than any individual could hope to achieve acting alone. That lesson was never more important than in the case against Sergeant Akbar.

With the prosecution team now in place, we were ready to proceed. We dove right into the case file. With a life hanging in the balance and victims seeking justice for their loved ones, we had to know everything about this case if we were going to prove Akbar's guilt to a jury. But before we could begin examining what Sergeant Akbar had done that night, we had to understand why he'd done it.

IN THE MONTHS and months spent reviewing documents, interviewing witnesses, and preparing for trial, the prosecution team learned a lot about Sergeant Akbar.

Most important, we discovered that Sergeant Akbar, a convert to Islam, simmered with hatred for the United States. In his diary, which he had kept for thirteen years, we found statements going back almost a decade in which he declared his loathing for America and for Americans. The manner in which he allegedly operated on that night in Kuwait showed careful planning and premeditation. This was not a man who simply snapped. This was not a man acting on a recent grudge. This was a man who knew precisely what he was doing, and he acted on a careful and deliberate plan.

As I absorbed the facts of the attack and the motivation of the attacker, my life slowly became consumed by the case. I was prosecuting a murderer and, in my opinion, a traitor to our country. Sergeant Akbar's crimes enraged me because he had betrayed his fellow soldiers. Everyone who has ever worn the uniform for their country knows that American soldiers fight for freedom. They fight for democracy. But most of all, they fight for one another.

When soldiers go to war, they pledge their lives to their fellow soldiers, in part because they know that every other soldier makes that same pledge to them. Sergeant Akbar broke that pledge. Sergeant Akbar considered the members of the 1st Brigade Combat Team his enemy that night. But they weren't his enemy. They were his brothers in arms.

Sergeant Akbar wasn't some poor, pathetic slob at the end of his rope. He wasn't some misunderstood kid whom society had overlooked. Sergeant Akbar killed his fellow soldiers on the eve of battle because he hated America and wanted to see America destroyed. He was and is a cold-blooded, ideology-driven, hate-filled murderer.

As a soldier, I knew that I would probably never do anything more important in my life than prosecuting this case. I felt that it was my responsibility and mine alone to ensure that Sergeant Akbar was held responsible for the lives he took, the lives he destroyed. If I failed in this mission, I could point the finger of blame at no one but myself. If the trial was lost, I knew I would have to face the families of Major Stone and Captain Seifert and explain to them why the system failed them—why I failed them. I know that Lieutenant Colonel Mulligan and Captain Benson felt the same way.

We knew what was at stake and it was with this burden on our shoulders that we walked into court on April 6, 2005, to begin the trial.

Before military judge Stephen Henley and fifteen officers and senior enlisted soldiers selected to be the jury, we presented our case against Sergeant Akbar. Captain Benson delivered the opening statement, carefully laying out for the jury exactly what we expected the evidence to show. Over the following weeks, we called witness after witness who described the carnage of that night and the events that followed. We slowly and carefully painted a picture of the soldier who harbored a deep hatred for America and a willingness to act on that hatred. We also explained in detail how several of Sergeant Akbar's commanders tried to help him in the days leading up to the attack. They even asked him if his Muslim beliefs would make it difficult for him to take part in the coming offensive. Each time, Sergeant Akbar assured his leaders and fellow soldiers that everything was okay. In fact, one time he even expressed his eagerness to engage in the mission.

But his words were all lies. Sergeant Akbar had no intention of participating in the impending assault on Iraq. He planned an attack of his own, against an enemy he'd chosen to hate. He waited until his comrades least expected it and he hit them when they were most vulnerable.

The evidence against Sergeant Akbar was overwhelming. Although he should have been far across the camp and away from the command tents that night, his handprint was found on the control panel of the generator light that was turned off just before the attack. A latent-print expert from the United States Army Criminal Investigative Laboratory in Atlanta confirmed this fact when he matched that print to one taken from Sergeant Akbar. After his capture by Major Warren, it was also discovered that Sergeant Akbar had a minor shrapnel wound to the back of his left knee. He had been wounded because he was standing too close to one of the tents when he tossed in a grenade.

Scientific evidence confirmed that DNA from blood splatter found at the crime scene matched the DNA of Sergeant Akbar. Although the wound to Akbar's leg was minor, it was a major development in our case. It not only placed Sergeant Akbar at the crime scene, it also placed him well within throwing distance of the grenade explosions.

If that wasn't enough, a firearms expert also found evidence that proved the bullet taken from Captain Seifert's body and the shell casings found in front of the tents by Staff Sergeant Phillips and others were fired from Sergeant Akbar's M-4 assault rifle. An explosive residue expert from the Army's crime lab determined that residue found on Sergeant Akbar's uniform matched the residue created by an exploding M-67 fragmentation grenade and an M-14 incendiary grenade. These were the same grenades used in the attack and the same ones that Sergeant Akbar had been guarding earlier that night.

If there was any doubt remaining after all this evidence, Sergeant Akbar removed it when he confessed to Major Warren that he was the one who attacked the tents.

Why did he do it? In the days following the attack, the FBI executed a search warrant on Sergeant Akbar's long-term storage unit located in Tennessee just outside of Fort Campbell. In his storage unit, they found a computer. On that computer, they found Sergeant Akbar's diary.

In my closing argument, I offered two very telling passages from his diary that helped explain his motives. In his second-to-last entry before deploying to Kuwait, Akbar wrote about the plan he was considering. "I may have to make a choice very soon about who to kill," he said. "I will have to decide if I should kill my Muslim brothers fighting for Saddam Hussein or my battle buddies." Then I read his final entry to the jury. In it, he made clear his intent to commit mass murder as he revealed whose side he was on. "I am not going to do anything about it as long as I stay here. But, as soon as I am in Iraq, I'm going to kill as many of them as possible."

The "them" he was referring to were his battle buddies. These last two entries expose the bone-chilling truth about who Sergeant Akbar is and why he did what he did. Sergeant Akbar saw himself as a Muslim first and an American second, if he saw himself as an American at all.

THIS IS A new kind of war. A war that does not recognize the traditional boundaries drawn on a map. In this war, the enemy might wear the same uniform, he might speak the same language as we do. The enemy we fight may be a fellow American citizen like John Walker Lind, who was convicted for providing services to the Taliban in Afghanistan, or even a fellow soldier like Sergeant Akbar. They amount to a faceless and deadly entity that hides in plain sight. That is why this new war requires that we be willing to strike at the enemy wherever we find him and that we be willing to devise and develop both the military and legal weapons necessary to defeat him.

The lesson of Sergeant Akbar's betrayal is that we must remain flexible in our response to the asymmetrical threat of ideological terror or risk not only the loss of more American lives but of our way of life.

The Akbar case tells another, equally important, story. The testimony about that attack didn't just describe a scene of horror and murder. It also revealed countless acts of bravery and self-sacrifice by the soldiers of the 101st Airborne Division. The story of that night is the same story that has been told about the American soldier throughout our nation's history. Men like Major Ken Romaine, Major Kyle Warren, and Staff Sergeant David Phillips exemplify the bravery and quick thinking in the heat of combat that Americans have come to admire and expect from our armed forces. Captain Mark Wisher, who cradled his dying friend in his arms, reminds us of the compassion that underlies their reasons for serving. And, most important, the sacrifice of Major Stone, Captain Seifert, Captain Holden, Captain Marton, and all the members of our armed forces who risk their lives for us without qualification or complaint stands as a testament to their courage and fortitude. They are men and women we can all be incredibly proud of and thankful for.

DURING THE TRIAL, Lieutenant Colonel Mulligan and I would take a break from our weekend work schedule to attend Sunday Mass at the Main Post Chapel located on Fort Bragg. I listened, as I always did, to that portion of the Mass in which the congregation is asked to pray for very specific intentions: an increase in vocations, an end to war and terrorism, that sort of thing. On this particular Sunday morning, however, we were asked to pray that civil leaders would turn away from the culture of death, including abortion and the death penalty. Lieutenant Colonel Mulligan and I exchanged a glance. I had never heard this particular petition against the death penalty offered in the three years I had been attending Mass at that chapel.

All my life, I have heard sermons from the pulpit opposing the death penalty and its inherent injustice and inhumanity. Not surprisingly, many priests and religious people believe that the death penalty is wrong and, under some interpretations, even a sin. I, for one, do not believe this. I believe the death penalty is an appropriate, legitimate, and just punishment for society's most heinous and irredeemable criminals. Whoever threw grenades into those tents, whoever calmly shot Major Romaine and then Captain Seifert in the back, whoever willfully planned and executed the attack in Camp Pennsylvania deserves to be put to death. I am 100 percent certain that Sergeant Akbar threw those grenades. Sergeant Akbar shot Major Romaine. Sergeant Akbar shot Captain Seifert in the back. And Sergeant Akbar deserves to die for what he did.

As a practicing Catholic, I often hear my fellow Catholics—including priests—say that the death penalty is immoral and can never be sanctioned by the Church. That's simply wrong—the Catholic Church has never ruled out execution as an acceptable form of punishment. The Church's catechism, prepared by then-Cardinal Joseph Ratzinger and published by Pope John Paul II in 1992, states on page 546 that "preserving the common good of society required rendering the aggressor unable to inflict harm." It goes on to say that civil authorities have a right to "punish malefactors by means of penalties commensurate with the gravity of the crime, not excluding, in cases of extreme gravity, the death penalty."

Surely the murders carried out in Camp Pennsylvania were extremely grave. Parents lost a child; children lost their fathers; a wife lost her husband. A fiancée lost the man she loved. And the United States of America lost two brave and honorable officers. Why? Because Sergeant Akbar hated America and wanted to see it destroyed.

Our criminal justice system provides several reasons for sentencing a convicted criminal. These principles are deterrence, public safety, societal retribution, and rehabilitation. The military adds the additional principle of maintaining good order and discipline in the military ranks. Any one of these reasons is sufficient for imposing a sentence on a convicted criminal. So even if the death penalty does not result in deterring a single person from committing the same offense, a death sentence for a brutal murder is still appropriate because we know it is going to deter at least one person—the murderer himself.

When he is finally put to death, Sergeant Akbar will never again have the opportunity to kill another human being. Then and only then will the community—including prison guards and other inmates—be truly safe from his deadly potential.

Society also has the right to punish an offender in a manner commensurate with the level of harm he inflicted on society. That means, simply, that we in society have the right to take from the killer an amount equal to what he took from us. In the case of murder, it is more than appropriate to require that the murderer forfeit his culpable life in exchange for the innocent life or lives he took.

As a prosecutor, I also want to point out an incredibly practical argument in favor of the death penalty. It encourages guilty defendants to agree to a plea bargain rather than risk a trial at which they might be sentenced to death for their crimes. An assistant district attorney can negotiate a plea to a life sentence without parole in exchange for taking the death penalty off the table. This saves the victim's family from a long and agonizing trial, during which they invariably grieve and feel victimized all over again. It also enables prosecutors to build stronger cases against members of a vicious criminal conspiracy by encouraging lesser players to turn state's evidence against those truly responsible for the crime. Without this powerful tool, some criminals will go free because prosecutors won't have all the leeway they need to get to the truth.

Our criminal justice system is not like our system of civil law, in which society can compensate a victim for his or her loss. Instead, the criminal justice system is designed to punish a criminal for the harm caused to victims. Loss of life for taking another's life seems an appropriate punishment. It is morally correct to condemn in the highest possible terms the crimes we deem to be the most reprehensible. Justice not only permits this type of sentence. It demands it.

But it's so expensive, I'm told. Getting a death sentence upheld and actually carried out requires so many steps and takes so long that it's cheaper to settle for life without parole. That's true, but applying our system of justice using a cost/benefit analysis is not only untenable, it is illogical. Imagine if we decided not to prosecute rapes, child pornography, or other heinous crimes because they simply prove too costly and time-consuming. Should we tell rape victims that the government has run the numbers and it is just not cost-effective to prosecute the man who brutalized them? Would anyone suggest that we tell these victims, "Maybe if you get raped again next year, we will have enough money in the budget to go after the guy?" That is absolutely absurd and anyone who thinks we should base the decision to prosecute or not prosecute a heinous criminal on the economic bottom line should be ashamed of themselves.

When I was prosecuting Sergeant Akbar, a friend told me he didn't think we should be seeking the death penalty. I asked, "Why not?" He answered, "Because it's not going to bring back the victims."

I couldn't believe what I was hearing, and from a really intelligent person. I explained the obvious—no punishment, not life without parole, not fifty years, not five minutes—would bring back the victims. Should we have a system that simply releases murder suspects because the criminal justice system can't bring the victims back from the dead? Of course not. We punish killers even though we can't bring back the dead for the same reason we punish pedophiles even though we can't restore the innocence of a child. We punish them because they deserve it and murderers deserve to die.

We should keep the death penalty as an option, in the same way we have other options like life without parole, or life with parole. All these sentences are appropriate options for convicted killers who place their own desires above the rights and the lives of law-abiding citizens.

When we sentence a brutal murderer to death, we do not condemn our own souls nor do we forfeit the moral integrity of our civilization. It is not the fault of society that the defendant is a brutal murderer, nor is it the fault of the prosecutor or the jury for seeking an appropriate sentence for a heinous crime. We are not responsible for the defendant's fate. The defendant is. The defendant could have avoided his or her fate if they simply chose to live peacefully with the rest of us. Since he or she made the choice to take away another human life, it is not unreasonable to require them to now forfeit their own.

We are only human and we cannot look into someone's heart and tell if they have truly repented and if they no longer pose a threat to us. We can only look at their actions and judge them according to those actions. We do not cast judgment on their souls. That is God's province and God's alone—and may He give His mercy to all those who truly deserve it.

OUR CRIMINAL JUSTICE system sometimes loses sight of who really is the most important figure in any criminal prosecution— the victim. In his sentencing argument to the jury, Lieutenant

Colonel Mulligan asked the members to sentence Sergeant Akbar to death for his crimes. His powerful and compelling argument described the pain and loss suffered by the victims and their families. As I sat there and listened to him, I couldn't help but think about how, even after a conviction, it is the defendant's life that is of constant concern to anti-death-penalty advocates. They tell us it is the convicted criminal's life that we must value when deciding how to punish him.

Lieutenant Colonel Mulligan's sentencing argument put it best. He told the jury that death was the just and appropriate sentence in this case because of what Sergeant Akbar did, because of how he did it, because of when he did it, and, most importantly, because of whom he did it to. To a hushed and somber courtroom, he spoke softly but directly. He asked the members to decide what a life is worth. But he didn't ask them to examine Sergeant Akbar's life; that had already been done in painstaking detail throughout the trial. Instead, he asked the jury to value the lives of Major Stone and Captain Seifert. He asked them to try to calculate the loss of a military career, or the use of one's legs when considering the lives of men like Captains Holden and Marton. He asked them to calculate what a little boy's life without his father is worth. To consider the emotional pain felt by a parent dealing with the loss of their eldest child, and of their only son.

I certainly agree that our system's focus on the criminal defendant is well directed and serves as the bedrock of our constitutional framework. In doing so, however, I do not think that our system should trample on the value of the victims' lives as we rush to cloak the defendant in some kind of constitutionally granted nobility. Convicted criminals are not entitled to the same level of compassion and understanding from society as the victims of their crimes. Criminals deserve due process. Victims deserve much more—they deserve justice.

SERGEANT AKBAR WAS convicted and sentenced to death for his crimes. Justice prevailed. I recognize that nothing I did in this case will ever ease the grief of the families of those two officers. Nothing will ever ease the pain of the two captains and those who suffered life-changing wounds, who will carry the scars of that night with them forever. But I was glad to play some part in making sure that a traitor to his uniform and his country received the same sentence he imposed on two of his fellow soldiers that night—a sentence he most certainly deserved.

After the trial was over, I congratulated Lieutenant Colonel Mulligan for his leadership and his talents as an attorney. It was remarkable, I told him, that during the long months of work on the case, he and I never butted heads or let our egos get in the way of the job.

The old hockey player reminded this old football player that we were both, once upon a time, athletes who played in team sports. "That's the key," he said. "When you play on a team, you realize that you're a piece in a larger effort. That's how you're trained. You see the big picture, and you realize that you have to work together to get the job done."

That's how an imperiled nation, a nation under attack, ought to be acting, too.

WHEN THE AKBAR trial concluded in late April 2005, I was thirty-eight years old and I figured I had just finished the most important assignment a military prosecutor could ever ask for. It seemed that whatever came next would pale in comparison to the previous two years. But then I received a message from Colonel Dunn. She was now deployed to Iraq and I had told her before she left that I wanted to deploy there, too, as soon as the trial ended. Her message was short. She said she had an assignment for me. She couldn't tell me what it was, but she promised me that I'd love it.

When I arrived in Iraq and found out what I was to do—I couldn't believe it. It was, in my opinion, a military prosecutor's dream. When Colonel Dunn told me, I thanked her for the opportunity and promised her that I would be happy to mow her lawn every week for the rest of life. She laughed and assured me that this wouldn't be necessary.

My new assignment proved to be every bit as unique and rewarding as Colonel Dunn said it would be. And for what it's worth, my offer to mow her lawn still stands.

Chapter Nine

* * *

The Central Criminal Court of Iraq—
Terrorism on Trial

AN HOUR AFTER I LANDED AT BAGHDAD INTERNATIONAL Airport, a suicide bomber blew himself up nearby, killing seven Iraqi police officers. At the time of the attack, I was in a convoy on my way from the airport to Camp Victory, the huge U.S. base that has sprung up adjacent to the airport. I was there no more than three or four hours when I heard a series of explosions in the distance—not close, but not far away, either. The enemy lobbed a couple of mortar rounds into camp, killing one American soldier and wounding nine others. I was just a day removed from civilized life on the home front.

There is no gradual acclimation to war. There is no quiet period of orientation, no downtime, no resetting of the body clock. There is no step-by-step immersion—war is not like the kiddie pool, where you wade in slowly and let your body adjust to the water temperature. War is angry waves and turbulent winds with a clutching riptide that will pull you under in a second. You have no time to prepare. War goes by its own schedule, its own calculations, its own dynamics. You adjust to war. War does not adjust to you.

While these attacks were disconcerting, I wouldn't describe them as a shocking reminder that I was in a war zone, either. I knew the risks when I asked Colonel Dunn to bring me to Iraq. I started a journal later that day, and in one of my earliest entries I noted that "my decision just feels right and I seem to feel better and better about it with each passing day." I wrote those words because I knew our mission was right. I knew that the larger purpose was nothing less than the cause of human freedom, and I knew our stake in the outcome of this war was nothing less than the safety and security of Americans both at home and abroad. Knowing this, I wanted nothing more than to do my part in whatever small way I could.

I deeply regretted the deaths of the Iraqi police officers and the U.S. soldier that day. Their loss was a horrible price to pay and their passing will be felt by their families for years and years to come.

But these attacks did not change how I feel about our nation's presence in Iraq. In fact, these attacks only served to reinforce my belief that we should be there. They defined for me an unmistakable truth about this conflict: Iraq is a dangerous and deadly place, not because of our presence, but because terrorists have descended upon that country to incite violence and create chaos. They want to prevent the establishment of a free and democratic system for the Iraqi people. The terrorists and insurgents responsible for those attacks claim to be saving Muslims from the infidel Americans when, in reality, they are the ones trying to enslave Muslims. Osama bin Laden says America is the Crusader nation and that we are assaulting Islam in Iraq. It is bin Laden and his followers, however, who are the greatest threat to the Islamic faith because they twist the teachings of the Koran in an attempt to justify murder and intolerance. As I write, bin Laden's second in command, Ayman al-Zawahri, has called for a holy war to establish Islamic fundamentalist rule from Spain to Iraq.

How is this any different from Hitler's murderous wishes to create an Aryan empire in Europe?

I SPENT THAT first night in Camp Victory, a sprawling city of tents and military hardware that featured some of the familiar comforts of home. There was a Burger King based in two trailers outside the PX. Inside the PX, you could buy everything from an air-conditioning unit to thong underwear. Just for the record, I bought neither.

As part of the Army's efforts to show the Iraqis that we mean it when we say that we respect their culture and that we are in Iraq not as conquerors but as liberators, Camp Victory has been given an Arabic name as well: Camp Al-Nasr. Several other Army facilities in and around Baghdad have also been designated with Arabic names. It was, on the Army's part, more than a mere gesture. It served as a significant acknowledgment that we were not trying to impose our values and culture on the Iraqi people. Yes, inside our camps we might enjoy pizza and burgers, but we also understood that we were not risking our lives to make Iraq safe for fast-food restaurants. We were fighting to make the country safe for Iraqis.

Behind the camp was a vast expanse of land that served as Saddam Hussein's personal hunting grounds, where he kept exotic wild animals including tigers. I suppose he hunted animals when he got tired of hunting down and killing his political opponents.

As I would soon learn, evidence of Saddam's cruelties and self-indulgence were not hard to find in Baghdad and all across Iraq. I would have personal encounters with several examples of the dictator's lavish lifestyle throughout my deployment. Each time I came across the remnants of his prodigality and ostentation, it reminded me of his insatiable quest for personal pleasure and power at the expense of the poor Iraqi people. It also confirmed another, more important point. It was proof of our victory over him and his two brutal sons. If some guy from New Jersey was smoking cigars on his balconies, as I was, that meant the liberation of Iraq from Saddam's cruelties was truly complete.

But don't get me wrong, I knew hard fighting lay ahead and that my job would be to prosecute the men and occasional woman who sought to restore the corrupt, tyrannical old order. But from the bustling base called Camp Victory to the liberated swimming pools and balconies of Saddam's palaces, the old order in Iraq had passed. Our job now was to help Iraq build something new, a task that would require the use of force at times, the rule of law, and the prosecution and imprisonment of those who had other ideas.

After spending the night at Camp Victory, I boarded a Black Hawk helicopter for the short ride to the U.S. embassy, located in one of Saddam's former palaces in the center of Baghdad. This particular monstrosity, called the Republican Palace, was used by Saddam more for office space than as a place to call home. It overlooked the Tigris River and was 1.7 squares miles in size. We flew at rooftop level into the center of the city, not out of any corny bravado, but because flying low made us less of a target. A chopper had been shot down a week earlier, so pilots were told to stay low so that they couldn't be seen long enough for the enemy to accurately fire at them as they approached the embassy compound.

The embassy was in the heart of what is called the Green Zone, a defensive perimeter that housed American and international diplomats, aid workers, and other personnel. Security was extremely tight but not impenetrable—ultimately, the Green Zone was an urban neighborhood, not a fortress. The enemy had to work hard to penetrate this area, but it was not an impossible assignment, as I quickly discovered. On my third night in the zone, as I got ready for a nighttime run around the embassy grounds, four mortar rounds exploded just outside the embassy walls, followed by a few bursts of rifle fire. Nobody was hurt. Nobody was deterred. Nobody was terrorized. It was, for the insurgents, an utter waste of ammunition.

When I reported for duty at the embassy, I was handed an M-16 assault rifle, which was more of a security blanket than anything else. Like I said, I am not a combat soldier. I figured the best chance I had of hitting an insurgent with my M-16 would be if I threw it at him. But I certainly felt safer having one strapped across my chest, although I am not sure if anyone standing next to me felt the same way.

My sleeping quarters were not in the embassy itself but in a trailer on its grounds. While the trailer certainly lacked some of the amenities of home, living in the embassy compound at least offered one nice advantage: access to Saddam's swimming pool. I took my first dip on June 4, 2005, my fourth day in Iraq. I smiled from ear to ear with every lap I did in that opulent, semi-kidney-shaped swimming hole. It was located directly behind Saddam's Republican Palace and featured a huge, multilevel platform diving board like you see during Olympic diving competitions. It also had an ornate fountain located near the center that was reminiscent of the Olympic torch. The irony of seeing these symbols of peace and cooperation among nations adorning the swimming pool of a brutal and bloodthirsty dictator did not escape me. Regardless, any opportunity for a brief dip in this watery oasis was a welcome, if nearly surreal, diversion from an otherwise stressful and harried existence.

I DIDN'T GO to Iraq to go swimming, but to prosecute terrorists and insurgents. So after my arrival, that's exactly what I did. With a full docket, there was no shortage of prisoners due to appear in the Central Criminal Court of Iraq, or CCCI as we called it. The courthouse we worked in was outside the Green Zone, which made the commute to work a little more tense than what I was used to, even when I was living in New York City and traveling by subway. The courthouse was located in downtown Baghdad and bore several marks of our successful effort to liberate the city from Saddam and his Republican Guard.

Each morning before heading to court, we would meet in our offices in the embassy. Anywhere from twenty to thirty people would be gathered together for the morning convoy brief.

A convoy usually consisted of five or six JAGs, a six-man Air Force Personal Security Detail (or PSD) team and ten to fifteen U.S. service members who were scheduled to testify as witnesses that day. The most senior JAG traveling to court was designated as the convoy commander. Before climbing into the four armored vehicles we used for traveling to court, the convoy commander and the head of the PSD team, Sergeant First Class Bill Glass, would give the convoy brief.

When I served as convoy commander, I worked closely with SFC Glass. He was a fantastic airman and skilled PSD team leader—a consummate professional. He arrived early each morning and reviewed the intelligence reports on enemy activity during the previous twenty-four hours. He kept tabs on the enemy's constantly changing tactics and relayed that critical information to all of us each morning. He briefed us thoroughly on all aspects of traveling by convoy in Iraq. He went over every last security detail, from how to react to enemy fire to the seating assignments for each vehicle. He made sure we all knew exactly which locations inside the courthouse would be used for rally points and defensive positions should we come under attack during the day, and the passwords we would need to safely enter one of these positions.

Finally, before heading out to the vehicles that would carry us to court, he would give us the JOC radio channel, call signs, and grid coordinates so that any one of us could call in the Quick Reaction Force for reinforcement and extraction as well as for air support if team members were killed or otherwise unable to call for themselves.

SFC Glass and his men, like Master-at-Arms 1 Robert Tiffany, Master Chief Curtis Webb, Master-at-Arms 2 Raphael

Henderson, and Senior Airman Eric Peña, were just some of the brave men who put their lives on the line every day to protect me and my fellow JAGs. As we went about our duties as prosecutors in the CCCI, these men shadowed us and protected us from the enemy. Their presence was essential to our mission because the courtroom we practiced in was completely open to the public, friend and foe alike.

In court all day, my fellow prosecutors and I had to be thinking about calling witnesses, presenting evidence, or listening to testimony from defendants. That meant we couldn't be taking notice of who'd just walked into the courtroom and if that person had explosives strapped to his chest or a grenade in his pocket. This inherent vulnerability made us easy targets for an insurgent or die-hard terrorist looking to kill an American. In this insecure environment of downtown Baghdad, far from the semisecure sanctuary of the Green Zone, we counted on SFC Bill Glass and his men to make sure we all returned to the embassy each day safe and sound. And we did—every single time. My fellow JAGs and I can never repay these brave men for protecting us and allowing us to return home safely to our families.

THE COALITION PROVISIONAL Authority created the CCCI several months after we overthrew Saddam. CCCI served as the primary court for trying terrorists and insurgents, whether they were captured by coalition forces or by Iraqi security forces. The court consisted of two chambers. One chamber, called the investigative court, handled the first phase of the process, which looked into specific accusations against individual suspects. The investigative court determined if a case should proceed to the second chamber, which was the trial court. At the trial court, charges were formally brought before a panel of three judges. U.S. military prosecutors brought captured defendants before the investigative court and then handed the case off to an Iraqi attorney who prosecuted it before the trial court.

My official job title was judge advocate liaison officer to the CCCI. The job as well as the process itself was quite a bit different from my experience as an assistant district attorney. Ultimately, however, the goal was the same—to identify threats to society, charge them, and then bring them before a court of law that decided their fates. Although we were responsible for putting together cases against terrorist suspects, identifying witnesses for the prosecution, obtaining evidence, and then presenting that evidence to an Iraqi judge, the judicial process in Iraq was still quite different from ours in America. We did not seek to impose our judicial system on Iraq. The Iraqi government chose the two-tier system, wrote the rules, and presided over the trials. We played by their rules, which meant we had to learn them first.

For example, to put together a case against a terrorist suspect, I had to produce two witnesses from the unit that captured the suspect, witnesses who could testify about the suspect's actions leading to his arrest or about any weapons found during a raid. The rules of the court demanded two witnesses—one to corroborate the word of another. Without two witnesses, I could not move forward on a case. It was just that simple.

The witnesses testified through an interpreter before a single Iraqi judge during the investigative hearing. This first phase of the process was a combination of a grand jury proceeding and a trial. It was like a grand jury proceeding in that it was the first screening of the case by an independent party to determine if there was sufficient evidence to warrant charging the defendant with a crime. It was also a lot like a trial because most of the evidence against a defendant was presented to the court at this stage. After first calling all of my witnesses during an investigative hearing, I would then offer any photographic, documentary, or other physical evidence to the Iraqi judge assigned to hear the case. With my last offering to the court, I would present arguments in support of my case. The defendants were present for the entire proceeding and their lawyers could cross-examine any witnesses I called and comment on any evidence I offered.

The defendants' right to confront witnesses did, however, have one notable exception compared to the U.S. system. If there were multiple defendants in a case, an accused terrorist or insurgent was not permitted to sit in the courtroom to hear the testimony of any other codefendant charged in the same case. This rule was quite helpful in prosecuting these criminals since many of them couldn't or didn't bother to get their stories straight while they were sitting in their prison cells awaiting trial.

In cases where no actual attack had occurred, establishing a suspect's knowledge or intent to carry out violence against coalition forces was a critical and immensely difficult part of my job. When a raid on a home or a farm led to the capture of arms and the arrest of the home owner, we had to try to prove that the suspect knew about the weapons on his property. In Iraq, the law presumes that farmers are intimately familiar with their property and that they inspect it regularly.

This presumption made our task a little easier, since many of the suspects we dealt with described themselves as farmers. In those cases, when a farmer claimed to have no knowledge of, say, a dozen artillery shells uncovered in his barn, Iraqi judges tended to be highly skeptical. As they should have been.

THE COURTHOUSE WAS an old clock-tower building in downtown Baghdad that used to be a museum of antiquities and the office of the highest-remaining Saddam loyalist fugitive, Izzat Ibrahim al-Douri. An investigative hearing took place before one of five Iraqi judges assigned to hear U.S. and coalition cases. The judge normally sat behind a modest desk with a clerk at his side to record the proceeding. The defense attorney would sit across from me while my interpreter sat by my side. The accused usually sat on a couch across the room, unchained but carefully guarded by two or more of the military police soldiers who had brought him to Baghdad earlier that morning from Abu Ghraib prison.

The Iraqi judge controls the overall process—asking questions of the witnesses, examining the evidence, and entertaining any arguments before determining if the case should proceed to trial. Unlike the system in the United States, all defendants in Iraq are required to testify. Actually, they have the right to remain silent. The only catch is, under Iraqi law, their silence can be used against them at their trial.

This may sound odd to Americans, but as far as I could determine, it was more of a cultural phenomenon than a miscarriage of due process. One of the judges explained it to me when I asked him about it one day after court. He said, "Captain McGovern, we Iraqis take great pride in responding to accusations made against us no matter what the consequences." He then explained that in his culture a man should want to respond to accusations made against him if they are false. "Should he remain silent, however," he continued, "it would indicate that he has something to hide." I guess that explains why most suspects readily testified before the CCCI, and the really hard-core true believers were more than happy to admit their guilt to me in open court. It was even a point of pride for some of them.

One case stands out in my mind. On August 15, 2005, I prosecuted a foreign fighter named Borhan Jalal Ibrahim. Borhan said he was born in Turkey and made his way through Syria into Iraq to fight in the jihad against the Americans. Borhan admitted to me and the court that he had spent eight months in the Syrian city of Halab training before crossing over into Iraq at the border town of Al-Qaim. He was captured in Falluja on November 20, 2004, only three months after arriving.

On that day, the Marines who captured him had noticed a Dodge Ram truck outside the house he was living in. The vehicle stood out to these young American kids for one simple reason—it had Texas license plates! These alert Marines figured that something was out of the ordinary. When they searched the home, they found a small bomb-making factory and a cache of weapons inside. When Borhan was asked to address the court, he turned to me and said he had come to Iraq to wage jihad against Americans and that he would kill everyone in the courtroom that day if he could.

AT THE CLOSE of an investigative hearing, the evidence was sent to one of three trial panels consisting of three judges. They read the written transcript of the hearing and listened to oral arguments from an Iraqi prosecutor and an Iraqi defense attorney. They also entertained testimony from the defendant again, if he wanted to change his story, or if he wanted to call any witnesses. As a U.S. military prosecutor, I had no control over—or even input into—this second stage of the process. The case was entirely in the hands of a local Iraqi prosecutor, who was free to request any sentence he deemed appropriate or to drop the charges entirely if he wanted to. In the end, the Iraqi judges made the final determination on the guilt or innocence of a defendant.

In Borhan's case, the Iraqi court found him guilty as a would-be terrorist murderer and sent him to jail. But, more important, the defendant received a fair trial and had his day in court before an impartial panel of Iraqi judges. He was afforded due process and given full legal representation. To me, these judicial hallmarks are the unmistakable signs that justice and the rule of law are truly returning to Iraq and that the days of Saddam's tyranny are finally and forever over.

Over the course of the next few months, I handled the investigation and prosecution of 286 cases and brought approximately fifty of those cases to trial or, should I say, to an investigative hearing. I spent day after day reviewing case files, identifying witnesses, and gathering evidence against 452 insurgents charged with killing or attempting to kill U.S. and Iraqi forces. Each case, each insurgent, each prosecution, offered object lessons about whom we fight, why we fight, and what we are fighting for.

My very first case involved another foreign fighter. This young boy from Morocco, named Azideme Buynam Abdel, was captured before he could carry out his designated assignment to become a human bomb in Iraq. His journey to achieve martyrdom is illustrative of the enemy we fight. He was attending an Islamic school in Syria when the imam of his mosque instructed the young men of the congregation to go to Iraq to wage jihad against the American infidels.

It was clear that his unholy handlers were grooming this young kid to be a suicide bomber because they kept Azidime isolated from other people and moved him from one location to another over a period of months. This is the usual maturation process for a suicide bomber. The enemy has to isolate these candidates before they're sent out to blow themselves up. The reason is simple. They don't want them forming any personal relationships—like friendships. If they did, it might actually cause them to reconsider their decision to strap on an explosive vest and die for Allah. Terrorist leaders like bin Laden, and the now thankfully deceased Abu Musab al-Zarqawi, want to keep these people isolated and alone so that they can fill their young minds with vitriolic rationales for murder and fanciful visions of the afterlife.

Young men like Borhan, who are chosen to be fighters instead of suicide bombers like Azidime, are trained in a very different manner. These men are not moved around and isolated from human contact. Instead, they are placed in safe houses with other fighters to train in guerrilla tactics and form the bonds that unite warriors.

We will probably never know exactly what techniques of brainwashing go into the education of a would-be suicide bomber like Azidime or a fighter like Borhan, but one thing is certain. The terrorists who recruit these men do so because they recognize the threat to their existence that the success of democracy and self-rule poses in Iraq. That is why they are fighting so desperately and so viciously. That is why they seek out vulnerable young minds and fill them with false promises of nirvana and paradise. They know, like I do, that democracy's success in Iraq and in the Middle East will put an end to the anarchy they try to create through terrorism.

Azidime wound up getting captured, brought before a court of law, prosecuted by a JAG from New Jersey, and sentenced to fifteen years in prison. That was a pretty ignominious end to one career as a holy warrior. It was also a pretty good ending for my first case and an even better one for the people of Iraq.

The presence of foreign fighters like Borhan and Azidime raises another interesting question for critics of our presence in Iraq. If they believe we are engaged in an imperial adventure there, that we had no business going there to defend our national interests, what of the governments that overtly or covertly encourage their citizens to journey to Iraq to fight Americans and Iraqis themselves? What are foreign fighters doing in Iraq? What interests do they have in Iraq's future, and what right do they have to intervene?

The United States is committed to bringing about a self-governing, democratic Iraq. The foreign fighters are committed to stopping that process, which means they are committed to hindering the Iraqis themselves from rebuilding their own country. Regardless of what critics say about America, the foreign fighters are clearly the real enemies and killers of the Iraqi people. They are the danger to the region—not us.

I WAS IN court every day, prosecuting cases ranging from possession of illegal weapons to planning ambushes to executing attacks on U.S. and Iraqi forces. Some suspects were foreign nationals, others were Iraqis. One case involved a rare female defendant who had been a confidante of Saddam's and a high-ranking member of the Ba'ath Party. Her main duty during Saddam's reign, it seemed, was the procurement of prostitutes for male party members. She now ran a car dealership and frequently traveled to Syria and Jordan on business, or so she claimed.

I thought she had an expansive idea of what her "business" was. It is my belief that she was laundering money in Jordan and Syria to finance terrorist operations in Iraq. Two of her brothers were already under arrest for allegedly attacking coalition forces. In the investigative portion of her trial, I produced documents that supported my argument that she laundered money in Syria and Jordan and then brought it back into Iraq to help finance the insurgency. She argued to the court that she was the victim of a slander campaign launched by her husband's ex-wife. I interviewed potential Iraqi witnesses who had firsthand knowledge of her illegal activities, but they were too scared to testify, citing fear of reprisals.

Without their cooperation, my case had little chance of success. I took a shot at it anyway and offered the documentary evidence to the court. However, without any eyewitness testimony to corroborate this evidence, it was an uphill struggle. No charges were brought by the investigative judge.

This woman's defense was a variation on a theme I heard repeatedly in court from defendants protesting their innocence. Many insisted that they had been framed by coalition forces, an argument the Iraqi judges rarely found persuasive. Other defenses had varying degrees of success, reflecting the complex nature of Iraqi society and of the volatile situation in Iraq itself.

Here were a few of the more common defenses:

"I was framed by a disgruntled neighbor." This defense was

often effective, depending on the amount of religious or tribal tension in the area. Distrust and outright hatred between Sunni and Shia Muslims was such an issue in some places that judges simply couldn't rule out the possibility of one neighbor framing another. In prosecuting weapons-possession cases, however, we could frequently point out that moving large amounts of artillery shells or other explosives onto the defendant's property was a huge and time-consuming task that should have been easily detected by the defendant.

"The explosives are mine but I use them to fish." Believe it or not, I heard this argument many times in court. And it actually had some merit, because in Iraq, some people really do use explosives when fishing. Now, this might not be an American's idea of an idyllic pastime—I mean, none of those nostalgic "Take Me Fishing" commercials on television show young kids using dynamite instead of worms. But in Iraq, throwing a grenade or a stick of dynamite into a lake and scooping up all the fish that float to the top is just another way to put food on the table. We made no judgments about this practice, but we were very skeptical of those who had huge amounts of explosives that, they said, were nothing more than a replacement for the old rod and reel.

"The weapons are not mine. I have no idea how they got on my property." Few judges, for reasons I mentioned before, ever bought this one. Not only were farmers in particular expected to know what was on their property, but the sheer size of some of the arsenals exposed these pleas of ignorance for what they were—hollow fabrications. For example, I tried a case against a defendant who was captured after our troops discovered, in addition to the usual assortment of assault rifles, a weapons cache consisting of thousands of rounds of .57-mm antiaircraft ammu-

nition, ten hand grenades, and all kinds of artillery shells that are commonly used by the insurgency as roadside bombs. It was hard for the judge or anybody to believe this defendant when he said he didn't know how such an amount of ordnance could be found on his property.

"I was forced to do it because the terrorists or insurgents threatened to kill me and my family." This was, for obvious reasons, the most difficult defense to refute. And, regrettably, it was entirely plausible. Where the facts supported such an assertion, I would make the decision to decline to prosecute the defendant. In one case, however, I was able to show that the three defendants were lying by pointing out on cross-examination the wide and imaginative inconsistencies in their testimony. I even had one case where a man was initially forced to let insurgents use his land but later became a willing and enthusiastic participant in the insurgency.

All in all, it was an incredible experience to be able to prosecute in an Iraqi court using Iraqi law. I proudly served with some fantastic Army JAGs like Major Walter May, Captain Nancy Lewis, and First Lieutenant Richard Gudis. It was also a rare opportunity to serve with fellow JAGs from our sister services like Navy Lieutenants Tyler Stone, Sean McLaughlin, and Danielle Kaminski. Marines like Majors Nicole Hudspeth, Ed Christiansen, and Captain Joe Galvin, as well as Air Force Captains Don Underwood, Matt Coakley, and Tony Casilli. They all lived up to the proud traditions of their services.

As I look back on my experience in the CCCI, I often compare the merits of their system to ours. Although their legal process is not one that I would recommend for our own country, it is a fair and objective one that affords the individual Iraqi citizen due process and his day in court. Unlike the American system, the Iraqi one is inquisitorial in nature and relies entirely on the fact-finding ability of judges. This system works because the Iraqi men I met and practiced in front of—including Judge Fathal, Judge Mahmood, Judge Sabri, and Judge Ahmed—were men of character and integrity who placed their country's well-being over their own. Indeed, these men literally risked their lives every day they came to court.

With such men leading the return to the rule of law in Iraq, I am confident that the Iraqi people will ultimately win their struggle against the anarchists and return their once-proud country to her rightful place in the civilized world.

AS PART OF my job, I sometimes traveled to forward operating bases to brief commanders and other JAGs on cases involving attacks on their individual units and to discuss better ways of collecting evidence in such attacks. On July 3, 2005, for example, I flew to a base near Kirkuk to discuss attacks with JAG Captain Chris Kessinger who was stationed there, and then drove via convoy two days later to do the same with commanders and JAGs at a base near Tikrīt, Saddam's hometown.

Again, I'd like to emphasize the commitment of these commanders and their troops to the rule of law and due process for those they captured for planning or carrying out attacks on our troops. I saw countless examples of soldiers and Marines showing incredible restraint in the face of their attackers. Even where the rules of engagement and laws of armed conflict permitted our forces to respond with overwhelming and deadly force, these brave men and women routinely refrained from doing so out of concern for the civilian population. This commitment, I found, was the rule, not the exception.

The ride from Kirkuk to Tikrīt took only two hours, but they were a long and tense two hours. The road was pockmarked with holes left by roadside bombs—evidence, as if I needed it, that I was in hostile territory. The war in Iraq, like so many other conflicts in recent years around the world, has no clear front lines. Our four-vehicle convoy wasn't behind enemy lines. The enemy had no lines. The roads, the towns, the cities and bases all across the country were a part of the battlefield. The insurgents were flexible, as they had to be given their small numbers. They adapted quickly and could strike at any time and in just about any place. This is the nature of the urban war in Iraq; it is the nature of war in the twenty-first century, and it is the nature of the War on Terror.

We arrived at the coalition base in the center of Saddam's city without incident. Our headquarters were in a massive palace—impressive from afar, shoddy from up close. The base had a breathtaking view of the Tigris River, but there was nothing pastoral about the circumstances. There was a reason why the base had been code-named Forward Operating Base Danger. It was, of course, built by and for Saddam. Similar reminders of Saddam's megalomania were everywhere, to the point where you actually grew weary of the sight of yet another palace in the midst of poverty and desolation. The only encouraging aspect of these morbid sightseeing tours was the knowledge that several of Saddam's most prized buildings bore witness to the effectiveness of our targeted air strikes at the beginning of the war.

While in Tikrīt, I met with Lieutenant Colonel Robert Moscati, the Staff Judge Advocate for the 42nd Infantry Division, to discuss the possibility of opening a CCCI facility in the city to hear cases involving attacks on troops in that area. The staggering volume of cases currently before the CCCI in Baghdad made this necessary. The plan was to open several new branches of the CCCI to hear U.S. and coalition cases from that area of the country. This would make the administration of justice faster and more efficient, which would reduce the prisoner population while also ensuring that defendants didn't languish in prison for months and months waiting for their day in court.

After several days in Tikrīt, I traveled to the now-notorious Abu Ghraib prison—along with thirty-seven detainees being transferred there from the Tikrīt area. I was going to Abu Ghraib—my first visit there—to discuss issues like the treatment of prisoners. News of the scandal at the prison had already broken, and it was with that context in mind that we went over details about the processing, holding, care, feeding, and transporting of prisoners from the jail to the courtroom. I wanted to make sure we were doing it the right way.

I know all we ever hear on TV about that prison portrays a scene of brutality and chaos. But what I found was nothing short of professionalism, leadership, and respect for human dignity.

The history of Abu Ghraib prison tells the real story of its horrors, and I'm not talking about the abuses that took place after our liberation. I'm talking about the inhuman torture that was part of the prison's daily regimen when it housed Saddam's enemies.

There's a difference between abuse and torture. If you can't acknowledge this, then you've been brainwashed by the media. When I hear TV talking heads refer to our supposed "torture" of terror suspects in Abu Ghraib, I want to put my fist through the tube.

It is one thing to be humiliated. It is another thing to be physically tortured and then brutally killed—killed slowly, so that you experienced horrific pain until you finally—and gladly—die.

That's an important difference, and it's the difference between the abuse meted out by a few of our soldiers and the systematic slaughter that was the rule under Saddam. And here's another difference. When our people were accused of abuse, they were brought to justice. When Saddam's murderers did their bloody work in that jail, they were probably rewarded for it.

Abu Ghraib is huge, and it had to be—not for our purposes, but for Saddam's. It can hold up to ten thousand prisoners, and it was generally filled to capacity under the old regime. The facility was divided into four distinct complexes, the most famous being the "hard site," where an isolated handful of U.S. troops stripped the clothes off some detainees and photographed them in embarrassing positions. I even visited the cell block made famous in those notorious photos.

I also walked the second-floor corridor known as the "Green Mile." This corridor holds the memories of acts far more horrific than any photographs taken by U.S. soldiers. During Saddam's tyranny, the tiny corridor often held as many as three thousand people in inhumane conditions. I heard a rumor, not easily dismissed if you know anything about Saddam's regime, that when the corridor became too crowded, Uday Hussein, the despot's son, ordered armed guards to shoot every third person. That was Saddam's answer to prison overcrowding.

Separate from the main facilities at Abu Ghraib sat Saddam's death house, where prisoners were tortured and executed. I visited a cell where prisoners were kept while awaiting their execution. Writing that looked like Arabic graffiti covered the walls. Some of the prisoners made small marks to count off the days they spent in this fetid, awful cell. One prisoner was there for sixty-two days; another, for seventy-three. Each day brought more torture—it's not hard to imagine that these prisoners came to wish or even beg for their own death. Written on the wall, in Arabic, was an Islamic death prayer.

The death chamber itself was equally gruesome. Attached to the ceiling of a stark, windowless room was a hook. Prisoners about to face an end to their misery were subjected to one last round of torture—they were hung from the hook and beaten to a pulp. Only then were they brought to another room, this one with a pair of trapdoors, where a hangman finished the job, not with a rope but with steel wire. One final brutal indignity for the condemned.

As I walked out of the dark recesses of Saddam's death house into the bright sunshine, I was reminded of a case I had been reviewing just a week earlier. The insurgent had been captured not by coalition forces, but by an Iraqi militia group aligned with a local sheikh. After being turned over to U.S. forces a week later, this particular insurgent begged the U.S. soldiers not to hand him back to the men who had detained him. For some insurgents, I guess, capture by noncoalition forces was not a pleasant experience.

Even acknowledging the misdeeds by some of our troops, there's little question that we treated those we captured fairly and humanely. I saw it firsthand; I was part of that process, and I am proud of our record of respecting human rights.

In American custody, even the insurgent I referred to earlier knew he would be treated far better than if he were in the hands of a local official or cleric. I'm not seeking to excuse accusations of terrible crimes committed by a few American service personnel. But after seeing Abu Ghraib, I was convinced that we were easily the most humane people in the region. Those prisoners who asked to remain in U.S. custody rather than be handed over to local militias were, in effect, acknowledging our adherence to basic standards of decency, even in war.

THE FOLLOWING DAY, I was back in Baghdad with a crowded docket. On July 13, 2005, I had three investigative hearings before the CCCI. One involved a defendant who claimed to have no idea why coalition forces had found thousands of feet of copper wire used to detonate roadside bombs and other evidence of bomb-making material in his house. That was in addition to the usual complement of assault rifles, small-arms ammunition, and various explosives. Actually, he did have an idea how they got there: he claimed U.S. forces had placed all these materials in his home to frame him.

Besides the absurd nature of his story to begin with, I was beginning to grow impatient with the incoherent, weasel-like, rambling, and ultimately unrepentant testimony of these cowardly killers. My cross-examination of this type of defendant usually amounted to a simple recitation of how the defendant's version of the facts made absolutely no sense. For the defendant's story to be true, I would begin, U.S. forces must have collected a huge amount of old, dirty, and unstable munitions from Russia, Syria, Iran, and elsewhere, loaded them all onto a truck, driven them to the defendant's house, and then placed them all over his property, taken pictures of them, and then apprehended the defendant.

If this illogical scenario was insufficient to convince the judge that the defendant's story was utterly implausible, I then explained to the defendant and the court that there was no benefit for U.S. soldiers in framing any innocent Iraqi. Our soldiers need to find the actual perpetrator of an attack for their own protection. U.S. soldiers are the primary focus of insurgent attacks. That means they are the "victims" of the very crimes they are investigating when they conduct a raid looking for a weapons cache or a bomb-making factory.

They are no safer if they frame an innocent man for an attack on a convoy or for possessing weapons on his farm. They would be just as susceptible to attack from the real insurgents the next day and the day after that.

Based on this inarguable fact, I would explain, U.S. soldiers have every reason to want to see that only the real insurgents are captured and prosecuted in the CCCI. That is the one thing that will ensure their safety. It will also avoid turning an innocent and formerly supportive Iraqi into one of the insurgents shooting at them every day. At this point, usually almost out of breath from my ranting, I would request that the court consider the defendant's tale of an Army-wide conspiracy to frame him and all of his fellow defendants as the moronic, self-serving, and convenient defense of a man caught red-handed.

Yes, I will admit that I was getting increasingly tired of many defendants' complete lack of integrity and their pathetic excuses. I, at least, had a little—not much, but a little more—respect for the true believer who admitted his guilt and took his punishment without whining like so many of these double-talking, finger-pointing criminals who were paraded before me daily.

You might wonder why I'm so disgusted with the enemy we fight. That's because on that very day of July 13, 2005, while I was listening to this defendant whine and moan about how he was the victim of an American conspiracy, a few miles away in Baghdad, a suicide car bomber approached a group of Iraqi schoolchildren who were happily accepting candy and toys from a U.S. soldier. When he got close enough, the bomber detonated the huge amount of explosives he carried with him. And so the children died. The suicide bomber didn't care that he would kill thirty-two Iraqi children so long as he could kill one U.S. soldier.

The following morning, at about nine o'clock, two huge explosions—much louder than the usual blasts that you get used to in parts of Iraq—rattled the windows of my office in the embassy. Two suicide bombers had blown themselves up at a checkpoint about two blocks from where I was working. They wounded about eighteen Iraqis.

Ask me again why I do what I do: I do it because I know the enemy, and I know we have to fight him.

CHAPTER TEN

★ ★ ★

This Is Not Vietnam—
"It is fatal to enter any war without the
will to win it."—*General Douglas MacArthur*

IF WE WERE AS POWERFUL AS OUR CRITICS SAY WE ARE, if we were as merciless as so many people seem to think we are, I would never have had a bad day in court. My rate of conviction would have been 100 percent. I wouldn't have had to spend hours listening to terrorists deny that the munitions found in their homes were theirs, or that, yes, the explosives were theirs all right, but they were fishermen, you see.

If we were what our critics say we are, I'd never have had to dwell on the ones that got away.

In July, I worked on a case involving a father and his two sons who were spotted leaving the scene of an attack on coalition forces. Eyewitnesses placed them in a white pickup truck. Their escape route was blocked, and they were detained. All three tested positive for the presence of explosive residue.

The U.S. troops asked the older man if he had recently been in contact with fertilizer, which might account for the residue. He said he had not. A soldier on the scene searched one of the defendants' sons and found a picture of the defendant wearing an Iraqi Army uniform from the days of Saddam. The defendant admitted that he had served in the military under Saddam, and that Saddam had given him land. Bomb-making materials consistent with those used in the attack were found in the back of the pickup truck.

An open-and-shut case. We had evidence and motive. The defendant told the court that he was simply a humble farmer—although one look at his manicured hands suggested a less harsh line of work. He protested loudly and in overly dramatic language. He offered no novel excuses.

I handled the investigative hearing, which went well. We sent the case forward to the trial judges. Surprisingly, the Iraqi prosecutor dropped the case, citing a lack of evidence. When I demanded an explanation from him, he refused to offer one.

It was a frustrating outcome, but instructive. There was not a doubt in my mind that the man was guilty. Justice, I believed, had not been served—it had been mocked. Nevertheless, I could do nothing about it, nor could the greatest military in the world. We played by the rules, even if our opponents did not.

As any fans of television's courtroom dramas will know, justice isn't justice if it isn't accompanied by the occasional farce. Just a few days after the farmer with the nice fingernails beat the rap, I was back in the courtroom working on a case involving a man who was captured late one night in possession of a detonation trigger for an improvised explosive device (IED)—the terrorists' favorite weapon. He'd been arrested several weeks earlier when coalition forces discovered an IED along a roadside. They focused on this location because it was an area where three other IEDs had been found in recent weeks. They spotted the defendant fleeing the scene in a car on an adjacent road, his headlights turned off despite the late hour.

He didn't get away. Troops stopped him and found the trigger device for the IED. They also realized that this guy had something extra in his tank, something that is often used to suppress the fears and anxieties that come with planting roadside bombs. He was given a sobriety test, which he failed, miserably.

He readily agreed that he was drunk. He said he had left his brother's house at about ten o'clock that night after pounding down a few drinks. As for that trigger device, he claimed it was nothing more than a special tool that a mechanic had mistakenly left in his car.

Although I didn't always take the opportunity to question a defendant, I cross-examined this guy, asking why he was out after the eight o'clock curfew. "I wasn't really out," he said. "My brother lives only two hundred meters from my house."

"So you decided to drive your car the two hundred meters to your brother's house, did you?" I said. "It didn't occur to you to just walk, did it?"

"I was so drunk I couldn't walk," he said. "That is why I had to drive." That was his only answer. I almost laughed but I didn't. It was a remarkable performance.

I turned to the judge and shrugged my shoulders.

"No further questions," I said.

A few weeks later, I prosecuted a case against a suspect charged with attacking a U.S. patrol near the town of Ba'qūbah. The troops who came under fire captured an insurgent as he attempted to flee the scene. A search of the area led to the capture of another insurgent who was identified as a member of a Ba'athist jihad group and a prime suspect in a mortar attack on a U.S. base in Tikrīt. On the day of his appearance in the CCCI, the suspect showed up leaning on a crutch and using some kind of colostomy bag. Amazingly, neither of these items was on his person when he was arrested. He told the judge that he was a former army officer who was disabled by a building collapse. He simply could not have been carrying a heavy AK-47, as the coalition forces stated.

The other defendant in the case, the suspect charged with firing on coalition forces, swore that he was just a simple farmer, etc. To prove that we had the wrong guy, he said he had been wearing a brown shirt on the day of his arrest. Eyewitnesses testified that the man who fired on the patrol wore a blue shirt.

I immediately produced a photograph of the suspect taken immediately after his capture. He was, in fact, wearing a blue shirt. Gotcha!

"That is not a blue shirt," the defendant said. "That is a brown shirt."

This reply stopped me in my tracks for a moment. I looked at the picture again to make sure it was a blue shirt—which it was. I then looked at the judge, who nodded in agreement with me that it was, in fact, a blue shirt. I didn't know whether to be annoyed or amused. I mean, at a certain point, you almost have to admire a guy who can lie like that in the face of overwhelming evidence.

"No further questions," I said.

★ ★ ★

I CONTINUED KEEPING a journal detailing the cases I worked on—often as many as three per day, involving multiple suspects. The language I used was short and direct, much like the police reports I used to read while working in the Manhattan D.A.'s office. I'd like to think that my notes about the defendant in the Ba'qūbah attack were a model of police-style prose. The witnesses, I noted, reported that when the suspect was captured, he was in possession of an AK-47. An interesting fact, but given the plethora of AK-47s in Iraq, not nearly enough for a conviction. Everybody, including the judges, owned an AK-47.

I noted, however, that the weapon was found to be "still warm to the touch." With these police-blotter details, we built our cases against terrorists who thumbed their noses at our rules and our complex and sometimes flawed system of justice.

When they captured Americans like Nick Berg, they cut off their heads. When we captured terrorists, we put them before a court and let judges decide their fate. I wonder if our critics around the world have ever reflected on this interesting contrast.

In early August 2005, I was tasked to advise the team that would prosecute Staff Sergeant Alberto Martinez, charged with the murder of his commanding officer, Captain Philip Esposito, and the company executive officer, First Lieutenant Louis Allen, two months earlier. The men served with the 42nd Infantry Division in Tikrīt, assigned to FOB Danger. Lieutenant Allen had been in Iraq for only four days before he was murdered.

Martinez was a supply sergeant who allegedly hated Captain Esposito and knew First Lieutenant Allen was coming in to be his new supervisor. Martinez is alleged to have planted a claymore mine outside Captain Esposito's quarters when the two officers were inside, and then to have tried to cover up his crime by throwing a few hand grenades to make it sound like the men were killed by mortar fire. Investigators didn't take long to determine that the men were killed by a claymore, not by mortar fire.

I flew to Tikrīt via Black Hawk helicopter on August 4 to meet with the members of the prosecution team, U.S. Army Lieutenant Colonel Meg Foreman and New York Army National Guard Captain Dave State. We immediately drove to the Water Palace in Tikrīt, where the two officers had been killed. Over the next three days, I spent hours at the site, reviewing photographs, interviewing witnesses, reading the CID report of the investigation, and exchanging information with the other members of the team.

The work in Tikrīt was much different from the fact-finding I did at the CCCI. Here, in Tikrīt, I was in the field, investigating a crime scene much like a detective rather than a prosecutor. I worked with an eye toward spotting any unusual or critical issues that would need to be addressed in the case before it went to trial. The team and I spent hours poring over documents, witness statements, and other evidence.

This was now the second time I had been involved in the prosecution of the alleged murder of soldiers by one of their comrades. I can tell you honestly that it is one of the hardest things I have ever had to do but also one of the most important. Soldiers have to be able to trust their battle buddies to their left and to their right. It is critical to the success of our military that soldiers can trust one another in the heat of battle. The thought that one of your fellow soldiers could be a threat to you is like poison to a unit at war. That's why it's critical to prosecute soldiers who turn on their comrades during war, but it's also why it is so draining on prosecutors. I was ready to return to Baghdad and to the insurgents and foreign fighters I'd come to Iraq to prosecute.

While I was in Tikrīt, I also tried to get moving on our proposal to have the CCCI court in that city start processing cases involving attacks on coalition forces. The city already had a CCCI court, but it heard only cases involving crimes committed by Iraqis on Iraqis. Before we could begin to hear cases in Tikrīt, I had to determine whether the local jail had the capacity to hold an increased number of detainees. After a tour of the facility, I figured the prison could, in theory, handle the increase in population, but since the twentieth century appeared to have passed by the jail's security, it would need a fair amount of work to make sure the invited guests stayed put.

I was trying to figure out just how to accomplish this assignment as I drifted off to sleep on the night of August 7, 2005. I awoke a few hours later to sights and sounds that were new to me—we were getting hit by a full-fledged sandstorm.

I suppose most of us think we know what a sandstorm is like. We've seen them replicated in the movies or described in print. Well, let me tell you, none of that can prepare you for what I can describe only as a blizzard, except in place of snowflakes, you have hard, gritty grains of sand. Not a pleasant experience. There's none of the charm associated with a snowstorm. And worst of all, when it's over, the sand is everywhere, from your mouth to your ears and in your hair. With limited opportunities to take a shower, the novelty of the experience wore off very quickly.

In the middle of the sandstorm, an enterprising insurgent

took advantage of the cover afforded him and set off a huge bomb just outside the base and only a few blocks from the prospective site of the proposed CCCI courthouse in Tikrīt. I had been scheduled to inspect the site later in the day, but obviously that mission would be postponed indefinitely, as would be my flight back to Baghdad. The storm pounded us for nearly forty-eight hours. Even traveling around the base on foot was extremely difficult. I could barely see a few feet in front of my face, and since the base had been built on a cliff overlooking the Tigris River, walking in these conditions was a bit hazardous.

Like a character from an old western, I made my way from place to place wearing a bandanna over my mouth and nose. I was an unusual sight, to say the least, as I staggered in the wind and sand whipping across the huge sprawling compound that was once the primary playground of Saddam and his sons.

When the storm finally ended, I finished my review of the local prison capabilities and provided Lieutenant Colonel Foreman and Captain State with some investigative suggestions regarding the Martinez case. Shortly after that, I boarded a helicopter bound for the embassy.

BACK IN BAGHDAD, I returned to my routine. When I wasn't in court, I was at my desk in the U.S. Embassy reviewing case files. As prosecutor, I had several choices when reviewing a defendant's file. If the witnesses were all Iraqi citizens and it seemed logical to let the Iraqi government take the lead in the prosecution, I could transfer the case to the Iraqi Ministry of the Interior. When there was insufficient evidence to prosecute the case in the CCCI and no reasonable expectation that further investigation would obtain additional evidence, I could decline to prosecute the case entirely. At that point, the case would be transferred to what was called the Combined Review and Release Board or CRRB. The CRRB consisted of Americans and local Iraqi community figures who determined if and when a detainee would be released.

More commonly, though, I had to determine if the case should take one of two familiar paths. I could either send the file back to our criminal investigators for further investigation, or if I had enough evidence, I could proceed directly to trial. If further investigation was necessary, I only needed to give the file and my instructions to our fantastic team of criminal investigators and paralegal support staff. The investigators would go out and find the previously undiscovered or overlooked evidence. Then they would hand the file over to our paralegal staff, who ensured that all the witnesses were located and given orders to fly to Baghdad so they could testify on the day of trial. These resourceful soldiers, sailors, airmen, and Marines not only made sure the prosecution train ran on time, but that we had all the available evidence and the technology to present it in court.

As I mentioned before, no one can win a trial alone. It takes teamwork and sacrifice from countless dedicated people like the great paralegals and investigators assigned to Task Force 134 and the CCCI. Thanks to the work of people like Senior Master Chief Anthony Hall, Master Chief Derrick Cote, Master Chief Michael Kittle, Master-at-Arms 1 Chris Guaydacan, Tech Sergeant Richard Cusack, Staff Sergeant Sarah Lykins, Sergeant Trista Neinast, Petty Officer Gayla Lang, Petty Officer Marian Pierson, and Specialist Thomas Bailey, I always went into court with all my witnesses, all the available evidence, and prepared for anything.

It was only with the help and assistance of these incredible Americans and a team approach to prosecuting the enemy that we were able to convict so many of these brutal killers.

The work of our support staff and investigators was not the only key to success at the CCCI. I also needed trustworthy interpreters committed to our cause in order to translate my questions and legal arguments into Arabic for the court. Most importantly, I needed them to translate the testimony of a defendant as quickly and as accurately as possible, in real time, so I could be effective on cross-examination. During my deployment, I worked with several interpreters both in and out of the courtroom. Some were Egyptian-born U.S. citizens like Soliman Maher, who returned to the Middle East in the hopes of participating in the growth of democracy in the region of his birth. Others were native Iraqis who managed to survive Saddam's brutal reign and were looking to join in the rebuilding of their country.

I came to know and trust one of the Iraqi-born interpreters more than all the rest. His first name was Ahmed and he came from a southern Iraqi village, the son of a teacher. During Saddam's regime, Ahmed and his family were branded as anti-Ba'athists and therefore unworthy of the blessing reserved only for party members.

For example, in Saddam's allegedly socialist regime, all citizens were entitled to a free college education. However, the local Ba'athist Party leader determined who attended the best and most prestigious universities. As you can imagine, Ahmed was not considered for the finest centers of learning in Baghdad or even the ones near his tribal home in the south. Instead, the Ba'athist Party leader sent him to the university in Mosul, one of the most northern regions of the country and far from his tribal roots. This decision ensured that Ahmed would receive little favor or assistance during his life and would have to constantly overcome the disadvantages that came from forgoing party membership.

This did not deter Ahmed in the least. He attended the university in Mosul and scored some of the highest grades in his class. He went on to become a professor just like his dad and spent the years following his graduation teaching other outcast kids in that same distant university he'd been banished to as a young man.

In Mosul, he also met the woman who would one day become his wife and the mother of his children. He made as good a life as he could for himself and his family considering he was far from his ancestors' home in the marshlands of the south and always under the thumb of Ba'athist thugs. All the while, he was learning English and hoped that this long nightmare called Saddam Hussein might one day end. After the fall of Saddam, Ahmed left his job as a university professor for the uncertain and extremely dangerous job of translating for U.S. soldiers in Baghdad.

Every day he made his way to the U.S. Embassy at a different time and used a different route from the previous day. He knew all too well what the insurgency would do to an Iraqi caught working with the Americans. He accepted this grim possibility for what it was—just another attempt by the terrorists to intimidate the population in order to prevent Iraq's steady march toward democracy.

In late August, as I finished my work in one of the courtrooms on the second floor of the CCCI courthouse, I heard a commotion coming from a hallway inside the building. A huge crowd had gathered to celebrate the pending release of two men, one of them a prominent Shiite cleric, who had been arrested for the murder of a rival cleric. The arrests in April 2004 had touched off a revolt led by Muqtada al-Sadr and militias aligned with him. The Iraqi government provided no information about why the two men were being released.

As the men were being escorted outside by court officers through a crowd of chanting and hysterical supporters, Ahmed took out his new digital camera and photographed them. It was his first day on the job, and he didn't know that the taking of photographs was prohibited in that part of the courthouse. The crowd's mood changed immediately—their chants had been jubilant before, but now they turned on Ahmed, who was standing about twenty-five feet away from me when I arrived on the scene.

As most things go in Iraq, the root of the crowd's anger was probably tribal in nature. The supporters of the cleric were all Shiites from the south. Although Ahmed was a Shiite and from the south as well, the crowd had little reason to know this and even less reason to care. They must have seen it simply as an offense to their leader's dignity that he be photographed while he was still in chains in the custody of the government. It could have been interpreted in their fanatical eyes as a final insult from a rival tribe or maybe even from a government they seemingly had little desire to recognize much less support. Whatever their motivation, members of the crowd encircled Ahmed quickly. This was the first time I'd ever seen a potentially deadly disturbance take shape in the courthouse. I feared for Ahmed's life, and worried what might happen to many others if things got out of control.

I put my finger on the safety of my M-16 and turned to the Air Force PSD guys who were with me. "Be ready for anything," I said.

I moved toward Ahmed. Somebody in the crowd had taken

away his camera and had him by the arm, like a police officer about to lead a suspect from a crime scene. Through another interpreter, I told this man that I was an American, and that the man he was trying to detain was with me. I tried to appear calm but firm. Truly, one false move or word could have inflamed an already dangerous situation. But I also wasn't about to let the crowd surrounding us drag an innocent man to an uncertain fate. I made this clear to the leader of the crowd. The M-16 across my chest added to the force of my argument, as did the presence of the fully armed Air Force PSD team quickly spreading out around me.

The man tightened his grip on Ahmed's arm and refused to let go. We had reached an impasse. As Ahmed's would-be captor probably knew, I wasn't about to start shooting and I had no intention of creating an incident that could easily spiral out of control. However, Ahmed was my interpreter and I was responsible for his life. As I stood there staring at this tall, thin fanatical-looking man with wild eyes, I was certain of only one thing. I wasn't letting Ahmed go.

I offered a compromise: I suggested that we bring Ahmed to the chief judge of the CCCI, Judge Loqmon, a man with whom I had had many dealings over the past few weeks. The man gripping Ahmed's arm thought about it for a second and then agreed. With Master-at-Arms 1 Tiffany and the rest of the PSD team clearing the way, we walked as a group to the judge's courtroom. I explained the situation to Judge Loqmon, who did his best to calm the crowd. Judge Loqmon was a thin, distinguished-looking man in his sixties with silver-and-black hair and a very powerful presence. He chastised the crowd quietly and they slowly calmed down under the spell of his soft and soothing voice.

Order now restored, I suggested that Ahmed delete the pictures—thank God for digital cameras—in the judge's presence. Everybody, to my relief, agreed that this was an acceptable solution. I was quietly delighted that a very dangerous situation had been defused. I used the little Arabic I knew to apologize to the judge and thank him in his own language, a gesture he clearly appreciated, and one I was mighty glad to offer.

This incident is a good example of the progress we are making in Iraq. It really tells me something when the leader of an almost riotous crowd from a far-off region is amenable to handing over a dispute to a judge like Loqmon, a man not of his religious sect or tribe. This would-be fanatic and his followers recognized and accepted the judge as a fair and impartial arbiter of their dispute, and despite their bluster, they willingly accepted his authority over them and settled this volatile matter peacefully.

WITH MY TOUR as a reservist in Iraq due to end, I decided that I didn't want to go back to civilian life, not with this war on. I put in a request to be put on full-time active duty in the regular Army. But Army rules being what they are, that wasn't so easy— I'd have to go back to the States before I could transfer from reserve duty to full-time regular Army.

In the meantime, I still had work to do. I filed a request to stay an additional two months as a reservist to finish the work I had begun. It appeared, for a few days, that I wouldn't get that opportunity. With no extension in sight, I started packing up. My pending cases would be reassigned to another JAG, and while I was confident about my replacement, I still had trouble letting go. It was a little like football, I guess. I knew I wouldn't be in Iraq forever, just like I knew I wouldn't be in the NFL forever. But in both cases, when the time came to leave, I wasn't ready.

I took the midnight convoy (aptly labeled the Rhino, for the vehicle's striking resemblance to the animal) and arrived at Camp Victory to wrap up my paperwork and prepare for a flight to Kuwait, and from there to home. But in a scene right out of a bad movie, I was handed my new orders just as I was about to board my flight to leave. Not only did I get my two-month extension, I was immediately assigned to serve as the U.S. military escort for the Iraqi minister of justice, Wakeel Hussein, and the Iraqi director of prisons, General Juma. I was to accompany the two officials on a one-week inspection tour of prisons in southern Iraq before returning to Baghdad and the embassy.

When most Americans think of Iraqi prisons, they immediately think of the scandal in Abu Ghraib. Without diminishing the allegations of mistreatment there, I think it's important to note that for the Iraqis themselves, the most important prison issues were the severe lack of jail space and an equally troubling scarcity of prison wardens and officers. As the U.S. military's liaison to the justice minister and director of prisons, my assignment was to help facilitate their efforts to solve these vexing problems.

I flew from Baghdad International Airport to Basra Airport in southern Iraq with the two Iraqi officials as well as three American civilian experts on prison management, Gloria Lloyd, David Wheeler, and Kenneth McKellar. In British-controlled Basra, the British prison officials briefed us on the need for more effective personnel inside the Iraqi prisons. When the old regime was overthrown, prison wardens, like so many other government officials, were removed from office. Unfortunately, the mass removal of these officials led to the promotion of local police chiefs who simply had no training in prison management. Our American prison experts recommended that the old wardens be brought back.

Adding to the potentially dangerous personnel situation in the jails was the severe lack of space. Our experts estimated that Iraq needed an additional twenty-eight thousand beds to house the prison population. Again, this seemingly prosaic problem was rife with security issues for coalition forces as well as for the fledgling government of Iraq. Prisons without proper security, and without decent facilities for inmates, were potential breeding grounds for a continued insurgency behind all-too-frail bars. It wasn't hard to imagine mass breakouts, which would be a public safety disaster as well as destructive to the cause of a stable, democratic Iraq.

We went to see the conditions for ourselves, and they were pretty much as advertised. Some Iraqi jails were well built but overcrowded. Some were poorly constructed but seemingly well run. Others still were just disasters waiting to happen.

We also visited a prison under construction by U.S. contractors, designed to house eight hundred prisoners. The project, however, fell behind schedule despite the urgent need for modern, secure facilities. An American contractor on-site explained why the work wasn't getting done on time: the project was plagued by work stoppages because of security guards from different and often hostile tribes. Some members of one tribe refused to work in an area where another tribe had worked until the project managers conducted a tribal cleansing ceremony involving the sacrifice of a goat.

As we walked through the remains of the biblical city of Ur, birthplace of Abraham, I couldn't help but be struck by the ancient and enigmatic past that has come to form modern-day Iraqi society. If Iraq is divided along any lines, they are first and foremost lines drawn by tribal allegiance. Tribe, more than anything else, drives the Iraqi people. It is why Saddam surrounded himself with so many of his own from Tikrīt, and it is why the crowd turned on Ahmed that day in the courthouse. You can talk all you want about how Iraq's problems lie in the differences created by opposing regions and the well-known mistrust between Shiite and Sunnis. But at the end of the day, it is in his own tribal roots and only in his own tribal roots that an Iraqi feels he can truly place his trust. That is, in my opinion, where the rubber meets the road and where most of Iraq's problems and all of her answers can be found.

WITH THE CLOCK ticking on my time in Iraq, I returned to the courthouse to prosecute my final few cases. While the details often seemed like a variation on a theme, each case, each defendant, offered yet another glimpse into the struggle we face. Soon after returning, I prosecuted two men who were spotted walking near the Iraq-Iran border with a donkey burdened with the weight of two mortar tubes, two antitank mines, three rocket-propelled grenades, nine ammunition magazines for an AK-47, and numerous sacks of electronic equipment. Upon capture, the defendants conveniently said they'd found this stuff in a shack they rented and were on their way to dutifully turn in everything to the nearest American soldier.

The picture this case paints is extraordinary—defendants clad in traditional dress, but carrying cell phones; donkeys climbing the rugged terrain of northern Iraq, carrying rocket-propelled grenades and bags filled with high-tech electronics gear. While I believe the war in Iraq is just, I would also admit that it is strange and at times surreal—and that's based on what I saw and heard in the courtroom, never mind what combat troops and support personnel must be seeing in the field every day.

In another case, I worked with a female soldier named Specialist Celeste Kivalu. She spotted a car and three men acting suspiciously while she was manning an observation post at a base near Balad, Iraq. The soldier used a special camera to film the three men as they placed an explosive device along a roadside, made their getaway in the defendant's blue car, dropped off one passenger—presumably the triggerman—stopped at a canal, where the other man cleaned himself and discarded the incriminating evidence, dropped off the remaining passenger, and then drove to his house. It was all on tape. The soldier did a fabulous job of catching these guys red-handed.

In court, Specialist Kivalu testified as to exactly what she saw the defendant doing from her guard tower that day, but I had instructed her not to mention that she had videotaped the entire thing unless specifically asked. Prior to trial, I made the decision to refrain from offering the video during my initial presentation of evidence to the court. This was not improper, as there are no rules of discovery in Iraq, and although the concept of trial by ambush is impermissible in America, it seemed completely appropriate and even poetically just in the current environment of Iraq. In fact, I had requested and received permission from Judge Sabri to proceed in this manner and it worked like a charm.

After I finished presenting my initial case, the defendant took the stand. He denied that he was involved in an IED plot. He said he was a lawyer and had been at court all day and returned home only moments before the soldiers arrived to take him into custody. He also claimed he didn't own a blue car, that his car was white. He went on to say he had never even been in a blue car in his life. All the while I just sat back in my chair quietly, trying to restrain my glee.

When he finally finished his testimony, he sat back smugly, confident—I'm sure—that the testimony of a prominent, male, Islamic lawyer from Iraq would be deemed far more credible by the Iraqi judge than the testimony of a female, American, Army reservist from Hawaii. That's when the fun began.

I recalled Specialist Kivalu and I played the video footage on my laptop computer for the judge and the defendant to see. Specialist Kivalu then repeated her earlier testimony, which tracked seamlessly with the footage unfolding before our eyes. It was one of those moments a prosecutor absolutely dreams about.

But did this shake the defendant up at all? Cause him to rethink his testimony? Encourage him to beg for mercy from the court and renounce his illegal ways? No, not a chance. He just drove on with his story, although this time the smug look on his face was nowhere to be found. He tried to claim that the man in the video wasn't him, although a close-up view revealed a person who looked an awful lot like he did. It also showed him to be dressed in the exact same clothes he admitted to wearing earlier and the same ones the soldiers photographed him in when they'd captured him at his house. It also showed him being led from his house, which was at the exact location he previously admitted to living at.

I suppose when you're caught dead to rights, what else can you do but deny the obvious and hope for the best?

The case against this man was made possible by the quick

thinking of Specialist Celeste Kivalu. She was only one of the many terrific women soldiers I met in Iraq and Afghanistan. I can't say enough times that I consider myself blessed by the number of strong women I've known in my life, beginning with my mother and my two sisters. My brothers and I were all big and athletic, but if you wanted to see real toughness in my family, you'd have to turn to my mother and my sisters. Betsy, as I mentioned, is a cancer survivor and my sister Patti has battled type 1 diabetes all her life. She has had to vigilantly monitor her blood-sugar levels and administer multiple insulin injections to herself daily while simultaneously trying to raise her four children. I don't know how she does it.

And my mother deserves a medal just for being able to raise nine children without losing her mind. I truly believe that the Good Lord never sends us more than we can handle, so when He sent a tough challenge like cancer or diabetes to the McGovern family, He chose only the ones strong enough to handle it—the women.

I mentioned before, in talking about Brigadier General Dunn, that the debate over women in the armed services is clearly over. But I think the point is worth dwelling on because I'm not convinced that Americans understand how important women are to our modern volunteer armed services. Without them, our efforts in the War on Terror would be immensely more difficult, if not downright impossible.

Brigadier General Dunn happens to be one of the best officers I have ever worked for. But I also worked with other women, officers and enlisted, whose patriotism, idealism, and professionalism inspired me and many other male soldiers. Take, for example, Sergeant Jennifer Roper. She's a single mom, a paralegal, and a combat lifesaver, which is one step below a medic. I met her at

Fort Bragg when we worked together in the legal assistance office, where she nicknamed me "Arnold Schwarzenegger" because of my football background. She even hung a picture over my desk of Arnold sitting in a tank and drew my name above it with an arrow pointing down to Arnold.

I still have the picture, but I didn't have the heart to tell her that my old coaches would have gotten a kick out of her idea that I was some big, strong bodybuilder type. They were likely to think of me more as "Teletubby" than the "Terminator."

Sergeant Roper and I went our separate ways when she deployed to Iraq. It had to be traumatic for her to leave behind her young son, who stayed with her parents while she went to war. Before deploying to Iraq with the XVIII Airborne Corps, she earned her jump wings at Fort Benning, Georgia, and became a full-fledged paratrooper, earning her air assault wings by rappelling out of helicopters at Fort Campbell, Kentucky.

She was stationed in Camp Victory outside Baghdad International Airport, where she was working as a paralegal in her office one day when the camp came under mortar fire. The first shell landed near her office, a direct hit on the sleeping trailers of some troops. Mortar attacks generally come in rounds of four shells, so when the first one hits, everybody runs for cover and waits for the next three to land. Only then do we attend to the wounded. But not Sergeant Roper.

She immediately grabbed her medical bag and ran toward the smoke and debris where the first shell had landed. As the other shells whistled through the air and landed nearby, she found a soldier who had been knocked out of his bed and badly wounded by the exploding shell.

"I broke my TV," this young soldier said. "I broke my TV."

As she wrapped the soldier's wounds, Sergeant Roper looked around and saw a television on the floor, smashed to pieces from the force of the explosion. It was brand-new. "I broke my TV," the soldier repeated over and over again. He clearly was in shock and on the verge of becoming agitated.

"Listen," she said in a hushed, conspiratorial tone of voice. "I'm a paralegal. You can make a claim for that TV. I know what forms you need. I'll fill them out and make sure that you get reimbursed for the damage to your TV." The soldier instantly calmed down, and Sergeant Roper finished dressing his wound. An awkward, even funny moment in the midst of battle. But a great example of the type of women serving in our military today.

That kind of thinking—that kind of bravery—is in the best tradition of America's armed services. And both qualities were displayed by a woman who was very much on the front lines, and very much in danger.

My short-lived work on the Martinez murder case put me in touch with another outstanding female JAG named Kelly Hughes, whom I also knew and worked with a little at Fort Bragg. I bumped into her at FOB Speicher on my way back to Baghdad from Tikrīt after meeting with the Martinez team. She was stationed near Balad and was the only experienced military prosecutor for a jurisdiction that included more than twenty thousand soldiers. During her year in Iraq, she protected soldiers and the military community by prosecuting criminals for all sorts of misconduct from rape to larceny to the possession of child pornography. Like Major Bovarnick in Afghanistan, she also advised soldiers from the commanding general to newly enlisted privates on the morass of often ambiguous legal and ethical issues that is the War on Terror.

She is all of five feet tall, but don't let that fool you. She is not to be messed with. She has a black belt in the Korean martial art of hopkido and is an avid skydiver who, not surprisingly, was voted the honor graduate of her class at airborne school. She was a gymnast and a soccer standout in Saudi Arabia, where she moved at age eight with her brother, Ted; mother, Dianne; and father, Jim, an employee of Chevron.

After high school, she traded in her athletic uniforms for an Army one and graduated from Colorado College as the nation's top ROTC cadet for 1995. She served several years as a Military Police commander in places like South Korea, and went on to become one of only a handful of soldiers selected to attend law school at the Army's expense.

At Campbell University Law School in North Carolina, she continued to excel as the managing editor of her school's law review, graduating in the top 10 percent of her class in 2003. If that wasn't enough, she also earned an MBA in the school's night program. In Iraq, she was almost killed by mortar fire and one of her convoy missions was hit by an IED. But no matter how dangerous the assignment or how difficult the task she was given, this intelligent, hardworking, and dedicated officer always accomplished the mission and served her country with pride and distinction. After returning from Iraq, she was assigned to be one of the prosecutors in the Martinez case.

I should admit to a little bias on the subject of Captain Hughes. As you may have guessed, she also happens to be the love of my life. I didn't know it on that hot and windy day in Iraq when we bumped into each other in the chow hall on FOB Speicher, but I was staring into the eyes of the woman who would some day change my life. After we both returned from Iraq, some good friends ensured that our paths crossed again. Although Kelly and I had known each other for years, this time it was different. I quickly realized that Kelly was the person I had been looking for all my life. Luckily for me, she felt the same way. We began dating and fell in love immediately. Kelly Hughes showed me that everyone deserves a second chance in life and, sometimes, that second chance can be the greatest thing that ever happens to you. It was for me, and on November 10, 2006, Kelly Hughes did me the honor of becoming my wife.

So you can see why I'm so passionate on the subject of women in the military. Those who believe women don't belong in uniform, or belong well behind the lines, simply don't get it. Women are making remarkable contributions in this wide-ranging war against those who regard women as inferior beings, as property, as third-class citizens subject to the whims of fathers, brothers, and husbands.

The presence of women in uniform truly does remind us of why we fight.

I LEFT IRAQ in September 2005, but not before prosecuting a few more insurgents, including one accused of launching a mortar attack that killed two U.S. soldiers and two others who were charged with shooting down a U.S. Kiowa helicopter—killing the pilot, Chief Warrant Officer 4 Matthew Lourey; and the copilot, Chief Warrant Officer 2 Joshua Scott, from the 1st Squadron, 2nd Cavalry Regiment, 82nd Airborne Division.

All three suspects had fanciful explanations for their presence near the two attack scenes. The defendant in the mortar attack, captured while driving away from the scene, denied that he was in the car at all. He claimed it had been carjacked from him just before the attack, only to be returned to him on the side of the road by the real insurgents just moments before his capture. Unfortunately for him, he had been spotted in the act by a U.S. helicopter crew that followed him the entire time until he was captured.

The defendants in the chopper attack said they were innocent bystanders who had been praying all night in their local mosque and had been framed by coalition forces. Their story was replete with tales of torture and abuse at the hands of the American captors, which had led, they claimed, to their confessions.

On cross-examination, I inquired if their alleged beatings included blows to the face and head, leaving marks and abrasions. Thinking they had fooled me and wanting to further embellish their stories, they eagerly confirmed that their interrogation left several cuts and marks on their faces. However, like the case of Specialist Kivalu and the IED-emplacing lawyer, unbeknownst to these idiots, their confession had been videotaped.

A review of the video by the judge convincingly revealed that these two malcontents were completely scratch-free and showed no signs of duress. In fact, one even smiled and laughed a couple of times during his confession. As the judge watched the videotape, he quietly nodded and then scolded the defendants for their lies when it was finished. Captain Nick Jeffers and First Lieutenant Kevin Murnyack testified against the defendants. Their testimony as well as the calm demeanor and professional behavior of the U.S. soldier who recorded the confession told the real story of what happened that day.

These last few cases instilled in me the firm belief that we serve the cause for peace and life while our enemies seek only death and chaos. Their utter lack of moral integrity, defined by their targeting of civilians and their barbaric methods of murder, tells the story of a dark and dangerous threat. We at home need to demonstrate the same courage shown by our brave service members in Iraq. If we do, the terrorists will not succeed in Iraq or anywhere else because their cause is bereft of both moral authority and intellectual honesty, which is how they will be remembered when the history of these times is written.

NOT LONG AFTER my return to the States, I paid a visit to Mr. Morgenthau to officially submit my resignation as an A.D.A. I brought a present for him—a U.S. flag that had flown over Bagram Air Base.

As Mr. Morgenthau and I talked, I noted the old framed pictures that hung behind his desk. They were photographs of a much younger Robert Morgenthau in his Navy uniform, taken during World War II. Needless to say, Mr. Morgenthau completely understood my decision and wished me well.

I was sworn into the regular U.S. Army by my old boss, General Dunn. As of this writing, I'm based in Virginia, and am training other JAGs for service at home and abroad. I'm a captain. And I've never been happier in my work.

AMERICA IS A force for good in the world. I saw it myself. The incredible team of prosecutors I worked with in Iraq, with the help of great paralegals and criminal investigators, went into court every day and, using Iraqi laws and procedures, convicted literally hundreds of insurgents and foreign fighters for attacks on U.S. troops and for crimes against the people of Iraq. I saw Americans and Iraqis working together side by side to send remorseless and brutal criminals to jail and oblivion, where they belong. These convictions were possible because of the testimony of U.S. Army soldiers and Marines who not only showed their courage and dedication on the battlefield, but in the courtroom as well.

Men and women with names like Captain Jeffers, First Lieutenant Murnyack, First Lieutenant Hauge, First Lieutenant Rocha, Command Sergeant Major Falkenberry, Sergeant Henke, Lance Corporal Barker, Specialist Kivalu, and countless others made sure the enemy was held accountable for their crimes. Together, these heroes and patriots proved the guilt of these cowards in a court of law and made it possible for us to complete the mission, achieve the objective, and ensure that justice was done.

OUR PRESENCE IN Iraq is necessary and our mission there is just. We must persevere and prevail in Iraq because we face a cruel and remorseless enemy who must be stopped before they inflict further harm not only on America but on the entire civilized world. The Islamic fundamentalists' objection is not with American policy. It is with the twenty-first century, with people who do not believe as they believe, who do not practice what they practice, who cherish life rather than death.

I've seen the face of the enemy, and I sent as many of these Islamic fascists as I could to prison for their brutality and their extremism. I believe that while many are determined and would kill again and again if given the opportunity, they are doomed to fail. They do not have the ideological back bone or military and economic wherewithal to impose their twisted vision on the Iraqi people.

Without question, they are capable of killing, and it clearly doesn't matter to them whether they kill American soldiers or Iraqi children. They will continue to kill because they believe America will eventually weary of the fight. I hope that never happens. I believe if more Americans had a broader understanding of the War on Terror, they would understand that good things can and do happen in Iraq, and in Afghanistan, and in other places where our military forces are working with our friends to wipe out the terrorists who seek to return us to the seventh century.

After my return home, I saw media reports comparing our situation in Iraq to the Vietnam War. I happen to believe that we were right to fight in Vietnam, but that's beside the point. The two wars simply are not comparable. The insurgency in Iraq does not comprise the sheer number of fighters and display the same level of sophistication of the Viet Cong and the North Vietnamese Army. The insurgents are incapable of pulling off a coordinated offensive like Tet. The best they can do is set off car bombs near soft targets and hope Americans grow weary of the fight. The body count in such attacks can be, and sometimes is, awful, but it is not evidence of a popular insurgency.

Not all Iraqis are happy to see American troops in their country. That's only natural—we are foreigners, after all. But then again, many of the most bloodthirsty terrorist leaders in Iraq also are foreigners. The difference is that we are there to protect Iraqis. They are there to kill them.

Those who believe we are in an unresolvable civil war simply refuse to see, or do not know about, the progress we are making every day in Iraq. Elections have been held, government ministries established, and a judicial system put in place. Iraqis have made huge and united strides toward the establishment of a democratic government—despite the presence of foreign terrorists who would happily murder people for committing the crime of voting.

I know full well that Iraq is still a dangerous place. I know that the loss of even a single soldier is a high price to pay for any national objective. But as we move forward together, Americans should remember that our own future is at stake in this fight. We cannot back down. We must prevail. Our freedom, and that of our friends and allies, depends on our steadfastness, our moral clarity, and our courage.

CHAPTER ELEVEN

* * *

Why We Fight

I'M A SOLIDER AND A LAWYER. I'M ALSO A KID FROM New Jersey who was lucky enough to play a few years in the NFL—long enough to miss it when it was over, but short enough to appreciate that there really is life after football.

Ever since I was a kid, I've been a student of history and an avid reader, but I admit that I'm no intellectual. I'm not a philosopher or a priest. I'm not a scholar in the doctrine of the just war, a topic that's been debated over the centuries by saints, theologians, and intellectuals from Saint Augustine to Saint Thomas Aquinas to Immanuel Kant.

I don't know what those brilliant men would have said about our war in Iraq. I know that by creating a set of moral guidelines, they sought to stigmatize wars of aggression and avarice, wars motivated by greed and the desire for resources or land. I've read what they have to say about the conditions that make it morally permissible to resort to war, and those that make it morally wrong.

I believe our involvement in Iraq meets the criteria of a just war. And after being there as a judge advocate general and after prosecuting hundreds of insurgents who would have killed anyone and his loved ones simply because he was an American or a Westerner, I have no doubt that our actions in Iraq are morally justified.

I know people will disagree with that judgment. And I understand that it's rarely easy to figure out whether a war is just or not, whether you're Thomas Aquinas or a soldier in a foxhole. Because the United States is a democracy, we get a chance to debate all of this. We can let our government know whether or not we think a given war is just, and whether it should continue. We did just that during Vietnam and during the Spanish American War. When we went to war with Mexico in 1848, an obscure congressman from Illinois named Abraham Lincoln made it clear that he did not consider the war just. Even some of the troops in the field weren't sure why they were fighting. Ulysses S. Grant, one of the many junior officers in that campaign who would go on to command armies during the Civil War, called the conflict with Mexico a "political war."

As Franklin Roosevelt said prior to our entry into World War II, America hates war. America hopes for peace. When we go to war, we want to be sure that our cause is just.

For that reason, as much as we hate war and wish we could live in peace, Americans should realize that the conflict in Iraq and Afghanistan fits their idea of a war fought for the sake of enduring human values. Our operations in both countries are legally and morally justifiable in a war that, as President Bush accurately described, was declared on us. We did not march into Afghanistan with dreams of conquest, like the British and Russians before us. Let's remember, too, that when we began our campaign against the Taliban and their guests, Al-Qaeda, the world was on our side. The only dissenters to our actions in Afghanistan at the time were some people at home and around the globe who believe that any demonstration of American power is wrong—and, by extension, any assault on the United States is understandable and, to them, perhaps even justifiable.

Many Americans who supported our actions in Afghanistan believe the situation in Iraq is different. I've heard people say that Iraq posed no threat to our national security, as the Taliban government in Afghanistan clearly did by offering Osama bin Laden and his ilk a base of operations.

I think that position is simply wrong. The murderous and now thankfully overthrown Saddam made it clear that he was an enemy of the United States and of his neighbors and even of other Iraqis. He demonstrated his willingness—his eagerness— to go to war to achieve his goals. I don't think Saddam thought a whole lot about whether his wars met Thomas Aquinas's definition of a just war. And who can doubt that if he could have hurt the United States in any way, he certainly would have.

I think the war in Iraq is as justifiable as our entry into World War II. Remember, when war was finally forced on us on December 7, 1941, we immediately declared war on Japan—but not on Germany or Italy. FDR and Congress waited for those two barbaric regimes to declare war on us first. But in devising our strategy for a two-front war, our military planners decided on a Europe-first war—even though Germany and Italy had not struck a blow against us, as Japan had. We decided, however, to attack the most dangerous foe, and surely the most evil.

Likewise with Saddam. He didn't attack us, although he would have if he'd had the means. But he was a clear and present danger to our interests. He surely could have provided terrorists with the tools to hit us again and again at home or throughout the world. And after 9/11, we realized we simply couldn't wait to be provoked. We had to take action against people who had no qualms about declaring themselves our enemies.

What's more, Saddam had a record of atrocities that argued in favor of his removal even if he was no threat to his neighbors and to us. His removal has not immediately led to peace in Iraq. But I have no doubt that Iraq will be better off without him, and we will be, too.

As I understand the just-war doctrine, as a lawyer, a soldier, and a graduate of four Catholic schools, I believe that nations are legally and morally obliged to prevent injustices like genocide, military aggression, and threats to civilians. That principle has guided the United States for over two hundred years, and it justified our interventions in places like Bosnia, Kosovo, and Somalia in recent years. It would also justify our involvement in Darfur, where the systematic oppression and murder of thousands of innocent men, women, and children warranted, I believe, intervention by nations that claim to stand for basic human rights.

I know not everybody agrees with my position. And as the media bombards us with pictures and accounts of the bad news from Iraq—with no perspective, no context, and no acknowledgment that good things are happening there, too—fewer Americans believe we should be there.

That's fine. In fact, that's great—it's what I love about America, and what you should love about America, too. We get the chance to tell our government that we—or some of us, anyway—don't like a war, or a tax, or a law, or a Supreme Court decision. Soldiers throughout American history have fought and died for our right to tell our elected officials precisely what we think of them. In certain privileged circles in today's America, it's considered impolite to point out the source of this basic freedom. America did not invent the human rights we enjoy, rights that our enemies wish to take away from us. Our government did not, in its generosity, give us the right to speech, the right to our opinions, the right to pursue happiness. Those certain, unalienable rights were given to us not by government but by God. Thomas Jefferson said just this in a radical American document, the Declaration of Independence. So we didn't invent these rights. We just have to fight for them.

What bothered me in the run-up to our intervention in Iraq were the protests in places like France and Germany. Their message was pretty clear—they were saying that we, the United States, are a bad actor in the world. They were saying that our power and our ideas are selfish, self-interested, and inherently evil.

And that is completely disingenuous. The French, of course, have made an art form out of sticking it to the United States. As a student of history, I read all about French President Charles de Gaulle's antics during the Cold War. He made a big show of taking France out of NATO and saying, in essence, that he wouldn't be bullied by those primitive Americans. All along, he knew that if the Russians decided to bust through the plains of Germany on their way to Paris, the United States would come to save his pompous French you-know-what. Why? Because that's the role we played in the world then, and that is the role we play now. We defend freedom when it is under threat.

I believe that the United States is a force for good in the world. I believe we accomplish good things for people, far more than any other country. We intervene in places like Kosovo and Somalia not because we have a strategic interest there, not because our actions will somehow lead to material rewards, not because we seek to influence their governments, but because we wish to do the right thing. And the right thing often involves a moral imperative that has nothing to do with self-interest. No wonder so many other countries don't understand us, or pretend that they don't.

We could have stood by and allowed genocide to take its course in Kosovo and Bosnia. At the time of our intervention in the Balkans, some of my friends, knowing my political views—I'm a Republican and a conservative—tried to goad me into condemning President Bill Clinton for ordering those operations. Actually, I thought President Clinton did the right thing in Bosnia and Kosovo, and the only thing I didn't like about the Somalia intervention was our hasty exit after our Black Hawk helicopters were shot down and nineteen Army Rangers and Delta Force soldiers were lost in early October 1993.

I believe we let people down when we talk about freedom but stand aside when we have the power to help others who wish for themselves what we enjoy at home. Yes, sometimes we do not act quickly enough, or at all, when horrendous crimes against humanity are committed. We didn't, and perhaps could not, stop the slaughter in Rwanda. We were slow to appreciate the horrors of Darfur. In my opinion, we should have intervened in both places. We would have been completely justified.

What I find interesting and not a little annoying are the recent demands for U.S. intervention in Darfur. Having said I believe we should have intervened, I think it's interesting to see who else thinks so. Most of those calls came from the same people who criticize our intervention in Iraq. I don't understand why one intervention is morally permissible but the other is not. I believe that we ought to intervene in Darfur. That, too, would be morally justified. But what would critics of U.S. power think of that? Would they see a U.S. intervention as yet another example of what's being called "American imperialism"? Or are the people of Darfur somehow more entitled to our help than the people of Iraq?

I think the people of both nations, and many more, are entitled to better lives and better governments, and I believe this is the cornerstone of American foreign policy. Other nations export terrorism and fear. We export liberty. And sometimes, we have to take up arms in liberty's defense. That's why we fight.

THE WAR WE'VE been forced to fight, not only in Iraq and Afghanistan but all around the world, is about ideology not terrain. It's the same fight we had with the Nazis, and the same fight we had with the communists. The clash is between two ways of life, two very different attitudes toward individual freedom and liberty. The war will determine which ideology will prevail, and which will be consigned, like Nazism and communism, to history's dustbin.

I believe there's very little difference between Osama bin Laden and two of the twentieth century's bloodiest despots, Adolf Hitler and Joseph Stalin. Like those two evil men, bin Laden pretends to stand for a larger cause—in his case, a militant, imperialistic, and ultimately murderous version of Islam. But what he really cares about is his personal power, and the use of that power to bend great nations to his twisted will. He doesn't care about whether we have forces in Saudi Arabia or whether the Palestinians have a homeland. Those are not the reasons he chose to attack us. In the end, he is no different from any other thug with big ambitions—he wants to be on top and to do that he has to take on the biggest guy on the block. That happens to be us.

Like I mentioned before, as an A.D.A. in the Manhattan District Attorney's Office, my specialty was prosecuting the war on drugs. In my mind, bin Laden is no different from the cheap, amoral drug dealers I used to send to prison. They're all in the business of power, they all use force to impose their will. They offer no alternative to what they seek to destroy. Bin Laden and the drug dealers and others like them are the Huns of the twenty-first century. And remember, when Attila and his band of barbarians sacked the Roman Empire, they didn't replace one empire with another, one system with another. All they sought was chaos and destruction. They were incapable of building anything new. Our enemies in the world today are equally impotent. They cannot match us in wealth, power, ability, and benevolence. All they can do is hurt us.

The question for the next few decades is this: Will we allow this man and his followers to succeed in destroying us? But before we can answer that question, we must consider another: Do we believe he means what he says when he calls for our destruction? Or do we believe that somehow we can reason with him, like Neville Chamberlain reasoned with Hitler at Munich?

I, for one, am not about to go looking for bin Laden's cave and try to reason with him in hopes that he'll see the light and choose not to attack us anymore. I hope and pray for peace in our time. But that time has not yet come, and may not come for many years. It certainly has not come yet, five years after the attacks of September 11, 2001. Our involvement in World War II lasted from December 7, 1941, through May 9, 1945—VE Day—and concluded on August 14, 1945—VJ Day. That's less than four years. Imagine that: the War on Terror already has lasted longer than our involvement in World War II. And there's no end in sight.

I think most Americans realize that we are in a struggle not of our choosing, against one of the cruelest enemies this nation has ever faced, and that all that we hold dear—our diversity, our freedoms, our pursuit of happiness—is at stake in this conflict. I also think that there are some people, at home and in the West, who believe that bin Laden isn't as bad as he's made out to be. These people see bin Laden as the inevitable result of our policies in the Middle East and around the world. The attacks of September 11, 2001, were, in this way of thinking, little more than our just deserts—chickens coming home to roost, as Malcolm X so humanely described the murder of John F. Kennedy.

This kind of thinking infuriates me. I don't care if you think a nation has an awful foreign policy—that hardly justifies hijacking a bunch of airplanes and crashing them into buildings filled with civilians. That's an intellectually bankrupt response, but then again, nobody with a brain in his or her head would argue that the jihadists have any intellectual currency at all.

It's a peculiar position: some people see bin Laden and his followers as some new proletariat striking out at evil capitalists in

America and in the West. Of course, it does no good to point out that the men who hijacked those planes on 9/11 weren't exactly downtrodden members of some new proletariat. They were middle-class, well-educated religious zealots. Not exactly the people Karl Marx envisioned as the leading elements of the great workers' revolution, but I suppose today's new Marxist terrorists will support any revolutionaries they can find.

Some would say that people who think like me are mean. But to me, the people who think we can reason with men like bin Laden are dangerously naive. They seem to think that if we, say, dropped all our support for Israel that bin Laden, sitting in his cave somewhere, would sit back and say, "Hey, that's great. Let's make peace with those infidels. They're not so bad after all." Presumably, he would then encourage his minions to sit around the campfire and sing "Kumbaya."

That's just not going to happen. We could concede every demand bin Laden has made, and you can be sure he'd find more demands. Or he'd declare himself satisfied, as Hitler did after he took Czechoslovakia. And then, while we celebrated the return of peace and business as usual, he'd come up with a fresh set of demands and grievances.

I will say this much about the terrorists bin Laden sends into the field with promises of eternal glory in the afterlife. The ones I've met are true believers. They've drunk bin Laden's Kool-Aid. They're not like Saddam, who tried to save his own neck and, thankfully, failed miserably. These guys will kill themselves if it means they'll get a chance to kill you. That's the difference between bin Laden and those he sends forth—they die, and bin Laden lives to order more men to their deaths. Bin Laden and his deputies do not demand of themselves the same zealotry that they demand of their followers. They're too smart for that. So they tell these fanatics, some of them in their teens, to strap on suicide belts and go blow themselves up and as many infidels as possible. Nobody ever seems to ask if Osama owns a belt of his own, and if he ever plans on wearing it.

I'll admit I've developed a grudging respect for some of the opponents we face in Iraq and elsewhere. I've seen them in court after they've been captured—their faces are stoic, and they do not hold back in an effort to spare their lives. They will admit that they wish to kill Americans, including myself and anyone else who happens to be in the courtroom with me, if they had a chance. To which my response is: Thank you very much for your honesty. But now your show is over and soon you'll be swinging from the end of a rope.

When I was in Iraq, I prosecuted two foreign fighters captured during battles with our troops. One was from Morocco, the other from Iran. They had different life stories, different versions of the Islamic narrative, but they had one thing in common: they were losers. The Iranian told the court and me that he dreamed of being a big-time soccer player.

That little fact, by the way, tells you something about the Iranian people. The mullahs can ban this and crack down on that, but the force of Western culture—and soccer is part of that—is greater than their ability to enforce their dour, repressive edicts. In any case, this would-be soccer star fell on hard times. He screwed up. He had no money. He found himself listening to the anti-American rhetoric and the false promises of eternal redemption being offered in exchange for jihadist sacrifice some of the radical Mullah's in mosques all over Iran were spewing out. All of a sudden the idea of dying for Allah and getting a chance to make it with seventy-two virgins seemed a lot more appealing than real life.

What's more, he was assured that if he killed himself properly and took enough infidels with him, his family would be cared for financially and honored by neighbors and friends. He would no longer be an embarrassment. Instead, he'd be a hero. So he crossed the border to fight the Americans and wound up in a court of law with me prosecuting him. As I stared at him in court, I thought to myself, "I've met his kind before." We think we're fighting an enemy whose ambitions and ways of life are a mystery. But many of the rank-and-file terrorists are not so different from the low-level drug dealers who pollute our urban street corners. They're losers who want desperately to feel important, and they don't care who has to die in the process.

FIGHTING A WAR requires that we know who we are and what we stand for. We also have to know who we are fighting, and why. Sometimes that's not so easy. A lot of doughboys during World War I probably weren't sure why they were in France in 1918. And as I mentioned before, Ulysses Grant wasn't sure why he was fighting Mexicans in 1848.

But in the War on Terror, our enemies have done us the favor of demonstrating, time and time again, who they are and why they must be stopped. I'll cite just two examples now.

In late 2005, terrorists in Iraq calling themselves the Swords of Righteousness Brigade took four Western peace activists hostage. That in itself tells you something about the nature of the opposition. One of the hostages was a man named Tom Fox, a fifty-four-year-old American who was associated with a group called the Christian Peacemaker Teams.

The capture of Fox offered those righteous warriors a chance to live up to their pompous name. After all, they had in their hands an American who opposed the war. It seems to me that when you capture a guy like that, you've been handed an unbelievable chance to score a huge propaganda victory. You keep him alive, you treat him well, and then, after the civilized world urges you to let this innocent peacemaker go, you do so. The former hostage then holds a news conference and tells the world that just as he suspected, the so-called terrorists are not evil men, like the Americans say. In their own way, they are no different from many of us. The former hostage then goes on to say how well he was treated, and that the American people could profit by reflecting on this episode.

That's not how the story unfolded. The righteous men tied up Fox, shot him in the head, and dumped his body near a railroad in Baghdad. When his corpse was found, it bore bruises and cuts, indicating that this peace activist was tortured before somebody put a bullet in his brain.

I don't have a particularly elevated opinion of the terrorists in Iraq, but even I was shocked by this one. I couldn't believe, from a strictly strategic point of view, how they could have been so stupid. But, of course, they are fanatics. They enjoy the act of killing infidels. Their spokesmen have said on more than one occasion that the difference between the militant Islamic world and the West is that the West loves life, and militant Muslims love death.

I saw that attitude myself when I was assisting a Marine major, Nicole Hudspeth, in preparation for the prosecution of one of the men charged with the murder of American contractor Nick Berg. You may remember Berg's awful story—he was a guy in his thirties who went to Iraq to help rebuild the country's telecommunications infrastructure. He was taken hostage while trying to help the Iraqi people, and his captors didn't care that his family opposed the war, or that he was not a soldier. They brought him in front of a video camera and cut off his head. The prime suspect in the beheading was none other than Iraq's top terrorist, Abu Musab al-Zarqawi.

When the video showing Berg's murder circulated on the Internet, I made a conscious choice not to watch it. I had heard enough about what it showed. I didn't feel the need to see this man's final, awful moments, or to see the glee of his death-worshipping killers. But when I was assigned to help prosecute one of the terrorists in the video after he was captured, I had no choice. The video was evidence, so I had to see it.

It was unbelievable in its horror. Again, as much as I thought I understood the nature of our enemy, even I was amazed by their brutality. Berg refused to submit quietly. He tried to fight off his killers, although he must have known it would be in vain. They had to pin him down so al-Zarqawi could perform the coup de grâce.

I'd like to know what cause could possibly justify this bloodthirsty crime. It's one thing to kill an enemy solider. It's another thing to brutalize him, to kill him in a manner designed to terrify others. Berg's killers were trying to send a message by posting that video—they wanted to frighten any American working in Iraq, or any American period. But I saw another message in that video: the enemies of my country were telling me that they are brutal people with no redeeming qualities. We have no choice but to hunt them down and kill them. The killers of Nick Berg and of Tom Fox remind us that we are dealing with people who delight in slaughter.

As soldiers, I and my comrades willingly agreed to fight these fanatics. We are engaged with the enemy, and he is with us. Fine: let the best cause win (it will). But our enemies don't abide by these kinds of rules. They avoid attacking our military. Instead, they seek out so-called soft targets—people drinking their morning coffee in an office building in downtown Manhattan. That's why I find them so irredeemable, and why I think attempts to reason with them are a waste of time. They will not agree to peacefully coexist with us. They are bent on killing us. They are intent on forcing the rest of us to accept their death cult, their ideology, and their warped values. There's a word for this kind of behavior: *imperialism*.

CRITICS OF AMERICAN foreign policy claim that we are modern imperialists, ultimately no different from the Europeans of the Victorian age who set out to conquer vast stretches of Asia and Africa. The model most critics have in mind, of course, is the British Empire of the late nineteenth and early twentieth centuries, which dominated a quarter of the globe. They see American influence overseas as nothing short of criminal, regardless of whether that influence is represented by the U.S. military, by Microsoft, or by McDonald's.

This is an unthinking, knee-jerk reaction to an undeniable reality. Yes, the United States has a vast presence in the world today. Yes, you can go to most large cities, even in the third world, and find evidence of American business interests and

American popular culture. Newspapers and television sometimes show kids in the third world wearing clothes or hats with the logos of American sports teams. People everywhere buy music and videos featuring American entertainers. Multinational companies like Nike, McDonald's, Microsoft, Starbucks, and Time Warner bring a little piece of America with them when they set up shop abroad.

Is this imperialism? Many critics say so. If it is, however, why won't critics point out that we are hardly the only people in the imperialism game—and, in fact, we are the victims of imperialism. After all, our domestic auto industry has suffered dramatically thanks to the success of Toyota, Honda, and other Asian competitors. Is the ubiquity of Toyota evidence of renewed Japanese imperialism? Critics say American financial institutions are mere extensions of American imperialism. But what about China? Can't we argue that China's willingness to buy American debt is evidence of Chinese imperialism?

In my mind, what all of this means is that we truly do live in a global marketplace. We sell hamburgers, computers, and videos in Istanbul, Paris, and Bangalore. And we buy Japanese cars, Italian shoes, and Swedish vodka. Welcome to the twenty-first century.

America is not an imperialist country. When we intervene in another country, the first question all Americans ask is: When are we leaving? The idea of imperialism is that you stay, you occupy foreign soil, you impose rulers and governments on people, and you exploit the land you control. We don't do that. When we believe we have no choice but to send troops overseas, we begin planning our exit strategy from day one. We have no desire to rule other people. But we do have national interests—like every other country in the world—and we do believe that we have a right and a duty to use our power to help people, not oppress them.

When American forces go overseas, whether to France during World War I, to Japan and Germany during World War II, to Korea in the early 1950s, and now to Iraq and Afghanistan, our goal is to dismantle an enemy. When we have achieved that goal, all we ask in return is for enough ground to bury our dead.

Some years ago, I visited the American cemetery overlooking Omaha Beach in Normandy. I remember walking past all those crosses and Stars of David, thinking about all these young men who probably never thought much about France, and here they are, resting forever in a green space overlooking the English Channel.

We invaded France to rid that nation of German occupation. We did so with brave French allies in the Resistance and the Free French Army. We liberated the French, swept across the country, and crossed the Rhine into Germany. In less than a year, we conquered vast stretches of Europe. And when the war was over, we rebuilt these ancient nations in one of the most magnanimous gestures in human history. We didn't play the role of conqueror. Instead, we came to the aid of a suffering humanity, to use FDR's phrase.

If you call that imperialism, well, what are we to make of the stated goals and tactics of our enemies today?

Of course, apologists for imperialist Islam will say, "Well, what about the Crusades? Wasn't that an act of Christian imperialism?" Yes, it was, and it took place a thousand years ago and we recognize today that it was a bad idea. We have a guy here today who is trying the same damn thing, and yet people want to talk about our supposed imperial ambitions.

There's no doubt in my mind who today's imperialists are. They're the people who say that we must convert to Islam or perish by Islam's sword. They're the people who believe all of us should live in accordance with the Koran, and that those who refuse must be killed. Bin Laden denounces us as "Crusaders," but he's the imperialist in this war. We're defending our ideas against invasion.

On September 10, 2001, nobody in the U.S. government had any designs on Afghanistan. You could probably make an argument saying that we should have. But it speaks to the sort of power America wields that we didn't make a move on Afghanistan even though we knew about bin Laden's training camps. Yes, we fired some cruise missiles in his direction, and almost got him. But that hardly qualifies as an invasion—although, to our critics, it probably was seen as a war crime. For most Americans, terrorism was a distant threat, and even then, the people most at risk worked in embassies or military installations in troubled parts of the world.

That attitude changed on September 11, but only because it had to—war was forced upon us, and we responded as any nation would have. That awful day supposedly was ingrained in our memory forever, but how quickly we seem to have forgotten the pain, suffering, and unity we experienced in the days and months following the attacks. And we certainly seem to have forgotten how right it felt when, after almost a month of consultation with our friends and allies, we started bombing bin Laden's positions on October 7, 2001.

Or is it possible that not everybody felt that way? Perhaps some of our critics believe that we should have left bin Laden alone, or tried to reason with him, or perhaps asked the United Nations if they would please send a party to Kabul to arrest bin Laden. When I hear people talk about so-called American imperialism in Afghanistan, I can only shake my head and wonder what planet they're living on. And yet, when Michael Moore produces a film that argues that we went into Afghanistan because the Bush administration wanted control over a pipeline, many stand and applaud, and the French shower him with medals.

In the end, when this struggle is over and the forces of civilization are victorious over the forces of terror and darkness, the Michael Moores will be forgotten. We will remember instead our friends, neighbors, loved ones, and others who saw the struggle for what it was and who did their part, not necessarily by joining the military, but certainly by speaking the truth, and by being stout of heart, clear of mind, and pure of intent. We may yet again be called upon to comfort a wounded city or region. We may yet again be asked to unite around grieving families of murdered innocents.

I do not wish for the realization of those scenarios. The men and women I met in Afghanistan and Iraq are doing their best to make sure we are as safe as possible. But the future is perilous, for our enemy is as patient as he is murderous.

But I believe Americans recognize this new threat to our freedom for what it is: another violent power grab by another would-be dictator. And I would say of bin Laden and his ilk what Winston Churchill said of our enemies during a speech to the U.S. Congress on December 26, 1941, three weeks after Pearl Harbor. To a hushed House of Representatives, the great orator growled: "What kind of a people do they think we are? Is it possible that they do not realize that we shall never cease to persevere against them until they have been taught a lesson which they and the world will never forget."

Some lessons are never completely learned. Sometimes we must learn them over and over again. And that is why we fight.